SOMEBODY'S GOTTA SAY IT

SOMEBODY'S GOTTA SAY IT

NEAL BOORTZ

HC

An Imprint of HarperCollins*Publishers*

HarperCollins books may be purchased for educational, business, or sales promotional use. For information please write: Special Markets Department, HarperCollins Publishers Inc., 10 East 53rd Street, New York, NY 10022.

FIRST EDITION

Designed by Kris Tobiassen

Library of Congress Cataloging-in-Publication Data has been applied for.

ISBN 10: 0-06-087820-7
ISBN 13: 978-0-06-087820-7

07 08 09 10 11 10 9 8 7 6 5 4 3 2 1

This book is dedicated to my loving wife, Donna, and my daughter, Laura, as thanks for the decades of abuse they have suffered due to my chosen career as a radio talk-show host. For every time they stood up proudly to someone wishing to vent about something I said on the air, for every interruption my wife endured while we were simply trying to enjoy a quiet night out, and for her compassionate understanding every time I felt bowed by the events of the day, my most heartfelt thanks.

This book is also dedicated, with my deepest gratitude, to the millions of listeners who have remained loyal, even though I might say things that they vehemently disagree with. I trust you have been entertained along the way. If not, why are you still listening?

CONTENTS

INTRODUCTION

You hold in your hands a book by a radio talk-show host.

How special.

What can I possibly say that you haven't thought a thousand times already?

Well, *something,* I hope. After all, it's my job to come up with things to say—things to get people talking. If you're like most people, on the other hand, you probably spend most of your time every day watching what you say, for fear that blurting out your insensitive thoughts might bring about adverse repercussions, whether at home, at work, or in your social life.

After all . . . everybody has to get along. Right?

Nope—not me!

You see, I'm one of the rare people you know who has a job perfectly matched to his personality type. It appears that I somehow failed to develop the convenient social skill of keeping my yap shut. Even before I knew I had a mind, I had a penchant for speaking it. And I've been developing my skills in that department ever since.

Of course, in a lot of ways, we're alike, you and I. When you wake up in the morning and listen to the news or read a newspaper, you probably think, *What in the hell are these people thinking?* The only difference is, you then cruise off to work and make a studied effort to keep your ill-tempered thoughts to yourself for the rest of the day. When I wake up, hear those same news reports, and think the same thing—*What in the hell are these idiots thinking?*—I'm lucky enough to be able to do something about it. Right away I'm making plans to rip them a variety of new ones as soon as I get to work. I don't have to worry about the consequences of having opinions. For me, it's part of the job description.

Such is the life of a radio talk-show host.

I am, it is said, an equal opportunity offender. If I come to the end of my four daily hours on the air and I'm not sure I have gravely offended at least one group—social, racial, socio-economic, ethnic, political, generational, regional—then I consider my work that day an abject failure.

I begin each show with a simple basic truth running through my mind. "These people out there doing these dangerous, stupid, sometimes hilarious, and often strange things have no right not to be offended, and I'm here to see that these non-rights are recognized and respected."

There are no taboos on my show. Race, gender, religion, national origin, political persuasion . . . it's all fair game. No political correctness here.

People may be able to hide their illogical, sometimes downright moronic behavior behind the shield of a convenient group identity in their everyday lives. But not from me.

There's only one real requirement for someone to land in my crosshairs: that you do something, either intentionally or through ignorance, that will contribute to the destruction of the greatest experiment in self-government this world has ever known—our country, the United States of America.

Many of my diatribes, of course, are aimed at liberals. These people actually think that America is great *because of government.* Such easy targets.

But they're not the only ones. Theo-cons, for instance. Religious faith is fine, even admirable. But when you decide that your ideas on religion are so indisputably correct that everyone ought to live by them, it's time for a little talking to.

The earth is only six thousand years old? Just spare me.

Then there are the suburban soccer moms blissfully driving their urban assault vehicles adorned with those "My child is an honor student" bumper stickers to the repair shop to get the tires rotated on their riding vacuum cleaners. Someone needs to have a serious talk with these women about the wisdom of turning their children over to the government to be educated, and since nobody else seems to be stepping up to the plate, I'm happy to do it.

(And what's this fascination with soccer anyway? Are these overprotective parents afraid to let their precious little cutest-child-in-the-entire-world play a game where they might get hit, or where someone might throw something at them?)

Not to mention the men who are afraid to venture out of their homes for fear that they might actually come face-to-face with (gasp!) "one of them homo-sexual guys" out on the street someday. I mean, *really*.

And I'm just getting warmed up. In the pages that follow, you'll encounter:

• Welfare artists

• Screaming car commercials

• Parents who allow their child to trick-or-treat for UNICEF

• People who leave dealer tags on the trunks of their new cars

• Abortocentrists (you'll figure it out)

• The "I'm not interested in politics" sheeple

• People who don't know what they don't know (a particularly vexing species)

- People who have no business waving an American flag on the Fourth of July

And that just scratches the surface. The life of a no-holds-barred talk show host is richly rewarding—thanks to the listeners, callers, columnists, editorialists, and just ordinary red-blooded Americans who make it so.

While writing this book, it occurred to me that I may have been blessed to grow up and to spend most of my life during the best of America's years. As much as I love this country, it's certainly hard to be optimistic about her future.

We've become a nation of people who care little for their freedom and who've grown completely dependent on their government. We stand ready to trade away almost all of our precious liberties in exchange for a slender slice of security, courtesy of the federal government.

I've been around long enough that I'll probably weather any foreseeable disaster our power-hungry political class and our complacent, dependent voters might visit upon us. The generations that follow won't be quite so fortunate.

Just look around you! Open a newspaper for once. They don't hurt, you know. Try reading something other than *People, Sports Illustrated,* or *Cosmo.* Flip the channel to something besides *Extra* or *Entertainment Tonight.*

Things aren't going all that well, folks, and if we don't wake up and smell the tyranny, our children and grandchildren will grow up robbed of their individual identity, marching in lockstep with their fellow poorly educated, complacent, government-dependent friends, toward that great socialist Valhalla dreamed of by the great thinkers of the political left.

The hardest thing about writing this book was deciding when to stop. Since I finished the main text (I wrote this introduction last) we've:

- Seen a government school have a twelve-year-old special education student arrested and charged with disorderly conduct for wetting her pants;

- Learned that the Mexican government is providing GPS devices to Mexican citizens to help them avoid American law enforcement as they illegally cross our border to become part of the Mexican invasion force;

- Found out that George W. Bush wants broad new powers to open our mail just to see what we're sending to each other;

- Discovered that police in Paris, France, have determined that preparing soup with pork for feeding to the homeless is a racist act because a homeless person who *might* want to eat some of that soup just *might* be a Muslim;

- Watched Barack Obamamania sweep the country, focused on a man with no compelling political experience and no real agenda to speak of;

- Learned that the Bush administration has negotiated an agreement with Mexico that would allow illegal aliens to collect Social Security benefits in this country without working and paying Social Security taxes nearly as long as any American citizen would have to;

- Discussed whether or not Keith Ellison, the first Muslim to serve in Congress, will emulate his peers by trying to bring the pork back to his home district.

And that's just two days' worth of news!

I began my career in talk radio in September 1969. (You see, there was this suddenly dead talk show host . . . but we'll get to that later.) I was a quintessential grade school wimp and high school dork who defied the odds and turned a completely unpromising and lackluster childhood, coupled with a less-than impressive effort at education, into a career as one of radio's longest-running talk show hosts.

And how did I pull that off? Simple—by getting on the radio day after day after day and saying things that most people are afraid to say out of fear of losing their jobs or becoming social lepers.

The modern era of political correctness[1] has clamped the tongues of many. But the emergence of talk radio removed those clamps, actually giving people a public forum to speak their minds—to the utter horror of the PC crowd.

One thing I've been rather proud of during my talk radio career is the number of conservatives who complain that I'm too liberal, and the number of liberals who say I'm too far to the right. The poor libertarians? They think I don't know where the hell I stand.

This book will tackle some of the issues and ideas that have been the focus of some very interesting talk radio conversations over the years: from poverty to prayer in the schools, from race relations to religion, from abortion to gun control, from the United Nations to the war in Iraq, and from the "gay agenda" to the war against Islamic terrorism. Some of the stories are lighthearted, presented here more for your amusement than anything else. Others are here merely for their *gee-whiz* factor. Still others will be included to give you pause, to make you double back to your strongest opinions, ask some questions, and perhaps—just perhaps—rethink your unexamined convictions.

One last thought.

As I looked through the final draft of *Somebody's Gotta Say It*, I wondered just what sentence, what passage the bed-wetting left was going to seize on to demonize me. There are plenty of candidates.

---

[1] Political correctness is an invention of the left as a precursor to wholesale restrictions on the right to free speech and expression.

They won't like my feelings on the poor, poor pitiful people who seem incapable of earning above the minimum wage, or my thoughts about the one group of beloved Americans who, in my opinion, present a greater long-range threat to America than Islamic fascists.

Some of my ideas will irritate the left, no doubt about it. They'll try to fight back. But they'll never be able to refute them with any degree of fact or logic. So, instead, they'll respond the same way they've done for years: They'll pull out ye olde "hate speech" complaint. Remember, if you should hear or read that *Somebody's Gotta Say It* is just another hate-filled screed from some right-winger, what you're really hearing is they hate the fact that crying "hate speech" is the best response they can muster.

Come on, guys. Is that the best you can do?

I know it must be hard not to control the conversational agenda.

Well, you can always write a book. Who knows? Someone might actually buy it!

As they say . . . somebody's gotta say it.

DEATH KNOCKS—ALONG WITH OPPORTUNITY

There was a time when I would have killed to get into talk radio. As luck would have it, I didn't have to.

The name Herb Elfman probably doesn't ring a bell, and there's no reason it should. His name is but a small, sad footnote in the history of talk radio, but a very important one in the history of yours truly. In fact, it can fairly be said that I owe my entire career to this long-forgotten pioneer.

Bear with me, now, while I put you through a short course in radio history. Don't worry, it'll get interesting.

Elfman, like many of us who eventually landed our own shows, actually started out as a caller. Way, way back in the 1960s, Elfman lived out in Los Angeles. For years he worked as a salesman,[1] apparently for a portrait photography company. And he loved listening to a local blowhard on KABC named Bob Grant.

Yes, that's right, *the* Bob Grant—the one who's been called "The King of Talk Radio."[2] Controversial, opinionated, and wildly popular, Grant went on to become a living legend at WOR in New York, blazing a conservative yet independent trail for more than a quarter-

---

[1] Like yours truly. Yes, I know, it's ironic. Funny thing is, I only learned that Herb Elfman had been a salesman while I was researching this book.

[2] Especially by Bob Grant.

century before retiring not too long ago.[3] Grant was years ahead of nearly everyone else in the business. Even Howard Stern has credited him as a strong influence. WOR's website goes so far as to call Grant "the inventor of controversial talk radio"—which is somewhat truer than Al Gore saying he invented the Internet.

But still, I must humbly set the record straight. The fact is, Grant learned the ropes from the meanest guy in the business.

Grant had been working as a radio newsman since 1949, but it was when KABC hired him as sports director in 1962 that he met Joe Pyne, the station's headliner. By all accounts, Pyne was a miserable guy, on and off the air, and his show was a train wreck: People listened because they just couldn't help themselves. This guy was so nasty, he used to tell callers, "Go gargle with razor blades!"

From time to time, Joe Pyne allowed Bob Grant to substitute for him. Then, in 1964, when Pyne left KABC for an equally noxious television gig that lasted several years on NBC,[4] Grant eagerly stepped in to fill his footprints.

Isn't it nice when things work out like that? I couldn't tell you from experience—my own big break wasn't anything like that. Which brings us back to Herb Elfman.

Elfman was one of Grant's devoted listeners in L.A., and became one of his infamous "pest" callers.

Now, you've got to understand, talk radio in the 1960s wasn't what it is today. It just wasn't a very popular format; the hosts literally had to beg for calls. So even a pest like Elfman had no trouble making it on the air.

For a while, at least.

Eventually, Elfman grew enamored of his status as a minor celebrity, and became increasingly strident in his opinions and on-air arguments with the host, until Grant finally had to ban him from the show.

---

[3] Guess who that leaves as the longest-running radio talk-show host in America?

[4] Joe Pyne died of lung cancer in 1970.

Undeterred, Herb Elfman then decided to become the host of his *own* talk show.

As fate would have it, Atlanta was one of the last major cities in the country to come around to having an all-talk radio station, and nobody was expecting much when it finally happened in late 1967. WRNG—"Ring Radio," as it was known—was located at 680 AM, the last available spot on the dial.

"Radio does so many things bad that it is hard to know where to start," columnist Paul Hemphill wrote in the city's evening newspaper when the news was announced.[5] And, fact is, he was right. Given what had come before, who was really expecting much from a new talk-radio show?

"There will be no music, just talk," explained another article in the *Atlanta Journal* just before the station's inaugural broadcast. "On-the-air personalities will discuss news events, feature interviews with people in the news, offer household hints, sports analysis and the like."

By then, Joe Pyne was a household name—and not a good one. "A lot of people have the idea that all-talk radio features a great deal of syndicated shows of the Joe Pyne caliber," the article continued. "But this is something that WRNG will steer clear of."[6]

And so it did.

For a while, at least.

WRNG tried hard to play it straight—so hard that two of its hosts, Micki Silverstein and Teddy Levison, actually won the prestigious George Foster Peabody Award for a documentary on police brutality.

Then, in February 1970, Herb Elfman came to town.

Until then, the closest WRNG had come to genuine controversy was a guest appearance by famous LSD advocate Dr. Timothy

---

[5] *Atlanta Journal,* October 19, 1967. Paul Hemphill went on to become the author of four novels and eleven nonfiction books.

[6] *Atlanta Journal,* December 2, 1967.

Leary—a hippie-era nutcase who would have come across as sane and reasonable next to Herb Elfman.

Yet, somehow, Elfman ended up on the morning show on Ring Radio. Not as a caller—as the host.

I was out there listening. I can't quite remember what I was doing at the time—either selling chemicals or writing speeches for the governor—but I was an Elfman fan. I was completely fascinated. So were a lot of other people.

I recently came across an old newspaper clip saying that Elfman "wooed his audience with conservative zeal," which explains, I suppose, why he appealed to me. "A churchgoer with a patriotic passion, Elfman castigated critics of the nation's institutions."[7] But that hardly captures it. Elfman was a wild man on the radio—driven and unpredictable.

One day I picked up the phone, dialed the number for WRNG, and Elfman put me on the air. Before long, I was a regular caller.

There was always something in the news, something to talk about—one side or another to argue. Richard Nixon, still in his first term, was struggling with the war in Vietnam abroad and rebellious youth on the home front. William Calley was being court-martialed in connection with the My Lai massacre. NASA was trying to figure out just what had gone wrong on Apollo 13. A grand jury was looking into Senator Edward M. Kennedy's conduct in connection with an automobile accident and the death of Mary Jo Kopechne. Airplanes were being hijacked—a lot. Women were burning bras. Sex was being discussed more openly than ever before. And Yoko Ono was breaking up the Beatles.

What a great time to be a talk radio host—and how I envied Herb Elfman!

We never actually became friends, but Elfman eventually invited me to a speech he was giving, and after that we had lunch together several times. This was long, long, ago, and memory fades with the

---

[7] *Atlanta Journal,* May 29, 1970.

years, but as I recall, he was a little pudgy, though his face had very sharp, well-defined features, and he wore his hair in a sort of buzz cut. He had only a little formal education, but was very knowledgeable about a wide variety of topics. Sadly, I can't say he had a particularly pleasant personality.[8]

Nevertheless, I invited him over for dinner one night. He came, alone, and the result was one awkward foursome: me, my wife, Herb Elfman, and Herb's personality. I'll never forget it: When he finished eating, Elfman pushed his chair back, stood up—and proceeded to deliver a speech, right there in our dining room. I can't reconstruct exactly what he said. But when I saw the movie *Network* a few years later, Peter Finch's Oscar-winning performance as lunatic anchorman Howard Beale reminded me of Elfman that night. We just sat there, agape, watching him orate at great length to his small and captive audience.

By then his radio audience was considerably larger. I know that because WRNG made the mistake of firing him. Elfman ran his mouth on the air about a contract dispute, complaining very publicly about negotiations the station considered private.

Big mistake—but not for Elfman, as it turned out. His loyal fans, who were legion, marched on the station and flooded the Ring Radio telephone lines as never before. Within a week of the dismissal, Elfman was rehired. He was popular enough to say and do as he pleased.

Until then, no one had imagined that talk radio could have such influence.

A very short time later, I was watching the late news on television, probably after *The Engelbert Humperdinck Show,* and one story caused me to bolt upright in bed.

Local radio personality Herb Elfman was dead. A suicide.

---

[8] Now, many years later, I believe that Herb Elfman was actually a painfully shy person. That's the big secret about many of us who end up as professional broadcasters, whether on radio or television: The big ego is all an act. Put me in a setting where I'm supposed to meet and greet and grip and grin; it's just torture. Without exception, I'm the quietest guy at any party.

As it turned out, Elfman had made a surprise trip to L.A., where he put a .22 caliber revolver to his head. Earlier that day, his wife had served him with divorce papers. He left behind four daughters and both his parents. The poor guy was forty-one, and finally at the pinnacle of success. After selling God-knows-how-many-thousand portrait photographs, his entire career at Ring Radio had lasted just a little over three months.

Herb Elfman's death, sadly, also meant he wasn't going to be on the air the next morning.[9] And I knew they couldn't run with: "Hey, the following three hours of silence are brought to you on account of Herb Elfman's suicide."

Luck is opportunity met by preparation. This man's death was unfortunate, but for me it was also an opportunity. I was prepared to seize the day. And why not? If it wasn't me, it would be somebody else. (Even my wife was shocked. And she knows me well.)

And so, the very next morning, when WRNG employees began showing up for work just before sunrise, they were surprised to find a man sitting outside the front door in a lawn chair he'd brought from home. That man, of course, was me.

"What are you doing here?" the station manager asked when he arrived.

"Oh, haven't you heard?" I asked. "Herb Elfman's dead. He committed suicide."

"Yeah, we know. Why are you here?"

"Somebody's got to do that show. I can do it."

No doubt shocked, the station manager politely informed me that he'd already arranged for a replacement. "Our afternoon guy. He's going to do the morning show. But thank you very much, Mr. Boortz."

I was determined to get a job—to climb over the body of a dead talk-show host, if that's what it took to get into the industry.

---

[9] This was back when radio and TV stations signed off for the night.

"Well, who's going to do the afternoon show?" I asked, stopping him again as he attempted to enter the building.

"The afternoon show is going to go off the air before too long because of the end of daylight savings time and the early sunsets," the station manager explained—rather patiently, all things considered. "So we're just going to put somebody in there temporarily. But thank you very much, Mr. Boortz."

"Good idea," I said. "Put somebody in there temporarily. I'll do it."

He regarded me with a look of exasperation. Then his expression changed, just a bit. He knew who I was—a caller—and he knew I'd applied for jobs many times before, without success.

Until now. "Okay," he said. "Come back this afternoon and you can do the afternoon show. But remember, it's only going to last about six weeks."

"Fine," I said.

About two weeks later, they moved me to the morning show. That was more than thirty-five years ago. And I've been doing talk radio ever since.

SCHENECTADY

It occurs to me that after just a handful of pages, I may already be giving you the wrong impression of myself, dwelling a little too much on my soft underbelly. I may appear to be a gentle, vulnerable soul with empathy for my fellow man.

This misconception must be corrected.

This isn't about politics or philosophical leanings. I just feel the need to give my readers a more balanced idea of who I am. And so . . .

It was miserable and cold in Schenectady.

(Good days in Schenectady aren't that great, but this one was truly horrible.) [1]

Even so, I was thrilled to be there. It was, in fact, one of the happiest days of my life. Fortune hadn't smiled so kindly upon me since the day Herb Elfman decided to answer his wife's divorce plea with a gunshot to his own head. This was the breakthrough I'd been waiting for, the one that was going to lift me out of small-time radio and into the big leagues. I literally couldn't wait to get back to our hotel room and tell Donna the news.

I'd just been offered a job hosting a late-night talk show at WGY, the flagship station of General Electric's prestigious radio chain.

"Our nighttime signal covers about twenty-eight states," I was told. "You're going to get great exposure. This is going to be just great for your career. And we're going to pay you fifteen thousand dollars a

---

[1] So much for a warm welcome at my book signing in Schenectady.

year to start." That wasn't bad money in the 1970s, especially for a guy who needed a job.

You see, WRNG—good old Ring Radio—had just fired me. I'd been there for six or seven years, filling the morning airwaves with rants on everything from Watergate to Jimmy Carter, but talk radio hadn't yet become a major force. For the most part, nobody was listening to anything but music. And the music was actually pretty bad during those years.[2]

A procession of program directors had come and gone at WRNG, but not one of them knew how to make talk radio work. The clueless PD who decided to get rid of me had been a regional director for the John Birch Society, which I mention only to give you an indication of his radio expertise. This guy, who later became a good friend, was adept at locating Communists pretty much anywhere, but not so good at programming a talk-radio station. So, in his infinite wisdom, he concluded I'd been talking for too long, and gave me a six-week notice.

I wasted no time sending resume tapes to just about every radio station between Atlanta and New York City. Then, a week later, I took my remaining vacation days and hit the road. My wife and I got in our car and started driving up the Eastern Seaboard, stopping at every station on my list.

At most of these stops a receptionist would say, "We don't have any openings." That's as far as I would get. Back to the car and back on the road. At a few stations someone in a position of authority did agree to meet me, but nothing of consequence came of it.

By the time we settled into a hotel room in Schenectady, I really wasn't expecting much. I left Donna in the room and headed over to WGN for the obligatory turn-down. But it didn't come right away. Instead I spent over an hour talking talk radio and politics with the station's head honcho.

He bought my line of bull.

---

[2] "Midnight at the Oasis"? Spare me. I'd rather listen to Snoop Dogg . . . and that's saying something, know what I'm sayin'?

The job offer was everything I'd ever dreamed of; by the time I headed back to the hotel I was walking on air. I couldn't wait to tell Donna the good news.

They still actually had hotel room keys back then, and for the life of me I couldn't calm down enough to unlock the door. Finally, I fumbled my way into the room, and found Donna standing at the window, looking out over Schenectady. The spectacle on a dark, dreary Schenectady evening wasn't exactly alluring; this is one room that would have been better off without a view.

"Hey, hon," I said, waiting for her to turn around so I could say, "Donna, I got the job!"

But the words never made it out of my mouth. When she turned around, tears were pouring down her cheeks.

"What's the matter?" I asked, stunned.

She looked at me and said simply, "I hate this place."

My response was immediate.

"God," I said, "it *is* miserable, isn't it?"

An expression of relief washed across her beautiful face.

"I'll tell you what," I said. "Let's get the hell out of here right now . . . we'll head back south and see what New York City is all about!"

"Can we?"

"You bet," I told her. "I'm going to go downstairs and check out right now."

I went downstairs and checked out. Then I walked over to the pay phone, called the program director at WGN, and thanked him for his generous offer.

"I can't take the job," I said. "I'm sorry, but it's just not what I'm looking for."

Donna and I drove to New York and enjoyed the sights for a couple of days. No job offers were forthcoming there, however, so we headed back to Atlanta.

When I got home, I decided to do something completely different. I enrolled in law school.

A few months later I heard from WRNG. The man they'd hired to replace me had found a better job. He was heading to San Francisco and some station called KGO.[3] Once again, WRNG had an unexpected opening.

"We made a mistake," the station manager told me.

"Well, yes. I knew that at the time."

"Will you come back?"

I didn't even have to think before answering, "Not for what you were paying me."

"We'll double it," he said.

And that was that.

I was back on the air. And before long, I had a law degree, too. I think that made me a double threat.

It took me twenty years to admit to Donna that I'd been offered that job in Schenectady.

---

[3] The guy's name was (still is, for that matter) Ronn Owens. Great talk show host, dominates the San Francisco market to this day. He's been propping up his program director for nearly three decades now.

THE WAR ON
THE INDIVIDUAL

It was winter 2002. The New England Patriots had just won their first of several Super Bowl championships.

Sports championships—especially a Super Bowl or World Series win—can pump up a community with a glowing sense of pride, putting a spring in virtually everyone's step. The people love their champions. And politicians know it.

I still remember the Atlanta Braves' first trip to the World Series in 1991. As soon as the series was over, there was a parade in downtown Atlanta. Hundreds of thousands of Georgians lined Peachtree Street to see their heroes ride by.

And there, to my intense disgust, smack in the middle of the parade, was virtually every local politician you could think of. We had the mayor, city council members, county commission members, some state representatives and senators, and a congressman or two riding in their little convertibles right down the parade route with the Braves players. There they were, waving to the crowd as if they had some share in the credit for the Braves' accomplishment.

As I sat there watching this thing unfold on television, I couldn't help but wonder: "What in the ever-loving hell are those political hacks doing in that parade?"

Did I raise hell about this on the air?

Do a hog love slop?[1]

You bet I did. And to this day you don't see Atlanta and Georgia politicians glomming onto parades celebrating our local sports heroes.

That's just me. Making our society a more wonderful place to live in, bit by bit.

It's easy to understand why politicians want to be associated with successful athletes. Politicians are controversial. Winning athletes aren't. People generally love winners. People most certainly don't generally love politicians. Whenever a politician can manage to be identified, even for a short period of time, with a winning sports team, it can be a huge plus.

So . . . the New England Patriots win the Super Bowl, and who is one of the first politicians to step forward to bask in their glory? Why, none other than the hero of Chappaquiddick himself, Senator Ted Kennedy.

Before we move on here, allow me to say something to the people of Massachusetts: What in the hell are you people thinking keeping that man in office?[2]

I've visited Chappaquiddick. I've been to the bridge. I've been down that dirt road you allegedly jogged, the one that leads to the paved road back to Edgartown. I've seen that channel you supposedly swam in the middle of the night. Pretty swift current there, Teddy! Who knew you were in such good shape? Especially after a night of hardy partying and that little jog!

I'm calling BS on you and your entire story. I think you let Mary

---

[1] You know, I'm going to probably regret using that "do a hog love slop" bit in this book. That, you see, is a largely Southern expression. Believe it or not, there are many radio stations around the country who will not carry my show because they think it's "Southern." Why would that be? Because it comes from Atlanta, Georgia. Trust me, the anti-Southern prejudice is quite alive and well out there, even among broadcast executives who should know better.

[2] Now this is the essence of *Somebody's Gotta Say It*. I'm not saying anything here that millions of Americans haven't wanted to say out loud for decades. I have the voice, so I'll say it for them.

Jo Kopechne drown in your car in four feet of water off the Chappaquiddick Bridge while you were wandering up and down that dirt road worrying about salvaging your political career.

I think that if you'd been half the man either one of your brothers were, Mary Jo Kopechne would have lived to marry and raise some children of her own.

I think there's much to that story that's never been told.

But back to the story of Ted Kennedy and the New England Patriots.

Soon after the Super Bowl victory, there's Ted Kennedy, preening before the media, ready to share his eagerly sought opinion on the victory. After a few harrumphs and a wheeze or two, Kennedy explained just how his eminence felt about the Patriots' stunning win:

> At a time when our entire country is banding together and facing down individualism, the Patriots set a wonderful example, showing us all what is possible when we work together, believe in each other, and sacrifice for the greater good.

And there it is. You probably didn't know it, but in this historic moment, we're all facing down individualism! We don't exist for ourselves anymore! We aren't here to responsibly take care of ourselves! We're all here to sacrifice for the greater good!

Is it just me, or do I hear the stomping feet of schoolchildren marching and chanting in unison in Red Square?

It's a war that's been going on for decades, folks—more than a century, in fact. And plenty of its leaders are on the record, with statements that echo Teddy's own. I'll share them with you now, along with a few rebuttals.

We'll start with Adolf himself:

> The main plank in the National Socialist program is to *abolish the liberalistic concept of the individual* and the Marxist concept of

humanity and to substitute for them the folk community, rooted in the soil and bound together by the bond of its common blood.

> —ADOLF HITLER,
> *quoted in* Hitler: A Study in Tyranny,
> *by Alan Bullock (New York: HarperCollins, 1962)*

How's that for starting off with a bang? From Hitler in the 1930s to Kennedy in the 2000s, strange bedfellows in the war on individualism.

It is thus necessary that the individual should come to realize that his own ego is of no importance in comparison with the existence of his nation; that the position of the individual ego is conditioned solely by the interests of the nation as a whole . . . that above all the unity of a nation's spirit and will are worth far more than the freedom of the spirit and will of an individual. . . . This state of mind, which subordinates the interests of the ego to the conservation of the community, is really the first premise for every truly human culture. . . . we understand only the individual's capacity to make sacrifices for the community, for his fellow man.

> —ADOLF HITLER, 1933

Another of Adolf's greatest hits—more anti-individualist claptrap from one of the world's preeminent mass murderers.[3]

But why?

Why is it so very important to some people that the concept of individuality be demonized, if not outright destroyed?

Because the destruction of individuality is central to the liberal's very concept of government, that's why.

---

[3] It should be pointed out here that Stalin and Mao both killed far, far more people than Hitler. I point this out only to cause you to wonder why liberals like to brand Hitler as the all-time champion of mass murder. Mao took out as many as 60 million. Could it possibly have anything to do with the fact that Mao was and still is, to some extent, a hero of the left? A mass-murder is a mass-murderer. They're all worthy of damnation.

There is the great, silent, continuous struggle: the struggle between the State and the Individual; between the State which demands and the individual who attempts to evade such demands. Because the individual, left to himself, unless he be a saint or hero, always refuses to pay taxes, obey laws, or go to war.

—BENITO MUSSOLINI

The most important thing to understand about liberals is that they think in terms of groups, not individuals. Their main concern is always for the "poor," the "underprivileged," the "less fortunate," the "children," and the "minorities." Their enmity is reserved for the "rich."

If you're a left-wing, collectivist liberal in the Ted Kennedy mold, here's the rub:

If you recognize the concept of individuality at all, then it follows that you must recognize the existence of individual rights. This means that at some point you might actually have to consider the idea that an individual has a right to property. The right to property is very problematic to the left. Does an individual's right to the property he has earned trump any rights that *society* might have to that same property? What if some liberal needs to use the police power of government to seize some of your wealth, and repurpose it for whatever that liberal deems to serve the interests of the "common good"?

Do you exist for yourself as an individual? Or do you merely exist as a member of some group, ripe for exploitation by a collectivist society eager to use you to satisfy some vague idea of just what would serve the "greater good"?

That's an easy question for a libertarian . . . a difficult one for a liberal.

Fascist ethics begin . . . with the acknowledgment that it is not the individual who confers a meaning upon society, but it is, instead, the existence of a human society which determines the human character of the individual. According to Fascism, a true, a great spiritual life cannot take place unless the State has risen to a position of pre-eminence in the world of man. The curtailment of liberty thus becomes justified at once, and this need of rising the State to its rightful position.

—MARIO PALMIERI,
The Philosophy of Fascism, *1936*

Do you remember the 2005 fight in the U.S. Senate over George W. Bush's nomination of John Roberts to the U.S. Supreme Court?

After Roberts's nomination, Democrats and other leftists went scrambling for a reason to oppose the Roberts's nomination. Anything would do, really, but for a while they seemed to settle on whether or not Judge Roberts was ever a member of the Federalist Society. First he was; then he wasn't; then the Federalist Society said they didn't disclose members' names. And on and on it went.

Oh, what an episode![4]

So what if he was? Why all the controversy about the Federalist Society? What was it about this group that had John Roberts distancing himself? Democrats and the media were acting as if he might be a member of the Communist Party—oh, wait, on second thought they'd probably approve of that.

Maybe we'll get a clue if we go to the Society's own website. There, leading the frequently asked questions about the Federalist Society, we find our answer:

Q. What is the Federalist Society?
A. It is an organization of 35,000 lawyers, law students, scholars, and other individuals who believe and trust that individual citizens can make the best choices for themselves and society. It was founded in

---

[4] Quick! Name the movie! It featured the one person in our modern history whom I truly believe to be a traitor.

1982 by a group of law students interested in making sure that the principles of limited government embodied in our Constitution receive a fair hearing.

There you go. The dreaded "I" word appears twice in that one answer! After all, we're supposed to be *at war against individualism* in this country! Ted Kennedy told us so! So a Supreme Court nominee who belongs to an organization that not only supports the idea of individualism, but that believes that individual citizens can make better choices for themselves than can government—why, that's about as close to blasphemy as you can get, isn't it?

Sure, for a liberal. In their view, government is there to relieve them of the oppressive responsibilities that actually go with being a practicing individual! Everybody knows that individuals shouldn't try to make important decisions and choices for themselves, after all. That crucial task is best entrusted to the government!

But wait! There's more! Look at the second FAQ on the Society's website.

Q. How does the Federalist Society carry out its mission?
A. The Society's main purpose is to sponsor fair, serious, and open debate about the need to enhance individual freedom and the role of the courts in saying what the law is rather than what they wish it to be. We believe debate is the best way to ensure that legal principles that have not been the subject of sufficient attention for the past several decades receive a fair hearing.

Now the liberals' problem with the Federalist Society is becoming a little clearer. What's all this nonsense about "enhancing individual freedom"?

We have so many politicians with us today with no appreciation for history. They just know that the *It Takes a Village* approach doesn't leave much room for individual villagers.

All our lives we fought against exalting the individual, against the elevation of the single person, and long ago we were over and done with the business of a hero, and here it comes up again: the glorification of one personality. This is not good at all.

—VLADIMIR LENIN,
quoted in Not by Politics Alone: The Other Lenin,
by Tamara Deutscher

And that brings us to school honor rolls.

If you want to exalt the individual, what better way than to publish that individual's name on an honor roll? Here's someone who worked very hard to excel, and now they're being recognized for that effort! Isn't that supposed to be a good thing?

Not if you're Paul Richards, the principal of Needham High School in Needham, Massachusetts.

For years, Needham had a practice of publishing the names of the honor roll students in the local newspaper. In 2006 a parent came to Richards with a complaint. This parent[5] had three children in the school. One of the children consistently made the honor roll. The other two didn't. This was causing stress in the family.

Remember, this is a government school we're talking about. So you can guess what Principal Richards did.

The honor roll will no longer be published.

No longer will individuals be recognized for their achievements. According to Richards, the honor roll represents "an unhealthy focus on grades."

Say what? Simply honoring an individual for working hard enough to excel in high school is *unhealthy?*

Lenin would have approved. Needham High will no longer exalt the individual, will no longer glorify one personality. Whining parents will no longer have to worry that one of their children will be singled out for individual achievement.

---

[5] I'll bet you five dollars against a donut hole that the parent referenced here is a woman.

And I have no doubt that all the stress in her family will miraculously disappear.

> We must stop thinking of the individual and start thinking about what is best for society.
>
> —HILLARY CLINTON, 1993

I'm sure that's exactly what Principal Needham thinks he's doing. I wonder if it's ever occurred to this government employee that the school he runs wasn't created to educate society . . . it was created to educate the individual!

The war against individualism isn't limited to government officials and politicians. Many private citizens, it seems, have taken up arms and joined the battle.

In an alarming letter he wrote to *USA Today,* published on November 6, 2003, one Chris Wolfe responded to a story in the paper about university administrators keeping conservative student groups off campus. Wolfe defended the administrators:

> Whether an organization or person is conservative has nothing to do with decisions to prohibit certain groups or ideas from the public forum. Instead, school administrators are forbidding an environment where hate, individualism and repression are encouraged.

Yes, you read that right. This letter writer was praising administrators for prohibiting conservative groups on campus—that is, curtailing their rights to free speech and assembly—on the premise that such groups encourage "hate, individualism and repression."

So now the evil concept of individualism is equated with hate and repression.

Such is the mindset of the liberal collectivist. Only groups are worthy of recognition and attention. The individual, an instrument of evil, hate, and repression, must be suppressed.

The smallest minority on earth is the individual. Those who deny individual rights cannot claim to be defenders of minorities.

—AYN RAND

As this book is published, we're heading into one of the most exciting political seasons in my memory. Democrats will be trying to strengthen their control of Congress while putting a liberal Democrat in the White House.

Their theme for 2008, we've already heard, will be "The Common Good."

You'll hear nothing from the Democrats about individual rights, nothing about individual achievement. The entire focus will be on group dynamics. You'll hear speech after speech about "the poor" and "the less fortunate." There will be repeated demands that "the rich" step up to the plate to pay "their fair share." Much will be said about income redistribution, completely ignoring that the act of earning a living is a uniquely individual pursuit.

The war against individuals will be one of the main fronts in this war. We can expect the Democrats to enter the battle with zeal. As for the Republicans? I'm afraid any defense we get of individualism from the hapless GOP will be lukewarm at best.

I can't speak for you, but I am an individual. I exist for me, my family, and my friends—not for the state. I have individual likes and dislikes, wants and needs. Like you, I am unique, not merely a stamped-out variation of some larger group template.

Government exists to protect my rights, not to order my life. And I damn sure don't exist to serve government.

Every single person in this country should loudly proclaim his or her status as a unique and rare human being. We should loudly reject the group classifications that the left tries to force on us.

If this book accomplishes nothing else, perhaps it will wake you up to the reality of the leftist war against your status as a sovereign human being. This has been going on since the days of Lenin, and Hillary Clinton and Ted Kennedy carry the torch today.

You are not a tool of the state. You are not to be used as political cannon fodder for the elevation of a politician or political movement. You belong to you, certainly not to the government. Reclaim your ownership of yourself, and let these politicians know that you recognize and reject their war on the individual.

What better time than in the midst of our quadrennial presidential beauty contest?

> When will the world learn that a million men are of no importance compared with one man?
>
> —HENRY DAVID THOREAU

Couldn't have said it better myself.

BECAUSE SHE'S EARNED IT

At the end of my broadcast on an unremarkable winter afternoon in 2005, I signed off as usual, said goodbye to Royal and Belinda, stuffed a handful of unused newspaper articles in my briefcase, headed out to the studio's parking garage, and got in my car to drive home.

Usually I'm in the mood for a bit of peace and quiet, but not this day. Instead I turned on the radio. I got out of the studio fast enough to hear the Godfather come out of his hourly newsbreak.

Before going any further, let me make something clear: I'm a huge Rush Limbaugh fan. Nobody does talk radio better, not even me.

Moreover, Rush has made me money by elevating our industry to the top of the heap. He saved me even more through the tax cuts he promoted as part of the Republican agenda. I love what he's done for our format, what he's done for America, and what he's done *to* the left.

Rush Limbaugh did for talk radio what Arnold Palmer did for golf. Everybody who does now or ever will earn a living in talk radio owes him no less than a big wet kiss on the mouth. (Thus far, he has steadfastly refused to accept my token of gratitude.)

Liberals hate him—just *hate* him—and I love Rush for that, too.

On this particular day, I had no doubt what his subject would be, but I wanted to hear his latest thoughts. As it turned out, he had a question, directed at those he often refers to as "you liberals."

Rush wanted to know, "Why do you want Terri Schiavo to die?"

The reason I remember this day, and this broadcast, so well is simple. I was firmly entrenched on the opposite side of the issue. In fact, I was pretty much hanging out there alone. Rush, Sean Hannity, G. Gordon Liddy, and the rest of my not-so-liberal radio colleagues were all reading from the same playbook: Terri Schiavo must be kept alive. Period.

The question intrigued me. Why *did* I want Terri Schiavo to die?

Yes, you that read correctly. I actually *wanted* Terri Schiavo to die. I wanted the courts to release her from the hell her soul was being forced to endure.

Why write about the case now? It's old news, right?

Wrong.

Terri Schiavo became a household name, but, sadly, she's far from the only person whose life has been artificially and needlessly prolonged through advances in medical technology. Only a few, like Karen Ann Quinlan and Nancy Cruzan, have become well known. But there are many, many others—and, as unpleasant as it is to contemplate, any one of us, or a loved one, could someday be in the same situation.

In the unlikely event you've forgotten the sad case of Terri Schiavo, allow me a very brief refresher here. She was young, just twenty-six, when she unexpectedly collapsed in her Florida home way back in 1990. For the next ten weeks Terri remained comatose. Eventually doctors decided she had lapsed into a persistent vegetative state. There was, they agreed, absolutely no chance of recovery.

Her loving parents continued to hold out hope—wishful, if understandable, thinking. What they were so earnestly praying for, however, was beyond the realm of possibility.

Eventually, in 1998, Michael Schiavo, Terri's husband and legal guardian, defied the wishes of his in-laws by petitioning the courts to remove her feeding tube. A fierce legal battle ensued, but when the issue came to a head, the aftermath of 9/11 was dominating the headlines, and the case attracted little attention from the national media.

It wasn't until 2003, after a federal court of appeals upheld numerous lower court rulings granting Michael Schiavo's petition to terminate treatment, that the national media truly discovered the Terri Schiavo case. Along with the wave of publicity came well-intended but misguided efforts to "save" Terri Schiavo. These efforts succeeded in keeping her "alive" (if that's the proper word) for another two years.

Over and over America was treated to a grim videotape on the cable news channels, a shot of someone dangling a balloon over Terri's expressionless face. Many who watched the tape believed that her eyes were following that balloon, and quite a few believed they could discern a crooked smile on her face.

Every credible medical authority, however, chalked up such movement to an involuntary reflex action. The lights had gone out in Terri Schiavo's mind, they explained.

Terri's family clung to their state of delusion. They talked of taking her to the mall for her birthday once appropriate treatments restored her to a state of awareness. Spurious medical experts were presented to offer opinions on Terri's condition and the hope for improvement. Other "experts" were brought forth to offer opinions that Terri had been beaten and abused, perhaps even strangled, by her husband.

Finally, Terri Schiavo's feeding tube was removed. Thirteen days later, she was at peace.

Two months after Terri Schiavo was pronounced dead, the results of the autopsy were made public. The autopsy confirmed that Terri was in a persistent vegetative state. She had suffered massive and irreversible brain damage. Huge parts of her brain had actually liquefied. And there was no evidence of any type of abuse at the hands of her husband.

The doctors also reported that Terri was blind. The part of her brain that controls vision was gone. She hadn't been following that balloon with her eyes. She never did smile in recognition of loved ones when they walked into her hospice room.

So, why did I want Terri Schiavo to die? Rush's question deserved an answer—not some glib response, but an honest, heartfelt answer.

Here it is: I wanted Terri Schiavo to die because she had *earned* it.

You see, I don't view death as the end of the journey of a human soul. I view it as a transition.

The God I believe in would not waste the total life experiences of a human created in his image on a total and complete final death—a dead end, if you will, with nothing to follow. I simply cannot believe that it's God's plan that the life experiences of a man—wisdom gained, lessons learned, and love experienced—should disappear after death as if they never happened.

Rather, I believe that there's something that follows the life we know on this Earth. In fact, I believe that most of the people who fought to keep the body of Terri Schiavo alive feel the same way.

These feelings give rise to some questions of my own—questions for the devoutly religious people who tried so passionately to keep Terri Schiavo on those feeding tubes.

Do you believe in God's promise of everlasting life? Do you believe that the reward for a life well spent on this earth is a life with God in heaven after you die? If you do, then a few more questions, if you will. . . .

Do you believe the human soul can make the transition to everlasting life while the human body that carried that soul clings to life on this earth? If you do, then you must surely believe that Terri Schiavo had earned and was already enjoying her reward in Heaven even as her empty body continued to breathe. Under those circumstances, why was it so important to you that the unneeded body of Terri Schiavo be kept alive?

But there is another possibility. What if the human soul is so inextricably connected with its earthly body that the complete transition simply isn't made until that body ceases functioning, until genuine death occurs? Under *those* circumstances, how could you so ardently desire that the soul of Terri Schiavo spend five, ten, perhaps thirty years or more trapped in a useless and nonfunctioning husk, unable to move on to whatever reward awaits her? Wasn't fifteen years enough?

Where did your concerns truly lie? With the eternal soul of Terri Schiavo, or with her earthly body?

Most of us are aware of the stories related by people who have near-death experiences. Usually, such things occur during a surgical procedure, severe trauma, or other medical emergency. These people describe a sensation of leaving their body at the very time the heart stops beating and the brain ceases functioning. They tell of floating above their body while watching doctors below working hard to resuscitate, to bring them back to life. As the heart once again starts beating and as the brain resumes its functions, they tell of a sensation of falling back into their own body to resume life.

Of course, we don't hear from the patients upon whom resuscitation efforts are not successful. We don't hear from them because they've left us. They're gone on to experience whatever lies beyond. We call it death. I suspect that from their perspective they would call it a rebirth.

Is it possible that the soul of Terri Schiavo was floating—held in some prolonged and excruciating limbo—waiting for doctors to stop interfering with the process of her death? I believed it was—possible, at the very least—and that's why I supported her husband's desires to have her feeding tube removed.

Terri Schiavo wasn't murdered. She was allowed to die.

Death was not the end for Terri Schiavo. It was a beginning. She was finally being allowed to enjoy the reward we all seek—a reward she deserved, a reward she earned.

During the entire Schiavo affair, I received 15,683 letters and e-mails from outraged listeners, informing me in no uncertain terms that they were "never going to listen to me again." After the autopsy results showed that Terri was gone long before the plug was pulled, about three of these people wrote back to apologize.

As for the rest of you . . . no problem. Your apology is accepted, too.

I'M NEVER GOING TO LISTEN TO YOU AGAIN

Being the computer genius I unquestionably am, I've developed a little algorithm that I use to compute current listenership levels for my show. One of the factors that must be plugged into this hideously complicated program is the number of "I'm never going to listen to you again" e-mails I've received in the previous seven days.

At great expense (borne by the publisher of this fine book), I recently rented some time on a university supercomputer to run the program. The results? As of July Fourth weekend, 2006, I had actually accumulated a negative number of listeners.

Now, how could that happen? It's no mystery. The reason is my big mouth. I just can't help saying what I really think instead of what I think people want me to say.

During the last week alone, I've committed the following sins on my program:

1. I refused to support a Constitutional amendment to criminalize flag burning.

2. I refused to state unequivocally my total and complete acceptance of and belief in the Genesis story of a six-day creation, and instead offered my belief in the theory of evolution. I even went so far as to suggest that our world, and all that is in it, is older than six thousand years.

3. I refused to exhibit a hatred and/or fear of homosexuals and to go into a screaming scripture-quoting hype-panic over the "homosexual agenda."

4. I congratulated the infamous Ninth Circuit Court of Appeals for their correct ruling that classroom recitations of the Pledge of Allegiance were unconstitutional because of the phrase "Under God."

5. I dared to suggest that government schools might not be the best place for compulsory religious observances.

Shame on me. It can now be said with certainty that I am damned to eternity in hell.

All in a week's time.

Actually, any one of those transgressions would be enough to get the INGTLTYA (I'm Never Going to Listen to You Again) e-mail flowing. Load them all into one week, and Internet servers shut down trying to handle the increased outraged e-mail load.

More results from my computer research:

If every single person who has ever sent me an INGTLTYA e-mail or letter were still tuned in to *The Neal Boortz Show,* I would have somewhere around 32 million listeners and Sean Hannity would be screening my phone calls.[1]

I would guess that the people who write me these INGTLTYA e-mails and letters expect me to be distraught when I receive them. Not so. First of all, I know that these listeners, by and large, aren't going anywhere. Their e-mails are the adult equivalent of "You won't play nice so I'm going to take my ball and go home." The child is right back on the playground the next day. If, by chance, they are serious, then they're not the type of listeners I revel in anyway.

---

[1] Sean never gets INGTLTYA emails. He has a much more pleasant personality than I. People will tolerate a difference of opinion with Sean because he's so damned likeable . . . not to mention irresistibly cute.

I've always liked the old saying, "If two people agree on everything, one of them isn't necessary." One of the most boring things you can listen to in talk radio is two people, a caller and the host, in complete agreement on all points.

"You're amazing! I listen to you all the time!"

"No, you're amazing. I'm glad you called!"

"I'm so excited to be talking to you."

"Thank you! I'm so excited you called!"

"I agree with everything you say!"

"That's fantastic! I'm glad to hear that!"

"You ought to run for president!"

"You're right, I ought to run for president."

Gag me! Where's the dump button?[2]

My longtime executive producer, Belinda Skelton, is under longstanding instructions to favor callers who disagree with me. Callers who want to argue get on the air a lot quicker than those who just want to tell me how wise I am. After all, the obvious isn't always entertaining. I should add, though, that callers who want to take me on are going to be held to a high performance standard on the air. For those who fail to keep things entertaining . . . another caller is just a button away.

Oh, and while we're talking about buttons: I have a quick message for those of you who send me the whiney little e-mails saying, "You always cut off people who disagree with you." Know what? You're right. I do. But the truth is, I cut off *all* the callers. How often do you hear a caller say, "Well, Neal, that's really all I had to say. Bye-bye!" That's right—never. If we waited until every caller had said all he came to say, we wouldn't have ten listeners.

---

[2] If there's one caller comment that is absolutely, drop-dead guaranteed to make any radio talk show cringe and bang his head against the wall, it's the hyper-irritating "Long time listener, first time caller" bit. I wish I had a button that could send a load of llama spit through the telephone of the next person who pulls that one on me. Can you imagine how many times I've heard that? Thankfully, most listeners can only say it once.

Most people out there are mature enough to tolerate opinions offered by a talk jockey with goodwill and a bit of curiosity. Those who aren't write INGTLTYA e-mails. It's a reflection on them, not on the host.

Take another look at the five INGTLTYA topics I mentioned above. We have flag burning, creation vs. evolution, homosexuality, the Pledge of Allegiance, and prayer in the schools. Do you notice a common thread there? All but one of them, flag burning, deal with religion.

I can tell you without equivocation that throughout my three-plus decades of talk radio, the most vile, nasty, evil, cruel, vicious, irrational and just plain mean e-mails and letters I've received have come from people desperate to proclaim their status as devout Christians. Virtually all of the INGTLTYA messages have come from people who are upset because I've expressed an opinion that isn't consistent with their view of what a good, God-fearing Christian should be.

Now, I've expressed opinions on the air that were critical of Israel. Not one INGTLTYA letter from a Jew. Since 9/11, of course, I've expressed many negative opinions on the air about the wonderful, peaceful religion of Islam. I've called for racial profiling of Arabs in security lines at airports. Through all of this, I can honestly say that I've received not one e-mail from a Muslim listener that I would consider even rude, much less hateful. I've said ugly things about the Americans with Disabilities Act, referring to the "tyranny of the disabled." Nasty messages? None.

Liberals may call me a fool, a moron, a neo-con, a hate-filled conservative cretin, a chicken hawk, or a Bush sycophant, but seldom has a liberal told me he was tuning out because of my views on some issue.

Nope . . . it seems that the INGTLTYA message market has been completely cornered by those who call themselves Christians.

Do I pay a price for my failure to toe the fundamentalist Christian line on the air? You bet I do.[3] One of the major players in talk radio in

---

[3] Or, as they say in Texas, "Do a hog love slop?"

America is Salem Communications. Salem has talk radio stations in several major markets where my program isn't carried. Several times in recent years program directors of these stations have explored the idea of adding my show to their lineup (something to do with increasing their ratings), only to be told by top management that there is no way in . . . well, let's just say that no way in the *world* that Boortz is ever going to be on their station.

Look, I'm not slamming Salem here. The website for Salem Communications clearly states: "Research has shown that our News Talk format is highly complementary to our core format of Christian Teaching and Talk." Now, I consider myself to be a Christian. In high school, everyone expected that I was going to be an Episcopal minister. I admire devout Christians who live their lives as an example for all to follow.

For the life of me, though, I can't figure out why so many of them are forgetful when it comes to that "judge not lest ye be judged" thing.

With my views on things like abortion and homosexuality, though, the fact is that there's no room for me on a Salem station. A Christian I may be, but I'm not their particular type of Christian.

The folks who run Salem are good radio people. I know many of the executives there, and on a personal level we get along just fine. Mike Gallagher, one of their hosts, is a good personal friend, and the other hosts in their stable are certainly quite talented. Salem owns the stations, and they're more than entitled to program them along any philosophical or religious lines they wish. I just think it's worth pointing out that my show would be carried by far more stations, and my listening audience would be exponentially larger, if I just went along with the fundamentalist program. All I'd have to do is oppose a woman's right to chose, demand prayer in the schools, and tremble in fear of the (gasp!) "gay agenda."

No thanks. I'll just be honest with my listeners. Those stations that want to carry the show are welcome to do so, and the listeners who care to can just hang around to see what I'm going to do next.

Let's start by talking about burning the flag.

FLAG BURNING

Here's a tough question: Just why does our First Amendment protect freedom of speech?

Okay, maybe that's unfair. Chances are you went to a government school, so the subject may never have come up. Not your fault. Let's take it step by step:

Do you suppose the founding fathers[1] decided we needed to protect speech so that people would be free to say things other people were just bustin' to hear? Oh, sure. They took time out to ensure that people would be free to say things that would make everyone feel warm, fuzzy, secure, appreciated, loved, and respected!

Wrong.

This whole freedom of speech thing is about protecting speech that the masses[2] might find not to their liking. It's there not to protect expressions that make you feel good, but to protect expressions that make you want to pound someone to a pulp.

Which brings us to desecrating the American flag.

Look . . . I take a back seat to no one when it comes to my love for

---

[1] The PC term these days is "framers." They weren't framers, they were the men who wrote our Declaration of Independence and our Constitution. The framers put wood borders around them and hung them in courthouses around the country. Perhaps I ought to write a chapter on what our Constitution would look like if it had been written by the founding mothers. Read on. We'll see if I have the %(# to do that.

[2] Sometimes referred to as the "dumb masses." Be sure to say it slowly and distinctly.

this country. I believe that every person born in this great land is blessed beyond measure. Never in the history of civilization has any country or system of government done more to lift more people out of poverty and enabled them to live in freedom than has the United States.

Do we have our detractors? You bet! When you're weak, it's only natural to hate those with power, and there is no question that the United States is the most powerful nation on earth, both militarily and economically.

A poll of Western Europeans taken in 2006 showed that 58 percent wished for a weaker America. Thanks a lot, Euro-wimps. Sure, you want a weaker America, right up until you find your own sweet little collectivist, welfare-state posteriors threatened by a force you're incapable of or unwilling to deal with. Then suddenly a strong United States becomes your all-time best friend.

The Euro-weasels believe that weakening America will make them stronger. That's like believing that shaving someone else's head will help you grow hair. Most Europeans are at risk of being under Islamic rule in the not-too-distant future. We'll see how much they enjoy a weak America then.

For those of you who are tempted to agree with the Euro-wimps—those who are tired of America being, as they say, the world's policeman—a question: Who would you prefer?

Somebody, some country, some leader, is always going to step forward to be the world's policeman. Some nation is always going to be the world's strongest economic and/or political power. And if it's not the United States, who will it be but some dictator, some tyrant, some oppressive regime or dangerous ideology?

Of course, if you don't want that nation to be the United States, I guess that's fine. Go ahead, have it your way. But remember, power abhors a vacuum. So which nation would you choose to run the show? Which elected leader, which tyrant or despot do you want to lead the way? Who do you want the world's cop to be?

Okay, I'll give you a hint. Who are the two likely candidates besides the United States? Those would be Russia and Communist China. So . . . belly up to the bar of international intrigue and tell us what you'll have.

But back to this flag-desecration thing.

People don't burn flags to keep warm. They burn flags to make a statement. Usually that statement is one of anger, disgust, or hatred of the United States or something our country is doing. Well, guess what? That's what freedom of speech is for: It allows people to show their anger, disgust, or hatred for this country, just as it allows them to show their love and appreciation.

Here's my fundamental problem with those who want to ban flag-burning: to punish those who desecrate our national flag would be a sign of weakness, or an inability to take the worst criticism someone has to offer and come away standing tall. To accept that criticism, on the other hand, shows that we're strong—that we're able to take the punches and remain proud and unbowed.

When I've discussed this issue on the air, people go out of their way to try to make counterarguments. Some listeners have actually e-mailed to tell me that the Constitution says "freedom of speech," and that burning a flag isn't actually "speech," so it's fair game to be banned. These people actually believe that freedom of speech protects only *spoken words,* nothing else. I guess that means those bumper stickers, signs in your yards, and letters to Mom are all subject to government approval.

See? Didn't take long to destroy that idiotic argument.

America is strong enough to withstand expressions of disagreement, anger, even outright hatred. The very act of burning an American flag is an acknowledgment of our freedoms by those who profess to hate us. To criminalize these actions would be to affirm the worst things they say about America.

Some contend that our flag occupies a unique status as the symbol of our country, and that as such it deserves special protection. Now, there's your ultimate slippery slope. Special protection for this particular symbol today . . . and for what tomorrow? How soon before each religion steps forward to lobby for laws protecting its own symbols? Isn't that exactly what the peaceful, gentle religion of Islam is doing in Europe right now? In fact, the European Union is considering a law that would make it illegal to make a disparaging remark about the religion of Islam. Isn't that just amazing? Even as Islamic fascists are celebrating their all-but-assured conquering of Western Europe, the Euro-weenies are working on laws that would slam you in the brig if you said anything insensitive about them.

You see? The danger of outlawing freedom of expression on matters religious in Eurabia[3] is pretty obvious. Yet many of us are blinded to the danger of outlawing expressions of outrage in our own culture.

Of course, every two years there's a whole raft of politicians who pander to voters on this issue. A quick word to them: Campaigning for laws to ban flag desecration says one thing about your priorities—that your desire to get reelected outweighs whatever respect you have for our traditions of free speech and expression.

Now, having said all of this, let me add a personal note.

I would like to propose to the various states a little addition to their criminal code. The crime in question would be "kicking the crap out of anyone who makes a public display of desecrating the American Flag." The penalty for such a breach, I propose, should be a fine not to exceed $1.00 or five minutes in the custody of the police.

Rights or no rights, I'm just not wired to stand by and watch someone burn my flag.

---

[3] Okay . . . it might be a bit early to start referring to Europe as Eurabia, but the Islamification of Europe seems all but certain, and I'm an ahead-of-the-curve kind of guy.

EVOLUTION VS. CREATION

I must be an unadulterated fool for even bringing this up in this book. But since this is one of the most common causes of the INGTLTYA e-mails, it must be dealt with.

The principal reason we even get into discussions on creation vs. evolution on the show is that politicians are continuously trying to pander to devout Christians by having the Biblical theory of creation taught in our government schools. Call it intelligent design if you want to, but it's still straight from Genesis. And, as such, it has no place being taught in a government-operated school.

At least the courts consistently get this one right.

I believe that the earth is billions of years old, not six thousand. I believe that life evolved on this earth over that period of billions of years, not in six days.

I don't believe that any of this precludes the existence of God.

Thousands of years ago, people were curious about the origins of life. They asked those whom they thought would have the answers, their religious leaders, how they got here. Those religious leaders did not have the advantage of carbon-dating techniques or any of the vast scientific evidence available to us today. Nonetheless, they needed an answer for their followers.

Put yourself in the place of one of these ancient religious leaders. You've been asked where we came from and how we got here. You're supposed to have all the answers. Your leadership position is under challenge.

If you give the wrong answer, or one that's too difficult to comprehend, someone else might come along with a more attractive doctrine, and the next thing you know you're tending a flock of sheep in the wilderness somewhere.

So when that question comes, what's your answer? A simple "beats the hell out of me" isn't going to work. Besides, hell hasn't even been invented yet.

The whole story of creation, as set forth in Genesis, was simply the best that the religious leaders of those days could come up with, given the information and tools they had to search for the truth. There is absolutely nothing in the concept of evolution that prohibits the belief that the whole convoluted chain of events was set in motion by a supreme being. It would, after all, take a pretty bright and imaginative God to come up with us and all that we have around us.

If you want your children taught that this earth and all life on it was created in six days, just as Genesis says, then make sure that's the lesson plan in your Sunday school, or at home. With luck, when your children grow up they'll be gracious enough not to laugh at you.

Those who adamantly deny the theory of evolution will come up with arguments they claim to be based in science. Some of these arguments are even rather clever!

Take the argument based on the Second Law of Thermodynamics. (I'm no science textbook author, so bear with me.) Let's just say that the Second Law states that, absent the application of energy, a closed system will tend toward disorder rather than order. A jigsaw puzzle in a box won't put itself together until energy is applied from the outside—say, by a ten-year-old girl staying home from school with the sniffles.

Ah, but what of the Earth? the creationists will say. In the closed system of our world there was no outside application of energy, so how could the Second Law apply? How could the order of our universe have been extracted from its original state of disorder?

Two-word answer: the Sun.

Other creationists will tell you that there is no fossil evidence of evolutionary change. Sorry—they're wrong, too. There is such fossil evidence. For instance, we have fossils that illustrate how fish capable of living only in the sea were transformed into reptiles capable of living on land; and equally persuasive evidence of how certain reptiles were transformed into birds. It's there. Creationists just refuse to recognize it.

Subject: creation
Name: chris _____
E-mail: CM____@_____ .com

Who says those are transitional fossils. They are fossils of an extinct animal that had traits of 2 different classes of species, perhaps a species we are not even aware of. Think outside the box and shame on you for thinking you can understand or deserve to understand how God can do anything, you are his creation not the other way around you fool.

See what I mean? (Or, on the other hand, maybe you see what *they* mean. If readers are anything like listeners, I guess I might have lost a bunch of you right there. Maybe I should have made this the last chapter in the book.)

Whatever you believe, just remember one thing: There is nothing in evolutionary theory that precludes the existence of God or the role of God in the shaping of our universe and our earth. It all comes down to whether or not you're willing to accept the advanced knowledge that science and technology bring us.

I'm quite sure that a thousand years after it was proved conclusively that the Earth revolves around the Sun there were still many people roaming the earth who would swear that those who preach such nonsense are tools of Satan.

Some things never change.

HOMOSEXUALS AND THEIR (GASP!) AGENDA

Trust me, I know how to get my listeners worked up during my radio show. I know where the buttons are, and there are some days when I just love to push them.

Homosexuality is one of those buttons. A big one. In fact, other than religion, I really can't think of any topic that lights listeners up—and I don't mean in a good way—as reliably as homosexuality . . . especially when I suggest that scientific evidence points to a genetic basis for homosexuality.

For some reason, there are people who just cannot bear the thought that homosexuality isn't a choice.

The listener e-mails come pouring in whenever I start in about homosexuality, and boy, these are a loving bunch of folks. (Their grammar is just as bad.) Read for yourself:

Subject: my e-mail
Name: John _____

Boortz are you a homosexual? Is this why the strong defense of this perversion? Why haven't you read my e-mail which is clear homosexuals will NOT inherit the Kingdom of God, and they will inhereit the due penalty for their wicked behavior. Jesus may not have spoken directly of this subject, however God

inspired the writers of the Bible to speak on it. Unless they
repent they're doomed. Boortz do some research. You sound
foolish. Call 800–555–5555 and ask for John for a sound,
Godly, doctrinal conversation.

I really do hope that John didn't sit by the phone waiting for me to
call for his sound, godly, doctrinal conversation.

Here's something interesting: It's the men—only the men—who
get so infuriated when this topic comes up on the air.

I'm sure you've heard the old theory that the men who get so upset
and start throwing hissy fits when the subject of homosexuality
comes up are probably suppressing homosexual feelings themselves.
That's a bunch of hooey, right?

Wrong. Seems there's actually something to it! In the mid-1990s
researchers at the University of Georgia decided to put the theory to
the test.[1] The researchers used a questionnaire known as the Index of
Homophobia[2] to identify thirty-five homophobic men and twenty-
nine nonhomophobic men. All subjects were white, and none had
ever engaged in a homosexual act.

The men were hooked up to devices that could scientifically measure what we might say is the most important male sexual response.
Let's just say the gizmo measured swelling, and leave it at that.[3]

The text subjects were then shown three types of X-rated movies:
one heterosexual, one lesbian, and one gay. All were pretty graphic.

You already know where this is going, don't you?

---

[1] "Is Homophobia Associated with Homosexual Arousal?" Henry E. Adams, PhD, Lester W.
Wright, Jr., PhD and Bethany A. Lohr, University of Georgia; *Journal of Abnormal Psychology*,
Vol. 105, No. 3. August 1966.

[2] Perhaps you'd like to take the test yourself! Here's your link: http://www.bgsu.edu/down
loads/sa/file14259.pdf

[3] I'm told that the University of Georgia researchers had a pet name for this device. The "peter
meter." Clever people, researchers.

When shown the heterosexual movie, both groups showed a sexual response. Let's say they, er, liked what they saw.

Then came the lesbian movie. Again . . . both groups "registered" approval. Thus proving that all men are pigs. All men. No exceptions.

Then—*ta-da!*—showtime! Time for the homo-video!

Finally, the men were shown a movie clip depicting a homosexual encounter. And guess what? (I know you're way ahead of me here.) For the first time they did not show essentially identical responses.

The homophobic men seemed to make the dials on the peter meter jump quite a bit more than did the nonhomophobic men. In fact, 54 percent of the homophobic men showed definite excitement, while another 26 percent showed moderate arousal. Add it up: That's 80 percent of the homophobic men showing quite a little gay streak, if you will, when watching a homosexual video, while 66 percent of the nonhomophobic men showed nothing.

Say it ain't so! you might be saying. Sorry, no can do—because it *is* so. The researchers drew the only possible conclusion: This study demonstrates that most homophobic men have repressed homosexual desires.

Don't you just love it? Could there possibly be a better outcome of this study?

Is there a Nobel Prize for just deserts?

Subject: Best Friend
Name: Mike H_____
E-mail: m*****@msn.com

Is it true that Mark Foley and Barney Frank are your new best friends? I'm sure they are proud of you for pushing their sick lifestyle.

No wonder I get those INGTLTYA letters when I fail to exhibit the requisite degree of homophobia on the show. These men don't particularly like being reminded of their suppressed urges. (Lord, I hope I'm not turning them on!)

The scientific evidence points to homosexuality being a matter of genetics. Homosexuality is *not* a choice. (Though I do want to take note of the LUGs—"Lesbians Until Graduation," for those of you who aren't quite as in tune with the popular culture as your humble author. There seems to be quite a fad of high school and college-age women claiming to be lesbians and dating other girls. This is good for a little shock value, of course, but the truth is, these kids aren't gay. They're just yanking your chain.)

Subject: Homosexuals
Name: Chuck H _____
E-mail: _____@hotmail.com

There is not one shred of scientific evidence to support your claim that homosexuals are born as homosexuals. It is a complete choice. Just like adultery, murder, theft, cursing and all other sins. Man, in his own ignorance, chooses to do right or wrong. But in those choices, man has to give account for his actions. I have a sister and a nephew that are completely engulfed in the sin of sodomy. I love them both very much and I pray for them each day. Sorry, Neal. But you are wrong on this one.

Sorry, Chuckie, you're the one who's wrong. If you doubt it, crank up the computer and start Googling. You'll find plenty of studies that show rather conclusively that homosexuality is not a chosen sexual orientation.

This "homosexuality is a choice" nonsense can be put to bed with one question: Just tell me: At what point in your life did you decide that you were going to be a *hetero*sexual? Come on, surely you can remember such a big decision! Why, it must be one of the most important decisions you ever made! A decision that determined whether or not you would have children—whether or not you would be ostracized and hated by a significant segment of our population. Surely that must have made some kind of impression on your memory, no?

What was that decision-making process like, anyway? Was it when that little girl with the hazel eyes winked at you in the seventh grade? Did you go sit by yourself in the library and think: "Okay, Joe. This is it! Here I am, almost twelve years old, and girls are winking at me. I knew this day would come, sooner or later. *Hmmmmmmmmmm. . . .* Know what! I think I'll be a heterosexual!"

How long did you agonize over it? For an hour? A day? A week?

However long it took, it seems like you made the bold decision to be straight.

Well, good for you.

Subject: Homosexuals
Name: Vicki
E-mail: --------@earthlink.net

Hi Neal. Just heard part of your show today. You were discussing the topic of homosexuality and how it is not a choice, etc. I have to say you give the appearance of being a homosexual yourself as you keep harping on this topic like you are trying to make heterosexuals accept it without question and to change their beliefs just because your are trying to convince us its OK. Only people who are into what they are trying to defend, defend topics with such vim and vigor as you are doing. All you have done is convince me you are a homosexual yourself.

And what of those who "chose to be gay"? Why would they do *that?* Can you name one man who would choose to be homosexual after having just one bowl of chili and some onion rings at a Hooters restaurant? Who would say, "Yeah, that's very nice and all, but I really think I'd rather choose a lifestyle where I'm discriminated against on the job and in my church, and where I'm constantly derided and condemned by much of society. Instead of being a solid and respected member of my community, I think I'm just going to opt for a lifestyle where idiots assume that I'm a child molester"?

Come on—give me one reason you'd *choose* to be gay! You want to be a designer and live in Milan? Okay, touché. But just one more!

Fine, Neal, you say, *but you're missing the point. Homosexuality just isn't normal.*

Guess what? You're absolutely right! It isn't natural . . . for you. You are *straight,* remember? So any homosexual act would be abnormal for you.

Gay sex, on the other hand, is perfectly natural . . . for homosexuals!

Why does this have to be such a big issue? Why do so many men find it so difficult simply to allow others to live their lives in step with their own sexual orientation, while you do the same? (Oh, right, I almost forgot—that little Georgia study.)

Some people—former Pennsylvania Republican senator Rick Santorum comes to mind—actually adopted the policy that it's just fine with them if you're gay, just so long as you don't have sex.

Say *what?*

It's perfectly okay for you to be homosexual—as long as you keep it in your pants? As long as you don't mind being denied all the pleasures of a loving sexual relationship?

You know, because the straight guys don't think you're *doing it the right way.*

Think about that. What if a homosexual thought the way *you* have sex—with someone *of another gender*—was wrong? What if they suggested that it would be okay for you to go on being heterosexual . . . just so long as you didn't have sex?

Does that work for you?

If you're part of the problem here—and the problem isn't homosexuals, it's the people who campaign against them—then there's something you need to realize: As more and more people in this country come to understand the secret longings lurking beneath all that homophobia—the way those Georgia scientists discovered—you won't be able to stay in the closet much longer.

One more thing. If you eliminate people from your life just because you have a problem with their sexual orientation, you're going to miss out on knowing, and becoming friends with, some of the most funny, loyal, and dependable friends you could ever hope for.

That, too, is a matter of choice.

Subject: Are They For Real???
Name: Charlene L_____
E-mail: C_____@earthlink.net

Message:

Neal—Please tell me that the e-mails you are reading are just a joke. . . . I cannot believe that people are really that hate-filled!!!!

Yes, Charlene. They're for real. And we love each and every one of them.

THE NINTH CIRCUIT
AND THE PLEDGE
OF ALLEGIANCE

In June 2002, the infamous Ninth Circuit Court of Appeals ruled that the 1954 law—signed by President Dwight D. Eisenhower—that added the words "under God" to our Pledge of Allegiance was unconstitutional. In many circles, the condemnation of the Ninth Circuit and the ruling was immediate and overwhelming.

Me? I agreed with the ruling. And it probably brought on the greatest deluge of INGTLTYA letters in my career.

To begin with, I'm not all that fond of the pledge. Just what does it mean to "pledge allegiance," either to the flag or to "the republic for which it stands"?

Maybe the best person to ask would be the person who wrote the Pledge in the first place. His name was Francis Bellamy, and you may be surprised to learn that he was a socialist. Bellamy actually wrote the pledge as an *advertising slogan* to help in a campaign to sell American flags to schools. Its purpose, he said, was to teach obedience to the state as a virtue.

Now, I don't know about you, but this "obedience to the state" stuff doesn't rest all that easy with me. I see virtue in living your life responsibly and in such a manner that you don't become a burden on others. I see no intrinsic virtue in obeying the state. Adhering to the rule of law? Maybe. But "obeying" the state?

I don't feel any real need to defend myself here, but let me make it clear that I love this country. I am perfectly willing, on an individual basis, to pledge my allegiance to the United States. I'm just not in tune with the idea of forced patriotism. Either you feel it or you don't. It doesn't look right when despotic regimes like North Korea's Kim Jong Il parade thousands of little schoolchildren through the public streets wearing their neat little uniforms and chanting their love of their "Dear Leader." And to my mind, it doesn't look right when *our* government compels children to stand and pledge allegiance before all the readin', writin', and 'rithmetic starts.

When President Eisenhower signed the law adding the words "under God" to the pledge in 1954, he said: "From this day forward, the millions of our schoolchildren will daily proclaim in every city and town, every village and rural schoolhouse, the dedication of our Nation and our people to the Almighty."

Hold on a second. I thought our Constitution promised that our Congress would "make no law respecting an establishment of religion"?

So what was a president of the United States doing signing a bill into law that recognized the concept of monotheism—and, for that matter, that recognized one God in particular—while celebrating the fact that children in government schools would now be obliged to proclaim their national dedication to that God? At that time, most government schools actually *required* the pledge at the beginning of the school day. A government-mandated acknowledgment of our national dedication to God?

Come on, folks. You're not going to try to convince me that this doesn't run afoul of that "establishment of religion" thing, are you?

Well, the Ninth Circuit said it did, I agreed, and who knows how many tens of thousands of people turned off their radios and sent me their little INGTLTYA e-mail.

And that brings us to. . . .

PRAYER IN THE SCHOOLS

Let's start by correcting the record. Regardless of what you may think, or what you may have been told, no court—federal or state—has ever ruled that you can't pray in a government school. As someone once noted, as long as there are math tests there will be prayers in government schools. They're permanent fixtures, like drug-sniffing dogs and locker searches.

What the courts *have* ruled is that government employees working in government institutions cannot lead children—who, by the way, are trapped in those institutions by compulsory attendance laws—in government-prescribed religious observances.

Here's the trouble: According to the school prayer lovers, if you don't think our children should engage in a daily prayer in our government schools, you must be a horn-sprouting Jesus-hating heathen with a standing appointment at the fires of hell—a date that can't come soon enough for the make-'em-pray crowd.

Then again, the other side's not much better. If you *do* approve of prayer in our government schools, these types see you as a toothless, religious, snake-handling zealot with huge hair and plastic slipcovers on your furniture who speaks in tongues *(tall? venti? grande?)* to the poor girl at the Starbucks drive-through.

This whole controversy started with the United States Supreme Court's decision *Engle v. Vitale* (not Dick) in 1962. The New York State Board of Regents, which runs the state's government schools, adopted a policy on moral and spiritual training in government schools in the late 1950s. One component of that policy was this prayer, to be recited by government school students:

> *Almighty God, we acknowledge our dependence upon Thee, and we beg Thy blessings upon us, our parents, our teachers and our Country.*[1]

Along come the puddin'-stirring squad, in the form of the Board of Education of Union Free School District No. 9 in Hyde Park. The board took it upon themselves to instruct all principals to make sure that the prescribed prayer was recited by the students every day in class. It didn't take long before a group of parents were marching off to the local courthouse to file their lawsuits. They based their case, of course, on the provision in the First Amendment that "Congress shall make no law respecting an establishment of religion."

The local state court ruled against the parents, as did the New York Court of Appeals. So off to the U.S. Supreme Court they went!

The Board of Education, joined by other proponents of prayer in the schools, argued that no child was *compelled* to recite the prayer. The students were free to leave the room, or to stand there with their mouths shut.

You'd think these professional educators would have known a little more about the social dynamics of schoolchildren. Show me a child who leaves the classroom every day when the mandatory prayer is being recited, and I'll show you a child who's tormented endlessly by his classmates. In case it's somehow escaped your attention, young children can be cruel; all it would take is a few mornings spent waiting outside while his fellow classmates recited the mandated daily

---

[1] Clearly the Christian religion and public expressions of dependence on God were much more politically correct in New York in the 1950s than they would be today. The "Holiday Tree" had not yet made its December debut, and a "Spring Bunny" would be a plush toy with a Slinky inside.

prayer in unison to start a chain of events that would make that child's life miserable for years.

As you might suspect, the Supreme Court ruled in favor of the parents—that is, against a policy of government-ordered school prayer. This was the moment when, according to many Americans, God was taken out of our classrooms. It's a shame, isn't it, that such people are convinced that God needs a mandatory government permission slip to make His presence felt in a classroom (or anywhere, for that matter)?

In the Court's majority opinion, Justice Hugo Black wrote that governments (and that means government schools) can't create "official prayers for any group of the American people to recite as a part of a religious program carried on by the government."

Just what part of that doesn't make sense to you? Put your emotions aside for a moment. Do you really support the idea that the government should be leading children, who are bound by compulsory attendance laws, in a religious observance designed by the government?

Well . . . strangely enough, some people believe just that. Since the Supremes' decision in 1962, there have been attempts all over the country, at the state and local level, to reintroduce prayer in the schools. Some officials have attempted to circumvent the Court's decision, and our Constitution, by instituting "moments of silence." Others have referred to the prayer as a brief meditation. As fast as the ideas are run up the flagpole, the courts knock them down.

But that's history. I'm more interested in the principle of the thing. The whole "prayer in the schools" movement starts to unravel—starts to look, perhaps, a little sinister—when you really try to explore the proponents' motives. Just why is it so important to them that prayer sessions be returned to government schools? Ask them, and I'm sure they would tell you that they're doing it for their children. But is that really the case?

Let's say you have two grade-school children. Let's further stipulate that you are abusing those children (by sending them off to the government to be educated, that is). Now you start insisting that they be led in prayer in those schools every day. Why? Is this something that's neglected at home?

No, you say. You're a devout Christian. That's great—you're to be admired. Other than the child abuse thing, I'm sure you live your life in an exemplary manner. I'm sure the families up and down your block are lining up at your front door for family-living-in-purity lessons.

But just who are you pushing this prayer-in-schools thing for, anyway? Correct me if I'm wrong, but can't you pray with your children pretty much whenever you want? Can't you pray with them every morning when they awake? If you were so inclined, couldn't you have another prayer over breakfast, another prayer as they collect their schoolbooks, and yet another as they walk out the front door? Couldn't you walk your children to the bus stop and pray as the loser cruiser[2] approaches? (Considering some of the people they have driving those things, that might not be such a bad idea.) Then, once your children get home, can't you pray with them over their homework, before they go out to play, and again at dinner? And couldn't you lead them in a final rousing rendition of "Now I lay me down to sleep . . ." before the little rug rats crawl into bed?

Is the light bulb starting to come on? Are you starting to get a little uncomfortable with this line of reasoning?

Ah-ha! You got it! Of *course* those kids can get all the prayer they want. That's not what their parents are worried about.

For the zealots who are trying to make prayer another part of the day's activities at your government school, it's not about their children—it's about *your* children! They know that their kids are going to get every bit as much exposure to religion and prayer as they want them to. Why should they worry about cramming prayers into school hours, when they control the kids' lives every hour they're at

---

[2] School bus. *Sooo* uncool. You lose so many cool points riding a school bus, having Beyoncé carry your books wouldn't put you back in the black.

home, and every Wednesday night they can haul them off to the local parish hall to suck down a spaghetti dinner? When it comes to their own children's religious upbringing, these parents aren't the least bit deterred by what happens in their local government schools. And this is all to the good—their children are probably better off for their parents' involvement in their spiritual life.

Ahhh. But when it comes to *your* children, things are a little different.

Fundamentalist Christians are desperate to save your little tykes' souls, by whatever means necessary. But they can't force you to take your children to Sunday school or church every Sunday. You're unlikely to commit your child to a plate of spaghetti every Wednesday night with a stranger. You might even decide to defy God by sending your children to soccer camp in the summer, instead of sending them to summer Bible schools, as God clearly intended. And it goes without saying that they can't force you to pray with your children in the privacy of your own home. So what's left?

Well, here's an idea: Since it's impossible to get to your children when they're under *your* care and control, why not wait until they're under someone else's care and control—at the local government school?

So here's the theory I propose: The prayer-in-school proponents out there are merely looking for a way to use the government to present religious theory to *your* child. Those who don't see that as an abominable violation of the spirit of the First Amendment are either lying, or lacking a basic capacity for logical thought.

By the way, you'll note that my argument rests on one simple core idea: I don't believe it's our government's place to instruct or indoctrinate our children in any specific world religion—which, in our country, tends to be Christianity. In the eyes of many, this will make me anything from a heretic to a simple Christian-basher. (There's that word "bash" again . . . always trotted out when the facilities for logical conversation fail us.)

On the other hand . . .

I believe the courts were right in turning down organized daily religious observances in government schools. But we've clearly gone too far in our efforts to completely remove all references to religion from education.

I believe that our children would be well served by a good basic course in comparative religions in our schools. As some of you may have noted, we're having a bit of a problem with some of the world's other major religions. It might be a good idea if our young children were given an honest and unbiased lecture on the fundamental differences between Christianity, Judaism, Islam, and a few other major religions before they start developing their own prejudices.

But guess who would scream the loudest if such a program were started? Yup, you got it. The very same people who want Christian prayers said in our government schools every day.

There's also nothing wrong with students professing their own religious devotion in a school setting. If religious faith is important to that student, then recognizing and understanding that faith is an important part of getting to know that student.

Brittany McComb was the 2006 valedictorian at Foothills High School in Las Vegas, Nevada. Her valedictorian status afforded her the opportunity to make the valedictory address at graduation. Brittany was a devout Christian, which is good. She wanted to share her faith with her classmates during her speech, which is also good.

She never got the chance.

Brittany had to submit her 750-word speech to school officials before the graduation ceremony. When school officials saw that Brittany actually referenced her love of God in her speech, they got out their red pencils. Brittany's speech was heavily edited to remove most of her references to her faith.

Brittany was not to be intimidated. She was determined to share her feelings with her graduating class. This was not the school speaking, this was Brittany McComb. This wasn't an expression of the school's feelings, these were her feelings—the feelings of a teenager going through an important transition in her life.

What Brittany didn't know was that in the back of the auditorium, some school official had a copy of her speech in one hand and his other hand on the microphone switch. When it became clear to the official school censor that Brittany was actually going to say the "C" word, he was ready: Just as Brittany prepared to say the word "Christ," her microphone went dead.

That was it. End of speech.

I'm pleased to report that the graduates and their families were less than thrilled. The booing went on for several minutes. Good for them.

The story of Brittany McComb illustrates two things: the inherent stupidity and irrationality of government, and the problems that inevitably arise when you entrust your child's education to that government.

This kind of thing makes me almost apologetic for my stance on prayer in the schools, because I realize that there's an all-out assault on Christianity being waged in our country. I'm so sick to death of "Happy Holidays" and "holiday trees" that I could scream. One school in the northeast had to reinvent its "Breakfast with Santa" fund-raiser when a woman (who would have guessed it?) called to complain that Santa was a religious figure and the school was promoting Christianity. "Breakfast with Santa" became "Breakfast with Frosty."[3]

And the absurdities never stop. This past Christmas season, one local government permitted manger scenes to be installed in a government park—but without Joseph, Mary, or Baby Jesus. Just some sheep and goats and a bit of straw scattered around. When asked about the absence of the central figures in the story of Christmas, a government official said that it was really just a "desert scene," and that people should "use their imaginations."

Then there's Chicago. Every year there's a Christmas festival in

---

[3] My guess is that this nickname is used by many who know the woman who filed the complaint.

Chicago known as the Christkindlmarket. I don't speak German, but I believe that this loosely translates to "Christ Child Market." In 2006, New Line Cinema paid about twelve thousand dollars to be one of the sponsors of the festival and for the privilege of having a booth on-site. As luck would have it, New Line had a newly released motion picture running at the time called *The Nativity Story.* New Line was planning to play trailers for the film in their booth.

No way.

Some official with the Mayor's Office of Special Events told New Line that it couldn't display the *Nativity Story* trailers on the TVs in their booth. After all . . . someone might be offended!

As the days passed and the controversy grew, officials from the mayor's office scrambled for new excuses. On one day they said the display was too commercial. Then, when it was pointed out that other sponsors included corporate brands like Mercedes-Benz and Lufthansa, they changed their story: Now the film clips were "too aggressive."

One blogger on the website Chicagoist reasoned that sooner or later "we [could] expect another city official to clarify that their *real* problem with the ad is its portrayal of immaculate conception outside of the bonds of holy matrimony. This announcement will be followed by a press conference on Friday from the Board of Health, reminding all Chicagoans that they should avoid giving birth in mangers with cows and sheep, as they provide for unsanitary birthing conditions."

I could easily fill a few hundred pages with examples of ill-advised government attacks, if you will, on the Christian faith in recent years. We'll let someone else write that book.

Still, I can't help pointing out that in many instances, devoutly religious Christians have brought much of this upon themselves. Many Americans have come to see the demand for prayer in school as a none-too-subtle attempt to move toward government recognition of Christianity as our "official" state religion. And they're right: mandating prayer in government schools would be a step in that direction.

But allowing a valedictorian to mention her faith in Christ in her speech, or New Line Cinema to run trailers of their movie about the Nativity during a Christmas festival—that's a different story. Those are matters of free speech.

And anyone who can't tell the difference might do themselves good by picking up a copy of the Bill of Rights once they're done with their next Bible study group.

Of course, I know I'm never going to win everyone over. Take Andy, for instance:

Subject: oops!
Name: Andy _____
E-mail: ***********@********

NEAL: You need to get off your damn soap box against the Christian Religious Right. I am getting sick of your atheism. I called my local radio station that carries your show to complain and I was told they have already had numerous complaints on you already today. You have crossed the line! You are on your way out. You need to take lessons from Glen Beck, Rush Limbaugh, Sean Hannity, Jerry Falwell, Pat Robertson, Pope Benedict XVI, Dr. James Kennedy, Billy Graham, Michael Savage, Michael Reagan, Stephen Baldwin, Bill O'Reilly—oops—too late. You are gone and so is your "unfair" tax.

Well, he certainly told me, didn't he?

THE RAINBOW FRAUD

"A long way out in the deep blue sea there lived a fish."

Thus begins *The Rainbow Fish* by Marcus Pfister, an award-winning picture book that has been published in more than thirty languages and is beloved by children around the world.

Yep, you guessed it. I *hate* this *Rainbow Fish* thing. Someone ought to bait a hook, snare that insipid guppy, and cut it into bait at the first opportunity.

At this point, you may be asking, "Is this guy actually going to take some of the precious word allotment afforded him by the publisher to rant about a children's book?"

You better believe I am![1]

None of this will surprise longtime listeners of my radio show. Some of you may even remember, a decade or so ago, the broadcast in which I berated a harmless, sweet, innocent child at some length.

That particular on-air rant was triggered by a seemingly innocuous feature story in the *Atlanta Journal-Constitution* recounting the charitable efforts of a young schoolgirl in one of the city's northern suburbs. As I recall, the adorable tyke used to canvass her neighborhood regularly, collecting donations for one cause or another. A regular little eleemosynary moppet, she was.

Okay, I admit it: I may have gone just a wee bit overboard in discussing this little twit. Just far enough to make station's general man-

---

[1] In case you needed proof that I have too much time on my hands.

ager stomp, snarl, and snort—one of my favorite pastimes in those days.[2]

Whatever could have made the mean, bad man yell at this nice, friendly little do-gooder? Well, I'm afraid it was a philosophical disagreement. (Yeah, I know. With an elementary schooler. So sue me.)

You see, the girl explained her charitable inclinations with the brilliant assertion that "everybody ought to have an equal amount of stuff."

Say what? You're kidding me, right? This girl was a plant, the story was a fake. Someone was just lying to get me riled up on the air that day . . . right?

Nope. She was the real deal—a proud product of today's educational system. See what billions of dollars spent on government education hath wrought? All this time and money we've spent, and we end up with a sixth-grader who thinks, "Everybody ought to have an equal amount of stuff."

Did this brilliant example of government education and twentieth-century parenting think that her house should be no bigger or better than the house of any other sixth grader anywhere in the world? Ever been to Nicaragua, kid? How about Uganda? If you're going to pursue this "equal amount of stuff" stuff, your work is cut out for you.

Would this girl really be ready to give up toys and clothes once she discovered that everyone doesn't have just exactly what she has? What about her next trip to Walt Disney World? Would she give that up if she found out that some child somewhere couldn't go?

How in the wide, wide world of reason did she think we should actually get to the point where everybody *has* an equal amount of stuff? Should we appoint some sort of government agency responsible for measuring and quantifying stuff, and redistributing said stuff until everybody's stuff matched in quantity and quality? Should we

---

[2] Picking on this little girl was viewed as an egregious transgression, while telling the mayor of Atlanta to "Sit down and shut up, you son-of-a-bitch!" on the air was not! Go figure. He's probably in jail by now.

hire stuff police to do spot checks on everyone's home to make sure nobody has some stuff that someone else doesn't have?

· You see, I'm getting all worked up again. I'd better rein myself in. After all, the kid is eighteen years old by now, maybe older. I'm sure she left Barbie dolls and philanthropy behind long ago. No doubt she's spending like a crack fiend just to keep ahead of her classmates in the fashion department. So enough about Little Miss Equality.

But this does bring me back to that children's book: *The Rainbow Fish,* which won the American Booksellers Book of the Year Award in 1995.[3]

Marcus Pfister's anti-individual, anti-property rights tome was published in the United States by North-South Books. Marcus isn't from around here, though. He's from Switzerland, and that's where this noxious little book was first published.

Now, it just so happens I've been to Switzerland many times. Love the place. They make great pocketknives, they have cute railroads, and those Lake Lucerne steamers are to die for.

But in Switzerland you simply won't find the individual spirit and dedication to property rights that you find here in the United States.

Just what was it about this book that yanked my chain so hard? Here's the story . . . truncated, of course.

It seems there's this fish with really pretty scales—blue and green and purple and silver. (Big deal!) His other fish pals think he's really something special—so special that they call him *Der Regenbogenfisch.* Nice ring to it, don't you think? It's German for "Rainbow Fish."

The plot thickens when some little twerp-fish (probably a baby remora) swims up to the Rainbow Fish and asks him for one of his colorful scales. Since the Rainbow Fish has so many scales, the twerp-fish reckons he ought to just give one away.

Is this all starting to sound vaguely familiar?

---

[3] So now we know that the American Booksellers Association will give you an award for writing the most imbecilic, inane, obtuse, moronic, senseless, unthinking, flaky book of the year. Don't look for *Somebody's Gotta Say It* on the awards list.

Der Regenbogenfisch says *nein!* And the vile twerp-fish swims away to tell his fellow twerp-fish that the Rainbow Fish is being ugly.

All of the twerp-fish then start to shun the Rainbow Fish because he won't give away his scales. The Rainbow Fish, in a fit of depression, ends up in the dark cave of the cranky old octopus[4] asking for help.

Does the octopus have some advice? Why, of course!

"Give a glittering scale to each of the other fish," she says. "You will no longer be the most beautiful fish in the sea, but you will discover how to be happy."

As the octopus retreats back into the cave, the twerp-fish reappears and renews its demands for a scale. This time the Rainbow Fish caves . . . and gives one up.

Oh, joy!

From that point, the book devolves into a Great Giveaway Festival. As soon as word gets around that the Rainbow Fish is giving away his stuff, he's surrounded by twerp-fish and giving away scales left and right! Oh, how happy he feels! The more he gives away, the happier he is!

In no time flat, the Rainbow Fish is down to one special scale . . . and all the other freeloading twerp-fish have one too![5]

Think about that for a moment: *Everyone has an equal amount of stuff!* Paradise! Nirvana! A sixth-grader's irrational fantasy! I guess Little Miss Charity must have been multilingual: She obviously read this book before it was even translated into English!

So why do I hate this book so much? Because it's insidious. *The Rainbow Fish* is a children's book, folks. It's aimed at human beings who are still at their most impressionable age—the age when they still

---

[4] I have it on good authority—and remember, I'm very well connected in the entertainment industry—that the voice of the old octopus in the animated version will be provided by Hillary Clinton. If Hillary is otherwise occupied, there's always Helen Thomas.

[5] Just a reminder. This is not *giving back*. It is just *giving*.

believe that Mommy kissing your boo-boo will actually make it better.[6] The age of Santa Claus and the Easter Bunny.[7]

And now the propaganda machine is going beyond single-copy outreach to mass indoctrination: Someone has even gone to the trouble of producing a stage play based on *The Rainbow Fish* so that our little rug rats can be brainwashed en masse down at the local performing arts center! And the pathetic part of this whole sordid escapade is that too many American parents have no idea just what kind of message they're imparting to their tricycle motors when they drum this hideous little utopian fantasy into their impressionable minds night after night.

Obviously, parents need some help . . . and I'm just the person to offer it.

Here's the bottom line: *The Rainbow Fish* is, at its core, an anti-private property fable. It is your child's introduction to the idea that success is sinful, that the redistribution of wealth is the only foundation of a just society.

Children will believe pretty much anything grown-ups tell them—or read to them. Ask any child psychologist who isn't busy handing out phony diagnoses of ADD or ADHD and he or she will tell you that the lessons found in stories like *The Rainbow Fish* are taken to heart. The authors of such books are telling our children that there's something wrong with owning things that other people want. If you do happen to be the proud owner of such an item, they suggest, you need to give it away or you won't be liked. On the other hand, if you've squandered every opportunity we're all blessed with in this country and you have nothing to show for yourself, then it's perfectly legitimate for you to demand that those who have succeeded should fork it over.

---

[6] No . . . I'm not going there.

[7] Oops, that reminds me. This footnote is for the author. Don't forget to put a tirade about the "Spring Bunny" in this book somewhere. You can't say "Easter Bunny" anymore.

The Rainbow Fish—obviously some species of sucker fish—sets children up nicely for a life of wealth envy. In the wonderful world of the Rainbow Fish, you don't have to work to get what you want, all you need to do is demand it.

But the secret villain of this story, to me, is the octopus. Think, for a moment, about the role the octopus plays. When the Rainbow Fish starts being beleaguered by the jealousy of those around him, the octopus—a creature with many arms, remember—suggests that he should give away his belongings to those who have not.

You get it? The octopus is government—its tentacles reaching out in every direction to suck up the fruits of our labors, then telling us that we need to give up what we have left to those who have less.

If I may be so bold, I would like to suggest an alternative story-line to Mr. Pfister. Consider this: The fundamental problem of the story occurs when the Rainbow Fish recognizes that there's a demand for his colorful scales. Instead of deciding to give them away, why shouldn't he offer to *trade* them for something the twerp-fish might be willing to give up? Or perhaps the rainbow fish could even start a colorful-scale manufacturing business! After all, *The Rainbow Fish* is really a story of what happens when demand exceeds supply. Why not turn it into a marvelous opportunity to tell our children a story of free enterprise triumphant?

Even if Mr. Pfister had a sudden change of heart and revised his story in future printings, however, that would only be a drop in the bucket. It'll take a lot more than banishing the Rainbow Fish from the family aquarium to banish this "everybody ought to have an equal amount of stuff" idiocy.

I'll explain in the next chapter.

NICE PENCILS!

Now, Fork Them Over . . .

What? I'm picking on government schools again? Don't I have anything better to do with my time?

No, I don't. A day spent slamming the concept of government indoctrination is a day well spent.

I love this country, but I believe it's in deep trouble. I believe we're losing our sense of individuality and our love of liberty. Americans have little idea of the sacrifices that so many made to create this country where we live our lives of plenty.

Most adults have no idea of how essential our system of economic liberty is to the standard of life we enjoy today, and are unaware of how American free enterprise has already lifted much of the world out of poverty, want, and despair.

Furthermore, most Americans don't understand something as basic as the importance of private property rights in maintaining freedom and promoting prosperity.

And for this state of affairs I place the bulk of the blame on our system of government-owned and -operated schools.

I'll go one step further: Many of our government schools today, perhaps even the one to which you have surrendered your child, start in from day one trying to discredit the very concept of property rights.

How do they do it? Let's start by defining some terms.

Some of our brethren on the left denounce the idea of property

rights by saying human rights are always more important than property rights. It's a clever line, but it's really a kind of misdirection, like
a magic trick.

Why? Because property rights *are* human rights.

Think about it this way: Property has no rights. People have the
right *to* property, and that right to property, the fruits of one's labor, is
one of the highest human rights.

Chances are it's been quite a few years since you were in grade
school. Believe me, much has changed since those days. Back when
you were in school, for instance, it was probably okay to play tag during recess. Not so today. Why? Because tag involves (gasp!) *touching!*
And besides, in tag someone is chased, and someone does the chasing.
This teaches our precious little children *predatory behavior.* Now we
can't have that, can we?

As if that weren't bad enough, the campaign to abolish private
property starts with almost the first moment your child enters school.

Remember those weeks before school started for your brand-new
first grader? There you were, you and your proud new student, walking the aisles of the local Wal-Mart, your list of school supplies in
hand. Item by item you checked things off your list as you dropped
them into the basket: pencils and erasers, notebooks and pencil hold-
ers, construction paper and paste. By the time you made it to the cash
register, you had a full basket and a happy kid. As soon as you got
home, your budding Einstein took the supplies to his room and
spread everything out on the bed. This was *his* stuff, and it was important stuff, too—his very own tools and supplies, the things he'd use to
learn and grow. And tomorrow he would be taking them to school.
He couldn't have been more proud. On his last night before that
magic first day of school, just before he went to bed, your young student would pack all his stuff in his backpack . . . then unpack it . . .
then pack it again.

The next morning, it's showtime! Off we go, full of apprehension
and pride. Your young man is taking another grand step toward
adulthood! What could go wrong at school?

Plenty. Remember, it's a government operation staffed by government agents.

As soon as the students are seated, the bell rings, and as fast as you can say the Pledge of Allegiance, the indoctrination begins: Your child is about to be introduced to the wonderful concept of "the common good."

Ready for class? Nope, not yet. There's a small matter that must be attended to first.

The government teacher steps in front of her virtual hostages and promptly delivers the first raw lesson in the power of government:

She instructs her students to bring all of their precious new school supplies to the front of the classroom and put them into a huge box.

Wait just a minute here! *Why am I putting my stuff into that box? My daddy took me to Wal-Mart and bought that stuff for me! It's mine! You can't take it away from me!*

Oh, yeah?

As your child sits in stunned silence, the teacher tells him and his classmates that these supplies now belong to *all* of the class. What was once private property has been seized and transformed into *community property,* courtesy of the teacher's demands—demands that amount to a government mandate. There is no due process. No rule of law. After all, in school the teacher *is* the law. Your child's supplies are now everybody's supplies, and the teacher has assumed the responsibility of distributing them as needed.

Know this: This whole "dump all of your school supplies into this box" is no mere innocent exercise, no simple whim of a few individual teachers. It's a conscious policy, and it has a purpose that goes beyond simple expediency for the teacher.

Your child, and every other child in that classroom, is being taught that their private property rights end when someone in authority *says* they end. In this instance, that person in authority is the teacher—a government employee. And even if your child isn't able to understand that it's actually the government who's seizing his property, he certainly *does* understand that his property is being seized, and converted into everybody's property. Worse yet, he is told, very clearly, that this is a good thing.

And who is there to tell him otherwise?

I've talked about this property confiscation on the air many times. Some parents call in to scold me, convinced that I'm lying, that this doesn't really happen. But for every one who does, plenty others call in to confirm what I'm saying—to report that it happened to their own child! I've even heard from young parents who believed I was making it up . . . right up to the point when their own child returned home from his first day of school.

The most surprising thing to me is that some callers—even some parents whose children have had their school supplies confiscated—actually don't see the problem with the policy. Wake up, folks! The very concept of private property is under attack here, and government is leading the charge.

It is a simple truth that property rights are the very basis of human freedom. We come into this world with nothing but our bodies and our minds. Those are the assets we bring with us to the marketplace. And no society based on economic and social freedom has ever survived the loss of private property rights.

Nobody would seriously argue against the notion that we, as individuals, are the sole owners of our minds and our bodies. We present our physical and mental labor to the free enterprise marketplace and trade it there for wealth, usually in the form of money. It can be said that we have received that money in exchange for the expenditure of a portion of our very lives. When we convert that money to other forms of property, that property, too, represents a portion of our lives. That property is every bit as much ours as our very bodies and minds are.

To demand that we forfeit that property to the government—even so trifling a piece of property as a schoolboy's notebook—is to demand a degree of involuntary servitude from us all.

I know this may sound a little preachy, but the importance of the basic human right to property, and its role in the preservation of a free society, cannot be overstated. When the government schools we pay for are working to destroy that concept, from the very first day of a child's very first grade, it's our duty to speak up.

Today we see property rights under attack from all quarters—as anyone who's ever confronted the idea of eminent domain knows too well. Government, after all, has an interest in weakening the concept of private property rights. The more Americans can be conditioned to accept the idea that the government has the right to confiscate our property for "the common good," the stronger government becomes and the weaker we as individuals become.

Come on, you say, *my kid is only six years old! You don't expect him to realize what's happening and ask the teacher to respect his private property rights, now do you? What is he supposed to do, demand to be compensated for the seizure of his property?*

Of course not. Junior is a long way from understanding those concepts. But don't kid yourself: He certainly does understand, at least on a subconscious level, that his new teacher—someone he knows he is supposed to respect and look up to—thinks that the idea of seizing private property for general use is just fine. *After all,* the logic goes, *there are other people out there who might need some of your stuff. And it's just not right for you to have something other people don't have or can't share in, is it?*

All you need to do to correct this perceived injustice, according to these teachers, is to let your superiors even things out a bit by taking some stuff from you and giving it to someone else.

Karl Marx had his own words for this concept. "From each according to his ability," he said, "to each according to his need."

So what can be done to fix the problem? Well, I'll tell you what I did.

Actually, in my case, I didn't have to wait until my daughter, Laura, got into government school for this collectivist concept to rear its head. We learned this lesson in day care.

One afternoon I picked up Laura at her day care center. As she got into the car, I could see that her eyes were red; there were still traces of tears on her cheeks.

What happened? I asked.

"The lady," she said, had taken her candy.

You see, it was the day after Halloween and Laura had taken a bag of goodies to day care, to dip into throughout the day. As soon as the day care supervisor saw her bag, however, she seized it. She told Laura that it just wasn't right for her to have anything that every other child didn't have. If she didn't bring enough to share with everyone, then she couldn't have it at all.

As soon as I heard that, I spun my incredibly hot Ford Pinto around and headed back to the day care center. Once there, I asked for a private meeting with the director. I asked her if she was familiar with the concept of private property. She said yes. Then I asked why it was the day care center's policy to indoctrinate children into the idea that it was not right for them to have property that other children didn't have.

Blank stare.

Then I asked her how she would feel if the bank took her next deposit and distributed it evenly among its other customers, telling her it wasn't nice for her to have money that other people didn't have.

She got it.

The next time Laura brought some candy or cookies to day care, the supervisors left her alone.

For nearly all children in America, Day Number One at school—whether it's in an informal day care center or a public kindergarten—is also their first time in an independent social setting. It's their first chance to experience how the world is going to treat them. Until we do something to fix it, however, Lesson Number One your children learn that day may be that their rights exist only as long as the government allows.

And that's just the first week! Wait a little while, and you just might get that call from Teacher with vague, dark hints of a better world for your child if you'll just allow him to go on Ritalin.

SHINING A LIGHGHT ON ARTS FUNDING

Let's say you go into business manufacturing widgets. After dedicating a big chunk of your young life to designing these widgets and perfecting your manufacturing and production process, you come to a sobering conclusion: Nobody wants to buy them. Despite all the hard work you put in displaying them for the public, nobody's buying. Sure, people stop by and check out the selection; some snicker others walk away with furrowed brows. But no one leaves any cash in the till.

What do you do?

For most people, there would be only one answer: Close up shop, settle your debts if you can (or declare bankruptcy if you can't), and start looking for another way to make a living.

For others, however, there's a different option: Ask the *government* to use the one unique power that only government has—the power to use deadly force to accomplish any goal it sets for itself—to *force* people to buy your widgets.

After all, you've worked long and hard at this widget thing, and it's not your fault that the crass consumers don't understand how much more fulfilled their lives would be with a few of your widgets in their home. Since the consumers obviously aren't acting in their own best interests, you call on the government to help.

Come on, Neal. The government's not in the business of floating failing businesses, is it? Think again, folks. This very scenario plays itself out day after day, from the federal to the local government level, all over the country. The plunderers are people who call themselves "artists," and what they produce is a brand of garbage that's known—to them, anyway—as "art."

The problem they face is that their work just doesn't sell in the free marketplace. And so, rather than actually trying to get a real job where they trade some marketable skill for a wage, they ask the government to step in on their behalf. Their goal is to get the government to take the money it's seized from the taxpayers and spend it on these often grotesque works of art, which most taxpayers would sooner haul off to a Dumpster than frame over the couch.

In one of the most incredible scams ever perpetrated on the American taxpayer, tens of thousands of marginal artists across the country are now using the police power of government to compensate for their lack of actual marketable artistic skills.

My outrage over forced government transfers of money from those who earned it to those who produce unmarketable art was born over a poem.

To be more precise: a one-word poem.

In the 1960s, shortly after the National Endowment of the Arts was formed, the sum of $750 was seized from some hapless wage earner and transferred to the account of a budding literary genius.

Now $750 (a few thousand in today's dollars) may not seem like much, but in the early 1960s this money could have solved a lot of problems—or provided a lot of pleasure—for the person who earned it. But *noooooooooooo*. The government needed it, because it had to underwrite some fool who wanted his magazine to publish this one-word poem.

Are you ready?

Here's the poem:

Lighght

There, now, I've done everything I could to spruce up this work of art. I centered it on the page for you. I put it in a nifty little box with a nice border. I even sprang for a fancy typeface. Do you feel enriched? Enlightened? More in touch with the inner you?

Hasn't the American Way of Life has been improved in some grand way by the incredible experience you've enjoyed in reading that inspired poem?

Aren't you glad that our government confiscated some poor sap's wages to make sure this work of genius got published?

If so, why don't you take the time to tell me and the rest of us uncultured slobs out here where in our Constitution the Imperial Federal Government of the United States derives any authority to seize the property of a private citizen for such an asinine purpose?

Believe it or not, "lighght"—published in the *Chicago Review* in 1968—won Aram Saroyan[1] the NEA poetry award and $750 in taxpayer money.

Saroyan later scammed another $1,500 from taxpayers when editor George Plimpton decided to reprint it in the NEA-supported *American Literary Anthology.*

The money probably went to buy pot. (Wait—that's no baseless charge. A biography of Aram Saroyan at the University of Connecticut, where his papers are housed, notes that he smoked marijuana in the 1960s and never graduated from college.)

Not everyone was pleased with this NEA grant. When word got out about it, William Scherle, a Republican congressman from Iowa, demanded to know what "Lighght" meant. Was it a typo? A joke? A con game?

"If my kid came home from school spelling like that, I would have stood him in the corner with a dunce cap," Scherle reportedly said.

---

[1] Aram Saroyan is the son of William Saroyan. Aram's father actually took the time to write more than one word, spell them correctly, and string them together in coherent sentences, thus producing such modern literary masterpieces as *The Human Comedy* and *The Time of Your Life.* Artistic talent apparently isn't hereditary.

When one of Scherle's assistants contacted the editor of the *American Literary Anthology* to ask what Saroyan's poem meant, however, he didn't get a straight answer.

"You are from the Midwest," Plimpton replied. "You are culturally deprived, so you would not understand it anyway." Charming.

For what it's worth—and that's much less than $750 or $1,500—the question of the literary value of the one-word poem was eventually answered, in a way. Saroyan himself tried to explain the seven-letter word years later. This alleged poet said that by manipulating the spelling of "Light" to "Lighght," he found a way for his poem "to be, not mean."

Oh, yeah. Certainly clears it up for me.

He explained further:

"Part of the aim seems to have been to make this ineffable[2] (light) into a thing, as it were—to change it from a verb (the agency of illumination) to a noun that yet radiates as light does. The double ghgh seems to work in that way."

Aram, listen to me carefully and do exactly as I say. Put the pipe down and back away slowly.

You know, now that I've been thinking about it, I'm an artist, too! My art form is words! I craft words into carefully constructed sentences and paragraphs designed to inform, amuse, outrage, infuriate, and obfuscate! I'm only on about two hundred stations around the country. That makes me feel like my art is being rejected. I think I'll just go apply for an NEA grant for a few million to pay radio stations to take my show. That's how Air America did it! (Well . . . taking funds from Alzheimer's programs and Boys and Girls Clubs isn't exactly like applying for a federal grant, but they did have to pay radio stations to carry their programming.) Why shouldn't I give that a try?

Maybe because I still have some self-respect. Not a lot . . . but enough.

---

[2] I'll do the homework for you this time. *Ineffable:* "Incapable of being expressed or described in words." Well, I can certainly describe his poem in words. Open your dictionary to "S".

Was Aram's effort poetry or not? I have an opinion, in case you haven't guessed—but that doesn't really matter. This chapter isn't about the relative merits, or lack thereof, of Aram Saroyan or minimalist poetry.

If there's a market for this stuff—that is, if people want to read it so much that they're willing to pay money for the privilege—then I'm all for it. That's free enterprise in action! On the other hand, if a supposed artist is *not* able to support himself (and whatever expensive little habits he may have picked up in the swinging sixties) with the work he produces, then perhaps it's time for him to look elsewhere for an income. I hear Wal-Mart is hiring.

In what universe does the NEA justify reaching into my wallet or yours and stealing money for the purpose of enriching someone like Saroyan? Exactly how does this seizure of private property protect life, defend freedom, or support the general welfare of our nation?

Now, in case you suspect that I'm unable to see both sides of an issue, I can tell you at least one way that government spending on the arts benefits the public.

Whatever town you're in, it's easy to find a government office. Just look for the hideous sculpture by the side of the road—sure as you're born, that building lurking behind it is the local government outpost. (Step inside, and you're sure to find even more ugly welfare art.)

Years ago, the Richard B. Russell Federal Office Building was built in Atlanta. The taxpayers, of course, were forced to spend millions of dollars on ugly welfare art for the building. One work of "art" consisted of a large torn piece of canvas with paint splattered all over it. When contractors were doing the final cleanup, they came upon this work of art, mistook it for an old painter's drop cloth, and threw it in a Dumpster. When the artist discovered his precious piece of work in the trash, he threw what only could be described as a "diva hissy fit."[3]

---

[3] The word "hissy" comes from the word "hysteria." We trace "hysteria" to "hustera," the Latin word for "womb." We used to think that women were prone to mental problems because they had wombs. Now we know that it's the men who have the mental problems *because* women have wombs.

To anyone who cared to listen, he complained that the people in charge of postconstruction cleanup—and most of the ordinary citizens out there—just weren't sophisticated enough to appreciate his artistic masterwork.

Me, I think the people of Atlanta are the smart ones: To this day, that piece of dog squeeze hanging on the wall of the Russell building is universally known as the "drop cloth."

Every time a politician votes to dump a load of taxpayer money into the artistic community, that politician is telling you and every other taxpayer that he believes it's more important for the government to subsidize an unmarketable artist than it is for you to spend your money on things you need—things like health care, home payments, debt reduction, and your children's education.

Unbridled arrogance.

And don't for a minute think that the "Lighght" fiasco was an isolated incident. Oh, no. The NEA never fails to deliver.

Before we proceed, a warning: Some of the case studies that follow get pretty rough. I'm *trying* to get you angry. I'm trying to get you so steamed that you reach out to your elected officials and tell them that up with this you will not put. These examples, grotesque as they may be, illustrate how little respect these welfare artists, and the politicians who pander to them, have for you and the hard work you put into earning a living—before they get ahold of it.

Here we go:

- A grant of $30,000 to Philadelphia's Institute of Contemporary Art, sponsor of a traveling exhibition of photographs by the late Robert Mapplethorpe. Termed "homoerotic," the pictures included graphic sexual images such as a self-portrait of Mapplethorpe with a bullwhip sticking out of his you-know-what; a little girl with her skirt lifted to expose her genitals; and, oh yes, an especially lovely photograph of a man urinating into another man's mouth.

- A $75,000 grant to the Southeastern Center for Contemporary Art in Winston-Salem, North Carolina, for an exhibit by Andres Serrano that included a photograph titled "Piss Christ." That's the now-infamous photo of a plastic crucifix immersed in a jar of the artist's urine.[4]

- A grant to The Kitchen, a Manhattan theater, which sponsored a live performance by a porno star named Annie Sprinkle. While masturbating on stage, the performer actually commented, "Usually I get paid a lot of money for this, but tonight it's government-funded."

Angry yet? I am, but if you're not there yet, here are a few other outrages:

- $70,000 for a show called "Degenerate with a Capital D." This exhibit included the remains of "artist" Shawn Eichman's own aborted baby.

- $127,000 in 1990 and $125,000 in 1989 to the Center on Puppetry Arts, which happened to feature a puppet show depicting oral sex between puppets.

- $50,000 to Living Stage, which encouraged elementary schoolers to shout "Bullshit!" at the top of their lungs during a performance.

- $20,000 to an arts festival that included a display of sex toys and Bibles, which subsequently were set ablaze. The name of this one was "Bible Burn." Nice.

---

[4] Here's an idea. Apply for a government grant to study why the NEA is so fascinated with urine and scatology.

• $6,025 to Ann Wilchusky for "sculpting in space." As a pilot, I was particularly interested in this one: To this artist, "sculpting in space" involved the refined art of throwing crepe paper out of an airplane.[5]

• Several grants to a theater in New York where one Johanna Went performed with giant tampons, satanic bunnies, three-foot feces, dildos, and a giant vagina headdress which she squeezed as white liquid gushed from her mouth.

• $204,390 to the Franklin Furnace in New York, which put on a show featuring an eighty-six-year-old woman boasting of her sexual exploits, and one lesbian inserting her foot into another lesbian's vagina.

• $40,000 to the *Gay Sunshine Press* to produce "alternative" publications, including illustrations of sex between men and animals.

Oh, and this one I love.

Do you remember Andrew Cunanan? He was the serial killer from San Diego who murdered Gianni Versace at the front door of his home in Miami some years back. Well, three artists at the La Jolla Playhouse in California developed a musical around Cunanan and his exploits. That's right, a musical about a serial killer.

When three playwrights need some money, what better place to go than to the American taxpayers?

That's right, *the taxpayer-funded NEA* took a whopping $35,000 of its plunder and gave it to these playwrights. That's $35,000 taken from families who earned it, and who presumably had a good use for

---

[5] I have an eighty-seven-year-old friend who buys toilet paper in bulk. Every time he gets a chance he takes a few rolls of toilet paper and climbs into his Decathlon, an aerobatic airplane. He then gets up there a few thousand feet and starts tossing rolls of (biodegradable) toilet paper out the window. He'll then dive and swoop, shredding that toilet paper as it streams toward the ground. He's my hero. I won't tell you his name.

it, dumped into the laps of some welfare artists to help them create their musical about a murderer.

I wonder if poor Aram Saroyan felt cheated? After all, he only got $2,250 out of the NEA.

What's next? What about a live production on the life of O. J. Simpson? Now that the private sector isn't going to publish his book, perhaps he can apply for a government NEA grant. I can picture the marquee now: *If I Did It—The Musical!*

I wonder what *that* will cost the American taxpayers?

There are some artists who've actually figured out a way to make you pay for their work without actually getting their hands on your tax money. They force you to buy it with your own *after-tax* money!

That's the way it works in Naples, Florida. This artist moneygrab was launched as the "Percent for Art" plan, though was the name was later changed to "Dollar for Art." The plan here is to make real estate developers set aside one dollar for every square foot of new development to buy art. This applies to any private project totaling at least $500,000, and to all city construction projects.

The art has to be located on the site of the development, in full public view. What's more, the artwork must go through a three-step review process involving a Public Art Advisory Committee, a Design Review Board, and then the Naples City Council—two committees with no responsibility to the developer whatsoever, and then the local government. And you know who ends up footing the bill, don't you? Whoever buys the property. What a deal!

Cows have three stomachs, which they use to turn grass into cow flops. Now the City of Naples has a similar process—and I'm sure it will produce similar results.

THE LOUDER THE COMMERCIAL . . .

The Dumber They Think You Are

As you've no doubt figured out by now, politics isn't the only thing that moves me. I can get quite worked up, thank you very much, by other trivialities . . . such as loud and obnoxious radio and television commercials.

Time to take a huge bite out of the hand that feeds me.

I've been in radio since my senior year in high school. This means that I've been deriving income—sometimes meager, sometimes not so meager—from radio advertising for more than half my life. So I've developed a feeling for what kinds of ads work, what types don't—and what kinds of ads I absolutely detest.

Loud commercials. Screaming commercials. Commercials with explosions, with announcers reading over loud, drumming, raucous music.

HATE 'EM. Ohhhhh . . . I just can't tell you how much I hate 'em.

Here's the thing: The louder the commercial, the dumber the advertisers think their customers are. Think about it—those loud, screaming commercials, with their thumps, bangs, and heavy metal music, are almost always hawking cheap products to people with, let's just say, limited judgment about how they spend their money.

Take car commercials as an example. Listen closely to those car ads, and you'll soon recognize a universal truth: the louder the commercial, the cheaper the car. You never hear a Rolls-Royce spokesman screaming at the top of his lungs about inventory overstock, do you? The screamers are always trying to sell you something at the bottom of the automobile price range.

Okay, Neal, you say. *Point taken. But how do you get from there to "The louder the commercial, the dumber they think you are?"*

Here's where I step into it yet again. The truth hurts, and the truth is that the smarter you are, the less likely it is that you're going to be buying a car in the lowest price range. If you're smart, chances are you've parlayed that intelligence into a better-than-average living. And if you're making a decent living, why would you be interested in the cheapest, most underpowered, most bell-and-whistle-less cars on the market?

Conversely, the less sharp you are, the more you're likely to be in a low-paying job with barely enough money to buy a new car in the first place.

These auto dealers aren't stupid. (Trust me on this—in my lawyering days I represented quite a few.[1]) These dealers spend huge amounts of money on ad agencies and focus groups trying to figure out how to target the very socioeconomic group that's most likely to buy their cars. What they've learned is that higher-income consumers not only tune out those loud, screaming car ads, they're actively offended by them. Those with lower incomes, on the other hand, respond to them.

'Nuff said?

Much to the distress of our advertising sales weasels, who are constantly out there trying to sign these folks up to big-money advertising contracts, I've been complaining about these dealers' tactics for

---

[1] Okay . . . they might not have shown the best judgment in hiring me to be their lawyer; other than that, they're not stupid.

years. If I'll willingly suffer the slings and arrows for saying them on the air, I might as well repeat them here for you to ponder.

Advertising volume and noise aren't the only signs that a car dealer thinks you're an idiot. The promises they make in their commercials are another dead giveaway.

Screaming announcer: *"We'll pay off your old car no matter how much you owe!"* Yeah, sure they will. And they'll take the difference between what you owed on that car and whatever trade-in allowance they've given you, and add it to the amount of your new car loan. Come on, now—you didn't really think they were going to pay off your old balance just to be nice, did you?

Oh . . . you did? I'll bet you still have a Kerry/Edwards bumper sticker on your old beater, don't you?

Screaming announcer: *"All credit applications accepted!"* How wonderful! "Hey, Gloria! Blivet Motors is going to give us credit! Let's go get a new car!" Think again, hotshot! They just said they'd *accept your application.* That is, they'll allow you to apply. They didn't promise to grant you credit. Sure, they know how it sounds . . . but that little come-on is just a way to get you unsuspecting rubes in the door.

Know this: No truly reputable automobile dealer will ever use either of those two phrases in an ad—just as no truly reputable attorney would ever advertise on television.

One more thing before I quit picking on auto dealers:

Would you, the consumer, please tell me why you allow your local car dealer to slap an ad on the trunk of your new car before you drive it off the showroom floor? Why do you pay all that money to turn your $30,000 car into a car commercial on wheels?

I actually had one woman tell me she thought it was illegal to remove those stickers—much like the label on her mattress.

What was it I said about dumb customers?

THE RIGHT TO VOTE

Let's start here:

What right to vote?

You think you have a right to vote? Let me break this to you as gently as I can: You have no right to vote. None. *Nada.* It doesn't exist.

Oh, it may be true that your state's constitution contains guarantees your right to vote—*in state and local elections.* But that's really as far as it goes.

I invite you to pull out your dog-eared copy of the U.S. Constitution. (Come on, I know you have one. We're a country of laws, and this particular document is supposed to be the supreme law of the land—*le grande fromage* of all laws! Surely you have a copy handy! If not, just log onto the Internet—you can find it there in all its glory, in transcript or facsimile form.)

Okay . . . start reading. Where's that right to vote? You're so sure it's in there . . . show it to me! (Oh, and before you get all excited about the Fourteenth and Fifteenth Amendments—better reread them, because they're not what you're looking for. Keep digging.)

Give up? All right, relax. It isn't there. That's correct. The right to vote is *not* in the U.S. Constitution. There are provisions that prevent states from limiting any voting rights that might be present in state law based on your skin color, religion, gender (or lack thereof), or other protected status. But there's no provision that United States citizens are guaranteed the right to vote in national elections.

Don't want to take my word for it? Fine, I'm a talk show host, so I understand. (I also happen to be a lawyer. . . . I know, strike two.)

One person you *should* listen to is Michael C. Dorf, a professor of law at Columbia University and a prolific contributor to findlaw.com. In December 2000, he wrote a column titled, "We Need a Constitutional Right to Vote in Presidential Elections."

The good professor happens to be a liberal, and it seems he was a bit upset with the results of the 2000 election and the Florida recount debacle. Al Gore did, after all, get the majority of votes cast for president, so if it weren't for that pesky Electoral College, he would have been elected!

Dorf called the Electoral College "an undemocratic Eighteenth Century relic."[1] And then he really got on a roll:

> Amidst the divisiveness of the United States Supreme Court's second foray into the 2000 Presidential election, it is easy to overlook the significance of the Court's earlier, unanimous ruling of December 4, 2000. A close reading of the decision in that case, *Bush v. Palm Beach County Canvassing Board,* reveals a clear consensus for what will strike many Americans as an outrageous proposition: there is no constitutional right to vote in a Presidential election. The fact that the state in which you reside even permits you to vote for electors is purely a matter of legislative grace.

And there's the rub: In the current American system of government, the right to cast a ballot is not a right at all. It's a privilege offered to you by the states.

The states get to decide, for instance, whether or not you are going to be allowed to vote for president. Thus far not one single state has seen fit to allow you to do so. In all fifty states, you're not voting for the president at all. You're voting for a *slate of electors.* A few weeks

---

[1] This is how many liberals look at our entire Constitution. Anything that doesn't promote the concept of mob rule, which is the very essence of democracy, earns the "relic" designation.

after those electors are chosen, they get together over a few martinis somewhere and they—not you—decide how their votes for president are cast.

Here's the dirty little secret that Prof Dorf and just a few others already recognize: If your state decides it wants to appoint the VIP room bouncers from the state's highest-grossing strip club to be the electors in the next presidential election, then that is how it shall be. You get to sit back and watch,[2] but you have no say in how they vote.

At this point, I would be remiss in my duties to you, dear reader, if I did not suggest that strip club bouncers might very well have done a better job in some elections in the latter part of the last century than the actual electors chosen by the voters. Strip club bouncers, for instance, wouldn't vote for a man who has shown a penchant for using his position of power and authority to abuse women in the way at least one of our recent presidents has done.

I'm a realist. I recognize that if this question were to go before our current Supreme Court, they would probably conjure up a right to vote from some obscure Constitutional smudge. Perhaps they would say that since the citizens of some half-baked East European country are granted a right to vote, then it just must be assumed, in spite of any evidence to the contrary, that the right exists here as well.

So much for our Constitution being the supreme law of *this* land.

Let's face it: the modern Supreme Court would conjure up a Constitutional right to an iPod and free music downloads if there were enough social pressure to do so. Today's Supreme Court is more an agency for social change than it is a court of law.

The point I'm trying to make is that our founding fathers—the men who put this whole thing together—had no intention whatsoever of establishing anything close to a "one man, one vote" electoral system. They wanted to restrict voting on several grounds, some appropriate, some not. But they most certainly did not feel that the

---

[2] Watch the electors casting their ballots. Not the action in the VIP room. Unless, that is, you care to tip heavily.

mere fact of citizenship or residency should guarantee access to a voting booth.

Given the grade-A chumps our voters have chosen in recent years, maybe they were on to something.

So who *should* have the power of the ballot? Who should have the right to choose who gets their hands on that unique power that goes with what we love to call "public service"—or, as I think of it, the power to use deadly force to accomplish your goals?

In case you haven't picked up on it yet, I believe that the privilege ought to be limited.

There's a quote that I've been using for some time now that has been attributed to a number of different historians and authors, among them Alexander Tyler (or Tytler, if you please), Benjamin Disraeli, Arnold Toynbee, Lord Thomas Macaulay, Jack the Ripper, and others. Who actually wrote it? Who knows? Regardless of the original author, however, the idea itself rings true:

> A democracy cannot exist as a permanent form of government. It can only exist until the voters discover that they can vote themselves money from the public treasury. From that moment on the majority always votes for the candidates promising the most money from the public treasury, with the result that a democracy always collapses over loose fiscal policy followed by a dictatorship. The average age of the world's great civilizations has been two hundred years. These nations have progressed through the following sequence: from bondage to spiritual faith; from spiritual faith to great courage; from courage to liberty; from liberty to abundance; from abundance to selfishness; from selfishness to complacency; from complacency to apathy; from apathy to dependency; from dependency back to bondage.

Sound familiar? By your reckoning, aren't there an awful lot of voters in this country whose primary concern in casting their vote is to fatten their own pocketbooks? Isn't our country full of businessmen who vote for the candidate who promises the biggest government contract? And aren't there millions of Americans who base their vote solely on which candidate is going to funnel the most taxpayer-funded government benefits their way?

What about that bit about the progression of societies? Isn't it hard to deny that we're somewhere along the apathy-to-dependency stage right now? When was the last time you heard someone say, "I wish the government would just butt out of my desperate situation. I put myself here, I'll figure out how to fix it"? In your dreams, perhaps?

Admit it: If ever there was a society where people have discovered the magic of using the ballot box as an instrument of plunder, it would be the United States.

So when we start thinking about who really deserves the right to vote, there are some obvious candidates for restriction.

Welfare recipients, for one. As things stand, we allow people who live completely and totally off taxpayer money to reelect, year after year, the very people who arranged our money to be transferred to their outstretched hands in the first place. Are we nuts?

You remember, of course, the so-called "motor voter act." The official name is the National Voter Registration Act of 1993. This law even has its own website![3] Log on and you'll find, emblazoned across the top of the page, this headline:

"The Right to Vote Means Nothing . . . Until You Register."

(*What right to vote?* you may ask. Well, tell a lie often enough . . .)

We called that bill the motor voter act because it demands that every person applying for a driver's license be offered an opportunity to register to vote. Few know this legislation *also* demands that every single U.S. resident applying for welfare benefits *also* be offered the opportunity to register to vote.[4]

It might as well be called the Welfare Voter Act.

---

[3] www.motorvoter.com

[4] I would have used the words "every single U.S. citizen" here, but there seems to be little concern in D.C. about limiting the vote to citizens . . . especially among Democrats.

Did it ever occur to you that the politicians behind motor voter were actually motivated by self-interest? That they were simply scratching the back of a whole new voting bloc, who in turn were being offered a golden opportunity to dig even deeper into your own pockets by putting their favorite candidates in office?

Since we've established that voting in national elections is a privilege, not a right, why not at least do something to make people earn it? Why in the hell should we be approaching people who can't even take care of their own basic needs and saying, "Hey, how would you like to help us choose our leaders?"

It's completely absurd that the votes of people who have squandered every educational opportunity they have, who have failed to develop a work ethic, who have spent their time downloading a litter of skateboard riders they can't afford to raise, and who now depend on legalized plunder for their very existence, should count as much as the votes of people who work hard, who have agonized over their choices and made the right ones, who provide for their own family and plans for the future without having to dive into someone else's pocket.

Oh . . . I can hear the rumbles beginning now.

I can hear you getting all puffed up with your righteous indignation and your superior sense of morality, tsk-tsking about how insensitive I'm being. Save it. I'm immune to your moral exhibitionism. Deep in your own heart you know I'm right. You've busted your glutes to get where you are, and now someone who has made a life's work in living off the work of others gets an equal voice in selecting our leaders? On what level does that make any sense at all?[5]

Get rid of this "right to vote" mentality and start to apply some common sense. You'll agree, even if you're loath to admit it.

---

[5] As long as we're talking about welfare recipients and making sense, a while back the board of directors of Atlanta's Metropolitan Atlanta Rapid Transit Agency (MARTA) made the stunning decision to appoint a career welfare recipient as their chairman!! A welfare recipient running a billion-dollar transportation agency? Well, sure! Makes perfect sense to me!

A KNOWLEDGE TEST!

> It is difficult to conceive of a more worrisome relationship than that
> between ignorant voters and highly knowledgeable, well-organized
> political activists.
>
> —ILYA SOMIN,
> *"How Political Ignorance Threatens Democracy,"*
> USA Today *Magazine, November 1, 2004*

The sad fact is that most of the people in this country are completely
clueless—call it brain-dead, if you wish—when it comes to understanding how our government is supposed to operate and just who is
up there running the show.

More American men can name the two head football coaches at
their state's two major universities than can name the two people who
represent them in the United States Senate. More American women
can tell you who was crying on Oprah's shoulder yesterday afternoon
than can tell you who their congressman is.

If you don't understand the basic workings of our government, if
you can't name those who can confiscate your wealth at will, and if
you can't name the people who have a tight grip on the exclusive right
to use deadly force to accomplish their goals, then you have no business gumming up the works on Election Day. Stay home.

How ignorant are Americans when it comes to government?[6]
Maybe you don't really want to know. Read on . . . if you promise not
to slash your wrists:

One fair measure of the ignorance of the American electorate
is the number of people who blissfully send their children to the
government to be educated. For a more thorough evaluation of the
problem, you might turn to an analysis of the problem issued by
the Cato Institute on September 22, 2004. The report is titled,

---

[6] I believe the argument can be made that Americans are ignorant by design. What politician
truly wants a fully informed voter? And just who is it that controls our schools?

"When Ignorance Isn't Bliss. How Political Ignorance Threatens Democracy."

In his report, Somin points out that voter ignorance "raises doubts about democracy as a means of serving the interests of the majority."

Learned as Somin might be, he may have skipped a few history or civics classes. It is not now, nor was it ever, the intended purpose of our government to serve "the interests of the majority." Our Founding Fathers understood this quite well.

That's why we don't *have* a democracy. It's why the Fathers spoke in such fearful terms of the concept of democracy. It's why they gave us a republic instead—a government founded on human rights and laws, not on the dangerous principle of simple majority rule.

We can forgive Somin that confusion, however, because he's done such a dandy job of detailing the pathetic level of ignorance in our voting population.

Here are some gems from his report to lighten your day:

• You'd think most Americans know that Congress recently passed a law creating a massive prescription drug program for our Wizened Citizens. Well, 70 percent had no idea.

• While most people know that our budget deficit has increased, 60 percent don't know that that rise is largely due to increased federal spending.

• Can you name either one of your U.S. senators? Well, you should feel special—not just because you're reading this book, but because 70 percent of the people in your state can't. (And notice, I didn't ask for *both* senators . . . just one!)

• Wouldn't you expect any well-informed voter to know which political party controls the House of Representatives? Well, you'd be wrong. Before the 2002 election, fewer than one-third of voters polled could have told you that the Republicans were running the show at that time.

- Remember the election of 1994? The election that put the Republicans in control of the House and the Senate, and had Bill Clinton telling us that "the era of big government is over"?[7] One month after that historic election, 57 percent of Americans had no clue who Newt Gingrich was.

- In 2004, our economy showed some rather large job gains. Yet more than 60 percent of voters thought we'd lost jobs that year. They clearly weren't listening to my radio show.

- Try this one. Only *4 percent* of Americans can tell you the name of the person running against the incumbent congressman in their home district.

Pretty bad, huh? And that doesn't even scratch the surface of areas like the three branches of government and the roles they play in running affairs of state.

As Somin says, "The American electorate fails to meet even minimal criteria for adequate voter knowledge," adding that such ignorance "potentially opens the door for both elite manipulation of the public and gross policy errors caused by politicians' need to appeal to an ignorant electorate in order to win office."

Bravo, Professor Somin! I'm especially impressed by your statement that "efforts to increase the stock of knowledge possessed by voters are unlikely to be more than modestly effective."

Exactly!

So here's my radical proposition: Instead of trying to increase that stock of knowledge, why not *decrease* the number of ignorant voters!

---

[7] He lied.

Private businesses don't let ignorant employees decide company policy. Why should we allow ignorant voters to set public policy?

And don't give me that "right to vote" nonsense. I've shown you it doesn't exist. We are free to set some standards, as long as they don't discriminate against people for circumstances (like race, sex, or religion) that are beyond their control.

If the powers that be want me to devise the appropriate voter qualification test, I'll be more than happy to oblige. Put my test in place, and a good portion of the dumb masses will be sitting at home on Election Day.

No charge.

THE "INVEST IN AMERICA" APPROACH

Now here's an approach to limiting the privilege of voting that I'm particularly fond of. You buy shares of stock in America, and on Election Day you vote those shares. Simple as that.

How do you buy shares? Glad you asked.

Two ways.

You get your first share simply by enrolling—by being an American citizen. You get subsequent shares by paying taxes. Easy as that.

That process has worked for corporate America for generations. The more you invest in a business, the more you have to say about how that business is run. The more shares you own, the greater your voice in electing the board of directors.

So why not develop a system whereby the more you pay in federal income taxes, the more say you have in electing America's "board of directors"? One vote for being a citizen, then another vote for every $25,000 in income taxes you pay, averaged out over the previous four years. A citizen who averages $20,000 a year in income taxes gets one vote. A citizen who averages $100,000 a year in income taxes gets four votes.

And, yes, we can put a cap on it—say, five votes max—to keep Bill Gates, Warren Buffett, and Sean Hannity from running the whole show.

There you go, getting all puffed up again. Haven't you given up on this "right to vote" stuff *yet*?

If, as Henry Ford said, "the business of America is business," let's cherry-pick some ideas from the business world as to how to run our government.

No businessman would grab some derelict living in a homeless shelter (no doubt supported by his business's tax dollars and charitable contributions) and say, "Hey, pal! How'd you like to help me choose who runs my company?" If your average businessman can see the stupidity in an idea like that, why can't we?

But Neal, you may be saying. *What about my brother the screwup? Doesn't he get to vote?*

Sorry, folks, but that's my bottom line: I don't think stupid people *should* vote. The ones who are too irresponsible or ignorant to bother figuring out how our government works aren't doing our system any good. And the ones who are living off the fat of the land, courtesy of the welfare system, have only one motivation: to keep the money flowing.

After all, you wouldn't give your teenage son or daughter the opportunity to set family financial policy—to tell you where you can and cannot work, where you should make your investments, or what to do about retirement.

Why would you turn our country over to people you wouldn't trust to clean out your gutters?

ABORTION

You have reached the shortest chapter in this book.

As I've hinted already, abortion is a subject I refuse to discuss on the air, except in the simplest of terms.

Why? Because you have your opinion and I have mine, and though we may talk until we're blue in the face, neither of us is going to change the other's mind. There's absolutely no point in arguing about it.

Having said that, I've promised my listeners that I would address the issue, at last, in these pages. So here goes:

I don't like abortion.

In fact, I'm anti-abortion—especially when it's used for purposes of birth control.

But that doesn't mean you'll see me toting around a pickled fetus in a jar or blocking the doorway and cursing at a seventeen-year-old girl as she tries to get inside to see a doctor on what is probably the worst day of her life.

You see, it is possible to dislike abortion and still be pro-choice.

I'm not a woman. I'll never be pregnant. Thus it's not a decision I'll ever have to make. Nor should it be. And I wish to play no role in coercing a woman one way or another.

Lest you wrongly conclude that I've suddenly gone all soft-hearted—or, worse, bleeding-hearted—let me set the record straight. My concern isn't really for the emotional discomfort a woman must go through in order to undo a bad sexual choice. In fact, that experience probably *ought* to be unpleasant—at least enough to make her think long and hard before the next time she starts kicking back tequila shooters at Applebee's at two in the morning.

Okay, that's a little harsh. But you get my point.

No, my real concern isn't over preserving our precious "family values" or any of that other right-wing hoopla on the subject. In fact, I consider much of the debate about abortion—from both sides—to be a smokescreen, a distraction. The real threat, to you and me and everyone else in America, male or female, is the Imperial Federal Government.

I don't know about you, but I simply refuse to believe that my government should be powerful enough to pull out a gun and put it to a woman's head to force her to have a child she doesn't want to have. Because, believe me, the government won't stop there.

Oh . . . and one more thing.

The terminology is not "pro-abortion" and "pro-life." It's "pro-choice" and "anti-choice." Only those two terms present the controversy in a way that's fair to both sides. And you know what a stickler I am for being fair.

End of discussion.

GIVING BACK

Warren Buffett became a media hero by giving away some of his money. Never mind that he created an investment empire that enabled tens of thousands of Americans to earn money through investments and working. He was elevated to public sainthood when he started giving away the money he had worked for.

Ranked behind Bill Gates as the second-richest man in the world, Buffett created quite a stir with the announcement that he would give away some 85 percent of his vast fortune to charity. That's about $30 billion—by far the largest gift in the history of corporate philanthropy.

Sorry . . . but all I can say is, *Big deal.*

All right, I know you might think this makes Warren a very special guy. The media certainly thought so. After his announcement the media fawned over him as if he had discovered a cure for baldness, age spots, and body odor in one swell foop.

Nice job, Warren. But, still, you're going to be left with—what? $5 billion? $6 billion? $15 billion? So spare me your moral exhibitionism. Sure, you're giving away a lot of money, but even the leftovers will dwarf what most people make in their entire lives—hell, what the residents of most towns, all together, make in their whole lives. Your progeny won't exactly be worrying about paying the light bill.

So it's not as though you agreed to a premortem organ donation, now, is it?

There are many Americans out there who really do give till it hurts. They give so much of themselves and their earnings that they're left with financial struggles for the rest of their lives.

Figure this one out: If someone takes a fortune and gives it away, he's inevitably anointed as a hero. Statues are commissioned in his honor; bridges are renamed in tribute. If someone else takes a fortune and uses it to begin a hugely successful business—one that employs thousands of workers, bolsters our economy, and provides a useful product or service—he's either ignored or placed in the ranks of evil corporate capitalistic predators who drink the blood of minimum-wage workers as part of some IPO ritual that takes place only under a full moon.

Give money away: Good Guy.

Use money to make money: Bad Guy.

Warren Buffett gives money away. Bill Gates gives money away. All the rest of us just sit back and wait for the inevitable moment when some mindless journalist or pundit pops out of a hole some-where to tell us that these men are "giving back!"

They're not "giving back," you footstools![1] They're "giving"!

Sometimes just using the phrase "giving back" isn't enough. After Buffett announced his grand benevolent gesture, the nicely coiffed talking heads on ABC's *Good Morning America* were heard yammer-ing about how Warren Buffett was preparing to "give back" some of his "winnings."

Now there's a curious turn of a phrase: "Give back some of his winnings." There I was, all this time, operating under the clearly mistaken assumption that Warren Buffett had actually *earned* that money. I thought he worked for it. Now I learn that somehow—somewhere—he'd actually *won* it, and now he's going to *give some of it back!*

Perhaps the good Mr. Buffett will step forward and clear the air on

---

[1] This little piece of invective is in honor of my father. He used it often and to great effect. Imagine the payoff when someone asked just what a "footstool" was.

this issue. What's the story, Warren? Did you win that money? Was it *given* to you? ABC can't seem to make up their minds; maybe you can help us out.

To be fair, I don't believe Warren Buffett actually used the words "give back" himself. Bill Gates, however, has.

Specifically, Gates described his philosophy as one "of giving back my wealth to society." Now, Bill Gates has a lot of money. In fact, his time is so valuable that the mere act of breaking stride to bend over and pick up a $100 bill on the sidewalk would cause him to actually lose money. What shocks me is that, according to Gates himself, this extraordinary wealth was *given* to him—a nicely wrapped present, apparently, from our generous society.

We need someone to blame for this orgy of self-indulgent "giving back," so I'm nominating Ted Turner. Why not? He's an affable sort of guy—and besides, he gave a billion bucks to the United Nations. When you give that much money to an organization dedicated to anti-Americanism, you're fair game for just about anything.

Turner is another rich guy who just can't seem to bring himself to admit that he worked for his wealth: "Since I'm very privileged," Turner is quoted as saying, "I try to give back to the world what the world has given me."

But "giving back" his own money didn't satisfy Turner. He wanted to "give back" other people's money, too. And so, in 1997, Turner started badgering Gates and Buffett to jump on the charity band wagon with him. Thus my effort to hang him with the blame.

"What good is wealth sitting in the bank?" Turner asked. "It's a pretty pathetic thing to do with your money." (Almost as pathetic as losing it all in bad deals with Time Warner and AOL. But that's another story for another day.)

But take a moment to ponder Ted's question. *Does* money do any good sitting in the bank? Ted considers that a pathetic thing to do with your money. I consider Ted's perspective pretty pathetic. Let's look more closely.

A young couple needs a loan to pay some unexpected medical

bills. They go talk to their local bank. A brief credit and employment check looks good, and the young couple gets the loan. Where did the money for the loan come from?

From those pathetic losers who let their money sit in a bank, that's where!

A businessman goes to talk to his banker about a loan to expand his business. He excitedly tells the banker that his market study shows great potential for growth, as long as he expands and hires more people. The banker agrees, the loan is made, the business is expanded, jobs are created. New businesses are created to cater to the needs of the expanded company and the new employees. More jobs. More economic growth. Naturally, the entire community benefits. Again . . . where did the money come from?

From those pathetic losers who let their money sit in a bank!

Gee, Ted, maybe you're on to something, I don't know. But then, where would we get our next car loan? Unless . . . maybe you'd be willing to give us the money yourself? You know, *give a little something back to the world?*

A prominent business newspaper reports that my hometown of Atlanta will lead the nation's metropolitan areas in the creation of new millionaires over the next five years. Sounds like a good time to be living and working in Atlanta, doesn't it?

But wait!

It's not as though these new millionaires are actually going to *work* for their money. It's not just the leftist saps on *Good Morning America* who believe that wealth is won by the wealthy, or given to them. Check out this lead paragraph in a story appearing in the *Atlanta Business Chronicle:* "Multiplying millionaires will dramatically alter the way Atlantans live, shop, bank and give back over the next several years." Yup, there it is again. "Give back" is like kudzu—ugly and everywhere.

Newsweek has even established something they call the "Giving Back Awards." They've chosen fifteen "winners" who are helping other people by "giving back." The honorees included entrepreneurs such as Pierre Omidyar, who built a sizeable fortune with what is now known as eBay; Brad Pitt, who takes home big paychecks for being handsome; and Randy Rusk, a Colorado rancher.

Notice a trend here? You'd have to be stupid or a Democrat (sorry for the redundancy) not to. "Giving back" is now the conventional (leftist) wisdom. Nobody—especially not the evil, wretched rich—actually *earns* anything anymore. Fortunes aren't earned but won or freely given.

Why do liberals think this way? Because they find it impossible to acknowledge that people work for money. What about *you?* Chances are you didn't win whatever money you have, and I'm pretty sure it wasn't given to you. You probably traded some rather large hunks of your life, hour after hour, day after day, month after month, year after year, *working* for that money. Now some leftist ass or TV talking head comes along and suggests that whatever you have, whatever you've labored to earn, whatever you've sacrificed to save . . . is nothing but "winnings." Golly! How lucky you've been!

Words have meanings, and meanings create consequences. We try to tell our children that if they work hard and smart they can grow to be comfortable, if not rich. So when we tell our children that those who have actually accumulated some wealth didn't actually work for it, what's the message we're sending?

You can just hear the unruly teenagers now. "Come on, old man! Which is it? Do you want me to work hard, make good choices, and keep my nose to the grindstone so I'll have enough money to keep you and Mom out of the nursing home fifty years from now? Or do you want me to sit around and wait for someone to give it to me?

"Am I supposed to work for my money, or do I get to win it?"

We're creating a whole new language here, and it certainly isn't by accident. The left has never been fond of acknowledging the value of hard work, perseverance, and good decision-making in acquiring wealth. After all, any good leftist knows that wealth is distributed, not earned. Thus the extraordinary lengths to deny people the credit for the hard work that goes into wealth accumulation.

In 2006, Edward L. Rubin, the dean of the Vanderbilt University Law School, wrote a widely published opinion piece promoting the concept of wealth confiscation and redistribution.

"At present," Rubin wrote, "the top fifth of the population receives more than 59 percent of the nation's annual income, while the bottom fifth *receives* around 3.5 percent."

Ahhh . . . another weasel word to add to the list: "Receive."

Let me try to explain it another way. During the 2006 NFL season, the Atlanta Falcons had a particularly bad game against the New Orleans Saints in the Georgia Dome. As the team was leaving the field, the fans started heaping abuse on quarterback Michael Vick. Vick had just run more than 150 yards during the game; it certainly wasn't his fault that his receivers dropped about 300 yards' worth of on-target passes. So Vick did what any red-blooded American would do under those circumstances: When he heard the fans booing, he gave the mighty finger to the fans . . . twice, once with each hand. Now *that* was giving back. He hadn't earned that abuse, so he gave it back to those who had tendered it.

Later, the NFL declared that Vick should pay $20,000 ($10,000 per finger) for his little demonstration, and that $10,000 of that should go to charity. Vick then made a series of donations to some Atlanta charities. Can you guess what happened next?

You got it: The *Atlanta Journal-Constitution* headlined the story on its Internet site "Michael gives back."

This is more than a semantic argument, folks. I'm talking about a deeply flawed concept that leads to some deeply flawed thinking. My favorite example comes from a recent article in the *San-Antonio Express News*.

"Children raised in affluent families have their own unique set of challenges," the article states. "The wealth that rich parents share with them could hinder them from being fulfilled, productive members of society. If, indeed, they are mentored early, they can give back to future generations many times over."

Did you catch that? *Give back to future generations?*

That's a pretty neat trick, but as far as I know, even DeLoreans can't *really* travel back and forth through time. So it probably isn't worth your time to sit around hoping Doc Brown is going fire up the flux capacitor and drive through a hole in the space-time continuum to drop off a bundle of dough from some long-dead relative.

All this giving-back nonsense completely negates the reality that the people doing all of this donating actually earned what they're giving away through hard work, good choices, responsible decision-making, and perseverance. Something in the illogical and irrational way liberals perceive our world has rendered poisonous the very idea that anyone who has achieved great wealth actually did so through hard work.

"Oh," your typical liberal will say, "they didn't earn that great wealth, they inherited it!" Right. Tell that to Bill Gates and Warren Buffett. Neither of these men was born into poverty, but they certainly didn't *inherit* their billions. Gates, a college dropout, started Microsoft and the Windows revolution. Buffett, whose grandfather owned a grocery store, invested wisely—again and again.

The inconvenient truth for the wealth-redistributionist left is that fewer than 2 percent of millionaires in this country inherited their wealth. This giving-back hooey is just their attempt to negate the idea that people actually work for what they acquire. And it's affected our culture in deep-seated ways.

From our hideous government schools onward, we are hammered constantly with messages, both subliminal and blatant, that whatever we may have is ours not as a result of our own efforts; not as a result of the years of our lives that we have sacrificed; but because of the luck of the draw or someone else's largesse.

The goal of the left is to acquire and maintain political power. One of their most effective tools in this quest is their perceived compassion—compassion that's shown by spending someone else's money. If they are seen as confiscating wealth that was actually earned, that could be interpreted as, well, *unfair*. So they're happy to promote the fantasy that the money they're confiscating has been won in some grand game of chance. After all, that way they're just evening out the odds a bit.

And if the general perception is that the wealthy have been *given* most of their fortune, even better: Why not ask (that is, demand) that they give some of it back?

Here's a thought for Warren Buffett: If he finds himself in any hardship after all the giving back he's done, he should just let us know. Maybe we'll give him some of his stuff back to help him ease the pain.

Wait a minute! That actually *would* be giving back, wouldn't it?

WHAT KIND OF MINDLESS HORSESQUEEZE IS THIS?

I spent the first part of the 2006 Independence Day weekend at the Grove Park Inn & Spa in Asheville, North Carolina, playing a bit of golf, relaxing, and working on *Somebody's Gotta Say It*. While there, I was treated to several editions of the *Asheville Citizen-Times*.

This is a Gannett newspaper, put out by the same folks as *USA Today*. Needless to say, its slant is decidedly leftist. That seems to fit in quite well with the Asheville community, which, I'm told, is quite proud of its liberal leanings.

A quick glance at the letters to the editor seemed to bear out the rumors of yet another left-wing newspaper. It seems that the good citizens of Asheville are somewhat preoccupied with matters like raising the minimum wage. From the looks of things, Asheville is a city that embraces the idea that the government should force employers to pay their employees more than their services are worth to the employers. I wonder how many of these people willingly pay more than market value for an item when they're out shopping in Asheville's trendy little frou-frou boutiques . . . just because they want to put some extra money in the merchant's pocket?

As I've said plenty of times before, it's oh-so-easy to show compassion when you're showing it with someone else's money. Interesting, isn't it, that conservative communities tend to give more of their own money to charities, while liberal communities tend to give more of someone else's?

Anyway, the July 2 edition of the *Citizen-Times* carried a front-page questionnaire entitled "How Patriotic Are You?" Readers were invited to take a quiz of ten questions and grade themselves. Under this questionnaire there was a quote from one Randy Goodstadt, the chairwoman of social and behavioral science at the Asheville-Buncombe Technical Community College. To wit:[1]

> If people don't have a basic knowledge of history and civics, it means that people who are voting are complete ignoramuses, people who don't read a newspaper, who don't understand the policies of the people for whom they are voting. It's very scary. Very worrisome.

Well said, Ms. Goodstadt! Now perhaps you might hold a little training session with the folks at the *Citizen-Times*. Here are the ten questions they posted to test their readers' historical knowledge:

1. What is the date that the Declaration of Independence was signed?

2. What document is the legal framework of the United States?

3. Who wrote the words to the "Star Spangled Banner"?

4. What is the Pledge of Allegiance?

5. Where was the Declaration of Independence signed?

6. What is the number of original Colonies?

7. Who was the first president of the United States?

---

[1] You see, I did learn something in law school. "To wit" really means "that is to say" or "namely." I'm also fond of *res ipsa loquitur.* That means "the thing speaks for itself." I tried to market a line of men's underwear years ago when I was honoring the community with my legal skills called "legal briefs." Right there on the front it said *"res ipsa loquitur."* People didn't get it. You probably don't either. As they say: *Res ipsa loquitur, sed quid in infernos dicet?*

8. What is the minimum voting age in the United States?

9. Who is the current governor of North Carolina?

10. What is the motto of North Carolina?

Well . . . somebody's gotta say it, so here goes.

That is perhaps the most moronic, idiotic, shallow, meaningless, worthless, and plebian tests of a person's patriotism I've had the privilege to laugh at in my entire life.

It is just what you would expect from a left-wing newspaper.

Only two questions out of those ten are worth spending more than one nanosecond to answer: Questions 2 and 8. People do need to know that the Constitution is, or is supposed to be, the legal framework of the United States, and if you're at all interested in voting, it might serve you well to know that the minimum age is eighteen. The other eight questions are completely worthless; knowing the answers has absolutely no bearing on whether you're knowledgeable or patriotic.

Perhaps the *Citizen-Times* was having its annual Shallow and Meaningless Writing contest.

Now, you just knew I was going to have some suggestions on how to beef up this little quiz, didn't you? Let's take, oh, sixty seconds or so and see if I can come up with a better citizenship quiz than the *Asheville Citizen-Times*.

1. Forget *when* the Declaration of Independence was signed. (Hint: It wasn't July 4.) Instead, explain *why* it was signed. What were the signers trying to accomplish?

2. What happened to the men who signed the Declaration? Did they go on to be heroes and live happily ever after?

3. What does the Declaration of Independence say the people can do when a government becomes destructive to the ends of liberty?

4. Are we about there?

5. What would happen to anyone who tried today to alter or abolish our government if it became destructive to the idea that government derives its powers from the consent of the governed?

6. Which articles of the Constitution grant specific powers to the federal government?

7. Which article of the Constitution restricts the powers of the government to only those specifically set forth in the Constitution?

8. Which article of the Constitution do you imagine is the one most often ignored by the Congress of the United States?

9. Describe the circumstances under which Francis Scott Key wrote the words to "The Star Spangled Banner."

10. Do you believe people living in a free country ought to be compelled to recite a pledge of allegiance to that country? Why?

11. If you are required to recite a pledge of allegiance, are you really free?

12. Was the Revolutionary War supported by a majority of the colonists?

13. Should Washington have developed an "exit strategy" before he ever led his troops into battle during the Revolutionary War?

14. Where in our Constitution is it stated that anyone has a right to vote for the office of president of the United States? (If you've been following me, this one's a gift.)

15. How did our original Constitution provide for the appointment of senators?

16. Most foreign countries appoint an ambassador to be their official representative before the government of the United States. Who officially represents the fifty state governments before the government of the United States?

17. Explain the difference between a rule of law and the rule of man.

18. Explain the difference between a democracy and a constitutional republic.

19. Was our country founded as a country of majority rule?

20. Can you imagine what our country would be like today if the majority did rule?

21. Aren't you glad the majority doesn't rule?

22. If two wolves and one sheep vote on what they're going to have for dinner, what do you think the menu will look like?

23. Why does it matter in the grand scheme of things who the governor of North Carolina is?

24. Isn't a governor something you put on a state to keep it from moving ahead very fast?

25. What possible benefit could you gain by memorizing the motto of the state of North Carolina—or any other state, for that matter?

26. How many times can the word "democracy" be found in the Declaration of Independence and the U.S. Constitution?

27. How many times can the word "democracy" be found in the constitutions of any of the fifty states?

28. What does this tell you?

29. Define "civil war."

30. Was the war between the Northern and Southern states in the mid-1800s a civil war?

31. Who is third in the line of succession to the presidency?

32. Based on your answer to the foregoing question, would you demand that George Bush and Dick Cheney never eat from the same container of potato salad now that the Democratic Party is in control of the House and the Senate?

33. How did the political class manage to fool the people of the United States into supporting a Constitutional Amendment creating an income tax?

34. How do most people get their news on a daily basis?

35. Does the "freedom of the press" clause in the First Amendment apply to the broadcast media?

36. So, do most people get their news from agencies licensed to operate by the federal government?

37. Why were the words "under God" placed into the Pledge of Allegiance?

38. Do you think it's proper for the federal government to compel students attending government schools under compulsory attendance laws to acknowledge the role of God in the formation of our country? Would this constitute "effecting an establishment of religion"? If not, why not?

39. Do Americans derive their basic rights from the Constitution?

40. If we don't derive our rights from the Constitution, just why was the Bill of Rights added anyway?

41. Define a system of government where the means of production are owned and controlled privately.

42. Define a system of government where the means of production are privately owned but controlled by the government.

43. Define a system of government where the means of production are owned and controlled by the government.

44. Why do liberals have such a tough time answering question number 42?

45. What percentage of total income is earned by the top 1 percent of income earners?

46. What percentage of total income taxes collected by the federal government is paid by the top 1 percent of income earners?

47. Where in our Constitution does it specifically state that only U.S. citizens may vote for the office of president of the United States? (Caution: trick question.)

48. Name one right that a state government can exercise without interference from the federal level.

49. Where in our Constitution does it specifically state that only U.S. citizens may vote for members of the House of Representatives?

50. Look at the Bill of Rights. List any amendments in the Bill of Rights that were ratified for the purpose of limiting the powers of the government.

51. If our Constitution provides for equal protection under the law, why, then, does the Voting Rights Act only apply to certain states that were held in political disfavor in the 1970s?

52. List any amendments in the Bill of Rights that were ratified for the purpose of limiting the rights of individuals.

53. If the Bill of Rights was written to limit the rights of government and to guarantee certain rights to the individual, try to explain why so many people seem to think that the Second Amendment was written to limit the rights of individuals and guarantee the rights of government?

54. Does the First Amendment protect speech that some people might find offensive?

55. Explain how our republic was threatened when Janet Jackson showed the world that she likes to wear a Japanese throwing star on the nipple of her left breast.

56. What is the one exclusive power our government has that no individual or business can legally exercise?

57. If we were playing rock-paper-scissors and treaties with foreign nations duly ratified by our Senate were the paper, would our Constitution be the rock or the scissors?

58. Do you have the right to use force to take money from a stranger if you're going to give that money to someone in need?

59. Explain the concept of our government deriving its powers from the consent of the governed.

60. Now explain how you can tell the government to do something for you that, if you did it for yourself, would be a crime.

61. Should the government make something you might do a crime if that action doesn't violate another person's right to life, liberty, or property through force or fraud?

62. How many votes must you have in the Senate to be assured that a piece of legislation will pass?

63. Do you have a choice as to whether or not you pay Social Security taxes?

64. Why, then, do they call Social Security taxes "contributions"?

65. What is the average age of a country or society based on the rule of law and guaranteeing freedom, individual rights, and economic liberty?

66. Has the United States outlived its life expectancy?

If I didn't have so many other things to cover, I could expand this list until it filled an entire book. For instance, I could add a hundred or so questions beginning with "Where does the United States Constitution give the federal government the right to . . ." I think sixty-five questions are enough, though, don't you?

Here's a fun fact: Within days after I first posted this revised citizenship test on my website on July 5, 2006, I was flooded with letters and messages from government schoolteachers around the nation, telling me that this quiz, and the matters covered therein, would be the core of their next history and/or government class.

That's nice to know, and I thank you for the flattery. As for the rest of you, it might be interesting to spend one class session asking these questions. Who knows, someone might accidentally learn something.

THE TRAGEDY OF OUR GOVERNMENT SCHOOLS

Can anyone possibly write about our system of education in this country and make it even a mildly interesting read? I certainly hope so, and I'm always willing to give it the old college try, because I think that perhaps the most dangerous entity at work in this country today is our system of government education.

We love to talk about illicit drugs, crime in the streets, sexual predators, and pornography—all things we recognize to be damaging to our culture. We condemn these things while praising our system of education.

How screwed up is that?

Our government schools are killing the spirit of our children and, in the process, our country. They are destroying the greatest civilization mankind has ever known. The America you grew up in will bear little resemblance to the America your grandchildren will grow up in—unless something is done, and done soon, about education.

Early in 2006, I made a simple, off-the-cuff statement on the air that seemed to anger some people. *"Teachers unions,"* I said, *"pose a graver long-term threat to freedom, prosperity and the future of this country than do Islamic terrorists."*

As you might expect, the comment created a bit of a sandstorm.[1]

---

[1] Now if you want to believe that when I say "sandstorm" I'm really talking about sand, you just go right on ahead. Whatever floats your boat.

By the time I hit the air the next day, I'd had plenty of time to think about what I'd said, to consider the consequences of my off-hand remark. I knew there were many dedicated teachers out there who might have been offended by my words. I also knew that most parents were operating under the assumption that their children were getting a good education at their local "public" school.

So, after a great deal of soul-searching, and bearing in mind that I wanted to maintain at least a modicum of credibility with my listen-ers, I made a decision. I needed to address those intemperate remarks I had made as soon as I returned to the air the next day.

So, after going through the requisite *Rah-rah! It's me on the radio!* introduction, I reminded the listeners of what I had said the day before. I detailed the angry e-mails, and my consideration for the feel-ings of the good teachers you will find here and there.

Then I told the listeners that, after considerable deliberation and introspection, I had decided that what I had said the day before was *absolutely correct.*

I wouldn't retract a single word. In fact, I repeated it for those who might have missed it. Only **LOUDER.**

There is no greater long-term threat to our continued prosperity, economic liberty, freedom, and quality of life in the United States than that presented by teach-ers unions. And that includes Islamic terrorists.

Subject: Your comments
Name: Georgette _____
E-mail: G*******@comcast.net

Now you've lost me. I've been listening to you for years, but no more. Your comments bashing teachers today were inexcus-able. Right wing elitist fascist jerks like you need to be taken off the air. To compare teachers with a terrorist group is wrong.

I'm going to share your comments about teachers with the other teachers at the school where I teach, and I promise you that when we call your advertisers you will be wishing you had picked another group to pick on.

Your days are numbered.

Ohhhhhh! Georgette knows how to say "bashing"! She also knows that whenever you're criticizing a conservative (she wouldn't know what a libertarian was) you need to use the word "fascist" or "Nazi" or include a reference to Hitler, or you lose points. Isn't it nice to know that Georgette is a teacher?

But I digress . . .

Maybe Georgette does have a point. The comparison may be a bit unfair. After all, there is one glaring difference between teachers unions and Islamic radicals: Most Americans recognize the threat presented by the Islamofascists. Not so with the teachers unions. Far too many Americans still think the teachers are on our side.

A quick review, and I'll try to disabuse them of that notion.

Look at it this way: What can the Islamofascists do to us other than kill us? Their most effective weapon is violence. Unless they actually do decide to attack us with one of those long-rumored weapons of mass destruction, their power is limited. Yes, they can kill individuals—a hundred at a time, or thousands! They can hijack a plane, blow up a building, or strap a suicide vest to some poor sap. Yes, they can cause a momentary disruption in our economy, a ripple that fades within months or weeks or days. They can be cruel and wreak chaos and tragedy.

Well, guess what? We've been through all that before, and we survived.

We can recover from the destruction that may be visited on us by these Islamic radicals. But can we recover from the damage being done by our hideous government schools?

A massive terrorist weapon might destroy a city. Our government schools will destroy a generation.

There are millions of our children in government schools every day. Those schools are responsible for making sure that these kids learn what they need to survive as adults in the world.

Face it: they're failing.

That means that the future of those kids—that is, the next generation of adults, who will have to keep this country going for the next thirty or forty years—is in jeopardy. Those kids aren't getting what they need to cope in a free society. They are being educated to become perfect myrmidons, in love with government and suspicious of liberty.

Far too many of the high school graduates of today couldn't get promoted to the seventh grade thirty years ago. Without the government to care for them, they will face a future of chaos and want.

The failure of our children to learn . . . now *that's* a real danger to our society.

The real problem here is not so much the teachers unions as it is our system of government schools itself. But we can't fix that system as long as the unions are standing in the way . . . and standing they are.

THEY'RE GOVERNMENT SCHOOLS . . . NOT PUBLIC SCHOOLS

First, let's get our terms straight. Our so-called "public schools" are *government* schools. They're operated by the government, using government employees, on property owned and controlled by the government, using government funds. And they should be identified as such—if only to reveal the malicious wizard behind the curtain.

Supporters of this destructive system would object to such candor, of course, since most Americans know that to identify something as a "government institution" is to brand it as inefficient at best, destructive at worst. To refer to these schools as "public" is to associate them with rank-and-file Americans. We haven't been nearly bad or incompetent enough to have earned that negative association.

Child abuse is neither always obvious nor intentional.

The most rampant form of child abuse in this country is not only legal, but committed routinely. It is the act of taking what arguably is, or should be, the most precious things in your life—your children—and placing the responsibility for their education in the hands of the government.

There's no escaping the fact that our country has problems . . . huge problems. I believe, however, that these problems have a common cause—that being the ignorance and stupidity of people whose "education" (if you want to call it that) was inflicted at the hands of the government schools.

Year after year, our wonderful government education system cranks out hordes of young men and women who are completely unable to cope with, let alone understand, our culture, our history, our institutions, and what it takes not just to survive but to thrive in America.

We've reviewed the alarming facts already. Average high school graduates cannot tell you the responsibilities, or even the names, of the three branches of government. They can't tell you the name of the vice president, and probably don't even know that there is a designated third in line in the presidential succession.

They can't make change or do basic mathematical computations without a computer or calculator. They can't read apartment leases, balance their checkbooks, or read maps. They certainly have no understanding of capitalism or free enterprise, and couldn't write a one-paragraph description of what constitutes a profit. You would die of old age before you could find a freshly minted government high school graduate who could tell you the difference between a profit and a profit margin.

A disgusting portion of this government school effluent ends up in remedial courses in college before they can take on any actual college-level material.

A few years ago, I bought a dozen golf balls from a fine-looking young man at a driving range. The balls were cheap—ten bucks a box. I tend to lose a lot of golf balls. Unfortunately, the cash register was on the blink. Today cash registers are computers and they actually figure the sales tax.

You can see this one coming, can't you? The young man couldn't figure out what to charge me for sales tax. The $10 part he figured out just fine. But adding 6 percent to that figure had him almost in tears.

Finally he asked me for $12.50. He was nailing me with a 25 percent sales tax instead of 6 percent. It was an off day for all of us—for me, for him, for the tax system.

I didn't want to humiliate this young man by calling attention to his ignorance, so I told him I'd bought a box of the same golf balls the day before and the total was $10.60.

He breathed a sigh of relief and took the money.

And this is what we get after twelve years of taxpayer-funded education?

You're damned right it is, if we look to government to get the job done.

Our wonderful government educational system produces graduating classes of young Neanderthals with no sense of individuality, no sense of self-worth, and no understanding of what it means to live in a truly free society.

Internationally, our educational system is a laughingstock with a well-deserved reputation for mediocrity, if that. America may be admired for a long list of things, but our educational system isn't one of them.

Most of the rest of the industrial world is putting us to shame when it comes to education. Our children rank way below those of most European and Asian nations when it comes to testing on the basics. The European kids score higher on math, reading, and science tests than our children. It's an embarrassment.

In the spring of 2006, John Stossel hosted an excellent ABC special called *Stupid in America.* As Stossel reported, American fourth graders do well on international tests, but by the time they get to the high school level, American kids are well behind those in most other countries.

After the report aired, teachers unions called Stossel everything but a Child of God; they even demonstrated outside his office in New York. The lesson? Don't screw with teachers unions.

As part of *Stupid in America,* Stossel gave parts of an international test to students in an above-average New Jersey school. The same test was given to some students in Belgium. The Belgian kids made our kids look like morons. When the results were announced, the Belgian students themselves called the American students "stupid."

Why do we put up with these atrocious standards? Why do we allow our local governments to seize such huge amounts of cash from us in the form of school taxes, and then spend impossible amounts of money *not* educating our children, while we sit back like a bunch of numb-minded dolts and do absolutely nothing?

Aren't we better than this? Don't we want better for our children? At some point don't we start to understand that government has failed at the task of educating our children as badly as it has at almost everything else it's tried?

Oh, was that too harsh? All right, I'm listening. Think real hard and try to come up with one government program that works really, really well.

Social Security? Yeah, right. I know that Democrats like to call Social Security the most successful program in the history of our federal government, but it's failing, folks. It's going to be bankrupt before your children are old enough to collect benefits, and every attempt at any meaningful reform is demagogued by Democrats who are more worried about votes than about your retirement years.

Medicare? Medicaid? The Postal Service? Surely you jest.

Come on, I'm waiting!

To illustrate the folly of allowing the government to handle our most difficult life challenges, let's try a little experiment. Ready?

Pretend it's 1850. Try to put yourself in the mindset of someone living in the middle of the nineteenth century. Now, I'm going to ask you to consider four different tasks to be accomplished in the next 150 years. All I want you to do is sit down and think about how you would go about accomplishing these goals. I know, you won't live long enough to see them all come to pass, but surely you can develop the basic framework needed to get these tasks done.

Then, after thinking about it, I want you to tell me which task you believe would be easiest to accomplish. Here are your choices:

1. Figure out a way that I can sit in my living room in Thrall, Texas, and watch a performance of *The Nutcracker Suite* live, as it is happening, from the Bolshoi in Moscow.

2. Expand the average life expectancy of human beings by about thirty-five years.

3. Develop a method of transporting 350 people from Los Angeles to New York City in five hours.

4. Build a system of paved roadways from city to city across the country.

There you go. Remember, you're considering these tasks from the perspective of someone living in 1850. Which one of those do you think would be easiest?

Unless you just want to screw with me a bit, you're going to chose number 4—building a system of paved highways. Good choice. And you should know that this is the only item from that list that was actually accomplished by government.

Items one through three were accomplished by the private sector, by private individuals working in our competitive free enterprise marketplace pursuing private goals.

So, tell me, who decided that this government, which can't do anything as efficiently and well as the private sector,[2] is somehow the best-qualified entity out there to educate your child?

Diane Ravitch is a historian of education at New York University. In June 2005, she wrote a column for the *Wall Street Journal* about math education in our government schools. In the early 1990s, she noted, the National Council of Teachers of Mathematics issued a new set of teaching standards that "disparaged basic skills like addition, subtraction, multiplication and division, since all of these could be easily performed on a calculator."

Wonderful. Just wonderful. That's like saying that we don't need to teach history because any child in need of a historical fact can just look it up in a history book.

Helps explain that clerk at the driving range, doesn't it?

Ravitch's column noted that researchers Williamson Evers and Paul Clopton had compared a 1973 algebra textbook and a 1998 "contemporary mathematics" textbook commonly used in our schools. In the 1973 book, the index entries under the letter "F" included words like *factors, factoring, fallacies, finite decimal, finite set, formulas, fractions,* and *functions.* What about the 1998 book? *Families, fast food nutrition data, fat in fast food, feasibility study, feeding tours, Ferris wheel, fish, fishing, flags, flight, floor plan, flower beds, food, football, Ford Mustang, franchises,* and *fund-raising carnival.* Reading this, another "F" word comes to mind—as in "What the F are these people trying to teach?"

My guess is that the only reason you tolerate this hideous system of government education for your child is because you don't realize that there may be a better way.

We're going to work on that assumption, but before we do, let's put another misconception to rest.

---

[2] Okay . . . so that's not exactly true. Government can, I believe, wage war better than the private sector, but that would be due to the one unique power that government has that we, as private individuals, do not have; and that would be the legal right to use deadly force to accomplish its goals.

Would you think I'd finally gone off the deep end if I suggested to you that these government schools really don't exist for the purpose of truly educating your child in the first place? What if the people who developed our system of government-run, compulsory education had other goals in mind?

Allow me to suggest to you that our government schools were designed not to foster excellence through knowledge, but rather to insure that the American masses are relegated to an insipid, dull existence where they have barely enough knowledge and drive to sustain themselves in an anti-individualist society, but not enough of an education to understand how thoroughly our system of government is destructive of individual initiative and the quest for excellence.

May I also suggest that while these schools are busy robbing our children of their uniqueness and ambition, the collectivist left regards it as an added bonus that these schools just happen to provide employment for hundreds of thousands of loyal government workers—government workers who become good little government union members.

Are there people wiser than I who might go along with such a preposterous idea?

Why . . . as a matter of fact there are!

If you want to know what the people who designed this whole mess were thinking, John Taylor Gatto has done a lot of the homework for us. The author of *The Underground History of American Education: An Intimate Investigation into the Problems of Modern Schooling*,[3] Gatto was a teacher, and by all accounts a good one: He was named New York City's teacher of the year three times, and won the state title once. As blogger Russ Kick[4] writes, Gatto "became dis-

---

[3] New York: Oxford Village Press, 2001.

[4] The quotes attributed to Gatto's book came from Russ Kick's article "The Educational System Was Designed to Keep Us Uneducated and Docile." Posted on July 17, 2006 at http://www.thememoryhole.com.

illusioned with schools—the way they enforce conformity, the way they kill the natural creativity, inquisitiveness and love of learning that every little child has from the beginning." So Gatto began to dig into the routs of our education system.

Now here's something that Gatto turned up that should give you a big clue about how our schools were designed. In 1988 the Senate Committee on Education expressed concern that the nonstandardization of education brought on by local control was actually teaching the children too much! The committee report said, "We believe that education is one of the principal causes of discontent of late years manifesting itself among the laboring classes."

Are you grasping this? By their own admission, the legislators entrusted with our children's education were mostly concerned with making sure your children wouldn't learn so much that they'd become discontented little worker bees in their later years.

Think of the number of ways our government stifles initiative through tax and regulatory policies. Isn't it to the advantage of a government bent on suppressing individualism and individual initiative to rob its citizens of their drive to excel?

I'd tell you to go find Gatto's book to learn more, but in case you don't, here are a few more of the gems he's turned up. With luck, the 2 x 4 of undeniable facts will hit you hard enough upside your head to convince you that something is very, very wrong.

The outrages date back to the turn of the century. As psychologist and education "reformer" John Dewey wrote in the 1890s:

> Every teacher should realize . . . that he is a social servant set apart
> for the maintenance of the proper social order and the securing of
> the right social growth.

Oh, that's just dandy. Here we were, thinking that these teachers were there to teach our children—and now we learn they're there to maintain some sort of proper social order. As determined by whom? Interesting question.

Try this one: In 1905, Elwood Cubberly, the future Dean of Education at Stanford, defined schools as factories "in which raw products, children, are to be shaped and formed into finished products . . . manufactured like nails, and the specifications for manufacturing will come from government and industry."

There you go. Your child is merely raw material that is to be transformed into some finished product manufactured according to government specs.

Now, listen to the Rockefeller Education Board, which funded the creation of many government schools. Gatto quotes the board:

> In our dreams . . . people yield themselves with perfect docility to our molding hands. The present educational conventions [intellectual and character education] fade from our minds, and unhampered by tradition we work our own good will upon a grateful and responsive folk. We shall not try to make these people or any of their children into philosophers or men of learning or men of science. We have not to raise up from among them authors, educators, poets or men of letters. We shall not search for embryo great artists, painters, musicians, nor lawyers, doctors, preachers, politicians, statesmen, of whom we have ample supply. The task we set before ourselves is very simple . . . we will organize children . . . and teach them to do in a perfect way the things their fathers and mothers are doing in an imperfect way.

If those words don't bother you, then you're part of the problem.

We're talking about *your* children here. You need to give serious consideration to the possibility that you've willingly surrendered them to a system that was designed, and is being operated to this day, to see that all but the very brightest are safely passed through the system to become simple obedient Americans, ready to spend the rest of their lives working menial nine-to-five jobs while obediently paying their taxes and remaining subservient to the omnipotent Imperial Federal Government of the United States.

You may be an unwitting accomplice in the destruction of your own child's initiative.

That's a provocative charge, but deep down I know you recognize the truth. You know that our system of education is a disaster; now you might even suspect that it's all by design! Now all you can do is wonder whether the government educational establishment ever was, or ever will be, truly committed to educating our kids.

The ugly truth is that any actual educating that takes place in these hideous operations is merely a by-product of the process of creating safe, complacent citizens—while providing jobs for underqualified teachers, many of whom would have little chance of earning a comparable salary in the private sector. These people, led by their unions, are hell-bent on ensuring that no one comes along and upsets their monopoly apple cart.

The problem with so many Americans is that they will quickly agree that our government schools are horribly broken, and perhaps beyond fixing—except, of course, for the one where they're sending *their* children. Your child's school is doing a great job, right?

One Gallup Poll showed that more than three-quarters of Americans are satisfied with their child's government school. As John Stossel pointed out in his special, these parents—and that may well include you—just don't know any better. They have no idea how much better these schools would be if they simply introduced one element into the mix: competition.

Say the word "competition" around government school teachers, though, and you're likely to get your palm slapped with a ruler.

There is no greater sign of our delusion about the value of our government schools than those insipid MY CHILD IS AN HONOR STUDENT AT THE _____ SCHOOL bumper stickers. How sad.

I'll see your bumper sticker and raise you one: MY PAPILLON IS SMARTER THAN YOUR HONOR STUDENT. Come on, folks. Wake up and smell the ignorance. You might as well put a MY CHILD CAN TIE

HIS SHOES bumper sticker on your minivan. After all, it's entirely possible that many "honor students" can't.

As things grow progressively worse in our government schools, administrators and education "experts" are working hard to come up with even newer and more innovative ways to fix things. Try some of these ideas on and see how they fit your idea of a quality system.

In one government school system, teachers have been instructed to stop using red ink to grade papers. Red, after all, is an *angry* color. Our precious children have a negative reaction when they see red on their papers. We have to be sensitive to their precious little egos . . . so no more red.

Some schools have abandoned the grading system altogether. No more A, B, C, D, and F. Why? First of all, because you never want to tell a child he's failing. That could have such tragic consequences for his precious self-esteem. (Never mind that when this kid gets into the private sector, his boss will have no qualms at all about pointing out his failures—which he's certain to have if no one ever challenged him to improve his work.)

One school was so determined to get rid of the negative consequences of grading with letters that they changed to geometric shapes! Now there's an incredible advance in educational theory: Instead of As, Bs, and Cs, grade with circles, triangles, and squares! "Look, Mom! I made straight triangles!" What a delight when young men and women across the country can brag of never having received a square on their report cards. That ought to look impressive on a resume.

Florida, on the other hand, actually grades its government schools. If a school is particularly pathetic, it can even receive an F! Still, the Self-Esteem Police have a way of twisting the most embarrassing failures into knuckleheaded successes. Several years ago, a school in the Orlando area got an F for the previous year's efforts. When the children showed up for the following school year, though, the teachers and staff were wearing T-shirts emblazoned with "F is for Fantastic!"

Can you imagine what you'd do if your child brought home a few Fs on his report card, and excitedly told you that these grades were "fantastic"?

In the Gwinnett County government schools in suburban Atlanta, they've gone even further—they've turned our traditional grading system directly on its head. A Gwinnett County parent sent me a document entitled "Weekly Folder." "This document grades the student on conduct, work habits and behavior," the paper explained. Here, according to the legend printed on the Weekly Folder, is what those grades mean:

D = Exceeds Standards

C = Meets Standards

B = Does not meet standards

A = Significantly does not meet standards

Can someone tell me what the hell is going on here? D is the best grade you can get, and A is the worst? What possible purpose does this serve—other than keeping the parents and kids confused enough that they stop complaining altogether?

Agreed, then: Our government schools have been failures at educating. But you've got to admit, they've been marvelous successes at political indoctrination. And much, if not most, of their efforts in this direction have been leftist-inspired.

We are a nation that loves government. The more the merrier. Self-reliance is out; government reliance is in. Think about it: When people find themselves up to their necks in trouble, the current fashion is to start screaming for the government to do something to save them. It never seems to be up to the individual, always the government.

Have we come by this sense of government dependence honestly? Or is it the inevitable result of our government-controlled educational system?

Look at it this way. If your children go to a Catholic school, you can expect them to be taught that Catholicism is pretty much the way to go. Ditto if they attend a Jewish school or a Baptist academy. Why, then, shouldn't you expect your children to be taught the infallibility of government while attending a government school? Do you really expect a faculty of government employees to stand before your children and teach them that, as Henry David Thoreau once said, "That government is best which governs least"?

As a government operation, your local public school comes to praise government, not discredit it!

The next time you get a little bored, try a little experiment: Check your child's textbooks to see how our Bill of Rights is being presented. Harcourt Brace,[5] a major publisher of schoolbooks, published a social studies "activity book" that had a page addressing the Bill of Rights. This one is a real eye-opener.

Consider the Second Amendment. Now, if you've still got that copy of the Constitution lying around from our earlier activities, a quick glance will show you that the Second Amendment protects our right to keep and bear arms. "The right of the people to keep and bear arms shall not be infringed," it says simply and directly.

How does the Harcourt Brace textbook present that fact? Try this: "The Second Amendment says that states may enlist citizens for a trained militia [army] and provide and train them with weapons."

Can you believe that? That is a complete perversion—and a politically correct one at that—of what the Second Amendment actually says. Not one mention of "the right of the people . . . ," just a quietly vague reference to the government providing weapons to the army. How can this be viewed as anything other than a blatant attempt at indoctrination? It's clearly an attempt to disabuse these young minds of the idea that the Second Amendment has anything to do with our individual right to own firearms.

Is this the kind of education you want for your children?

---

[5] Now known simply as "Harcourt."

How about the Tenth Amendment? This amendment was written to limit the power of the federal government. It reads: "The powers not delegated to the United States by the Constitution, nor prohibited by it to the states, are reserved to the states respectively, or to the people."

Well, that's not the Harcourt Brace version. Here's your indoctrination: "The Tenth Amendment says that any powers not given to the federal government may be passed on to the state governments and the people."

"Passed on"? Where does the Tenth Amendment say anything about "passed on"? You can't "pass on" something you don't have, and the Tenth Amendment clearly states that these powers are "reserved by" the states and the people, not "passed on" to them. That's a huge difference, and clearly quite a little spin job by someone with an agenda. Step right up, folks: government schools preaching the doctrine of omnipotent government!

Since you won't hear about these guys in a government school, allow me to call your attention to a couple of characters named Marx and Engels, who in 1848 wrote a little tome called *The Communist Manifesto*. It's a much bigger book than this one, actually, and the authors are noticeably less funny than yours truly. Somewhere in its many pages, however, Marx and Engels actually list the ten things they feel are necessary to clear the way for a Communist society.

Several items on that list are pretty darn interesting,[6] but the one that's relevant to this discussion is Number 10—last but certainly not least:

"Free education for all children in public schools."

Now why do you think that's on their short list of things to do? Because they knew that the quickest way to bring about a change in the basic structure of society would be to seize control of the hearts and souls of just one generation. Take one generation, destroy their

---

[6] "A heavy progressive or graduated income tax," for instance.

love of true freedom, instill in them a reverence for government and a rejection of the concept of individuality, and you're on your way.

That, more than anything else, may accurately describe the role of our government schools today.

The upside, if there is one, is that the problem also can be fixed in one generation.

The fix? Competition. End the government monopoly on education and give the competitive free market a chance.

American history is filled with examples of the free market beating the socks off government institutions when given a chance to compete.

How long did it take *you* to switch from the United States Postal Service to UPS for shipping packages? I used to work in a Postal Service bulk mail facility. I can still remember one fall night as I was standing at the top of a platform. Boxes were coming up one conveyor belt. I would take those boxes, read the zip code, and then send them down the appropriate chute. I was taking great pride in doing the job accurately and fast.

Suddenly the conveyor belt delivering the boxes to me came to a halt. Another postal worker walked up the ramp to my position.

"Look," he said. "I'm the union foreman on duty tonight. You need to slow down. You're getting these packages sorted too fast."

"Why is that a problem?" Damn, was I naïve.

"If the supervisor knows we can work this fast, we won't be able to get as much overtime when Christmas gets here."[7]

---

[7] Okay, this is a long footnote. But I just had to tell you something I did during my stint with the Postal Service. (I think the statute has run out, so it's okay.) My physician at that time was Charles Watkins, a wonderful country doctor. Dr. Watkins had a nurse/office manager who was, shall we say, somewhat of a prude. A holy-rolling prude, if you will. One night I was sorting a shipment of mailing tubes that contained a calendar featuring a beautiful girl who had lost all of her clothes. As chance would have it, I came upon the tube, addressed to Dr. Watkins. I opened it, took out the calendar, wrote "Thanks for the great time in Vegas, Charles," and sent it on. Oh, those wacky postal workers.

Amazing. Intentionally doing a poor job in order to get more hours. Unions. Gotta love them.

Whether the task is delivering packages to Grandma, or well-educated children into the world, the problem is the same: Our government is a case study in bad motives and bad results. And the answer, in both cases, is competition—in the form of school choice.

Before we discuss how to proceed, though, let's take a little shopping trip.

To Moscow.

SHOPPING WITH
SVETLANA

My second trip to Russia was very different from the first, in that it took place after the fall of the Soviet Union.

This time, we *were* permitted to stay under the roofs of Russian citizens. It proved to be an eye-opening experience.

Donna and I were guests in the home of a fairly well-known Russian TV broadcaster and his wife. For various reasons, I don't want to identify them, so I'll call him Yuri and her Svetlana.

Yuri and Svetlana were part of the cultural elite. They were better off than many other Russians. Yet they still lived in a dwelling that wouldn't qualify as Section 8 welfare housing in most cities in America.

We slept in their—well, I don't know what it was. The living room was also their master bedroom. Sofa here . . . bed over there. Besides their very small sitting area—where our bed was—they had a kitchen and one small bathroom the size of an SUV's cargo area. All the pipes were exposed.

And remember, these people were the elite.

One night, Svetlana said she was going to cook us a meal at home.

"Do you want to go shopping with me?" she asked.

"Sure," we said, even though it was the middle of Russian winter. But I'd never been out grocery shopping with a Russian housewife in the middle of a Russian winter before. *Why not?* I thought.

Svetlana put a cloth bag over her shoulder, and we left. We went down the rickety stairs of the dilapidated apartment complex and into the cold.

Our first stop was a bread store. Buying bread, it turned out, was a hit-or-miss proposition. These were still the early days, and free enterprise—capitalism—hadn't yet seeped into the economy. There were no supermarkets, no one-stop shopping.

"We'll see if they have any bread," Svetlana said.

Luck was with us. The store had a couple of stale loaves, and we grabbed one.

Next we headed to a dairy store, in hopes of scoring some cheese. It was dimly lit and horrible-looking. Again, most of the shelves were empty, but we took the best of what was there.

After that we trudged on to the meat store, which had flooded a little bit from the melted snow. We actually had to slosh around in mud as we walked to the display case. We were able to put our hands on a couple of really terrible cuts of meat, from some creature that I suspect might have been pulling a garbage wagon just a few days earlier.

At the vegetable store, we finally struck out. Nada. There was nowhere else to go.

These were the government-run "grocery" stores that served Svetlana's neighborhood. You want to eat, this is where you buy your food. Piling into the car and going to a restaurant just wasn't an option. Oh, there was one little bistro in their neighborhood, but one evening meal for two there would cost nearly a month's worth of the average Muscovite's salary.

Nevertheless, Svetlana did an incredible job of preparing our repast.[1] We promised to return the favor someday, and we did. (More on that later.) For now, let's get back to the government schools, the real purpose of this trip down a cold Russian memory lane.

---

[1] Svetlana's pride and joy was a rudimentary microwave oven. She and Yuri kept it inside a cabinet, wrapped up, and brought it out only on special occasions.

What if grocery stores in the United States were all run by the government, the way our schools are?

A far-fetched proposition? I think not.

After all, people have to be healthy enough to work and make a living. The government could easily have decided it needed to make sure everyone has groceries, just as it decided it needed to make sure everyone has an education.

The process would be simple. A "nutrition tax" would be added to your property tax bill. From the proceeds of that nutrition tax, your family would be permitted to purchase a set amount of groceries from your assigned grocery store over the course of the year.

Your grocery shopping experience would be dismal. Selection would be limited; quality would be marginal.

In our government-run grocery stores, you wouldn't be able to choose between Dole packaged salads and American Garden packaged salads. There wouldn't be different brands of dairy products or meat or breakfast cereal. You would basically buy what the government deemed fit for consumption. My guess is that it would be bland, unimaginative, and tasteless at best.

The voters would probably elect local "grocery boards" that would make policy decisions on what would and would not be carried. Political hacks would run for positions on the local grocery board, with campaign promises of a wider selection and lower prices. You would know their promises to be empty, but you would cast your hopeful vote anyway.

Every neighborhood would have its grocery store, but not of the Mom-and-Pop variety. Your zip code would dictate where you were allowed to purchase food. That store, and that store only, would have your grocery account information. You would be permitted a certain dollar amount of purchases every week. If you wanted more, you would have to pay out of your own pocket. If you wanted to shop elsewhere, you would have to spend your own money.

It's a safe bet that the workers at these government-run grocery stores would be unionized. The workers would earn more than they could in the private sector, but that would be fine, since their jobs would be so *important.*

Now let's say someone—maybe me—comes along and says, "You know what? These government-operated grocery stores just aren't working out. We're getting an inferior quality. Nutritionally, we're not being served. We need a voucher system."

A voucher system, you say?

"That's right. We need the government to issue vouchers for groceries, so that people can take the vouchers for redemption at the grocery store of their choice."

Wow. Imagine that!

"And anybody can get into the grocery business. All you have to do is meet certain health and quality requirements. If you want to open a grocery store, go ahead. That way, people can decide for themselves. If they want to shop at a government store, fine. If they want to shop at your store, fine. They can just use their vouchers anywhere they want to shop!"

Well, that's just a little too logical, isn't it?

Of course, you know what would happen. First, the unions representing grocery workers would scream bloody murder. They'd condemn the voucher plan, arguing that it would hurt the poor. They'd claim that only the wealthy would be able to go out and shop for groceries.

Sound familiar? I'm not going for subtlety here. I'm reaching for the 2 x 4 again.

We would get the same arguments against vouchers for grocery stores that we get against vouchers for education.

A few months after our second trip to Russia, Svetlana and Yuri got to visit the United States. Needless to say, they were in awe.

"How could you afford this?" Svetlana asked when she saw our house.

"This is a middle-class home," I explained.

On her first full day in America, my wife, Donna, and I took Svetlana grocery shopping. This time, however, it wasn't in the harsh winter streets of Moscow. It was in a huge farmer's market in Atlanta. One of those giant, cheerful places where you walk in and see stacks and stacks of fruit and vegetables of every description.

As we entered, I peeled off to find a shopping cart. I returned to find Svetlana frozen in her tracks after taking only about five steps into the place.

She was just standing there, in disbelief, with tears running down her face.

"Who shops here?" she asked.

I told her the truth:

"Anybody."

Even for Russia's wealthiest citizens, nothing like this farmer's market existed in her homeland. To Svetlana, it was a paradise.

I will never forget the look on her face—the look of a citizen of the former Soviet Union experiencing her first taste of what capitalism and the competition of the marketplace can bring to the lives of an ordinary citizen.

There is no reason in the world this same magic can't be brought to our system of education.

That's our next chapter.

FIXING OUR SCHOOLS

There's a reason so many government school teachers send their children to private schools: They're in these schools every day. They know how bad they are, and they're willing to sacrifice to save their own children.

The answer to the problem of our failing schools is not to be found in spending more money, hiring more teachers, or tweaking the curriculum.

The answer is to be found in *freedom*. The freedom of parents to choose how their money is spent to educate their children.

As I've noted, many European schools outperform the government schools in the United States. To add insult to injury, though, consider this: Those schools outperform ours *while spending less money per child to do it*.

How do they pull that off? One fundamental difference between the two systems is that in many of these European schools the money follows the child, not vice versa.

European parents have a choice as to where their children will attend school. Once that decision is made and each child is enrolled, the government sends the money.

In America, your child is basically assigned to a school based on your home address. That's where the money has been sent, so that's where you send your child.

Step one, then, in improving our schools is to put the government schools in competition with one another. Allow parents to compare schools within a certain geographical boundary, and then decide on one for their children. Once the parent enrolls their child, the money will follow.

Sure, the teachers unions will howl over this. Let them. It's good exercise. But give the parents some element of choice.

The second step would be to involve private free enterprise. Don't just give the parents a choice among the local government schools, but offer them the option of selecting a private school as well.

This is what's commonly known as a school voucher system, and it's the teachers unions' worst nightmare.

If your local government is spending $9,000 a year for every child in government schools, just issue a $8,500 voucher to parents for every school-age child in their household. The local officials can keep $500 per child to handle administrative expenses. This money is for teaching, not for hiring herds of administrators.

The parent then takes that $8,500 voucher and goes hunting for a school.

I hear many complaints about the lack of parental involvement in their child's education. Well, what do you expect? After seizing your money, the government assigns your child to a school without consulting you, and with no regard whatsoever for your wishes. Then the government creates a curriculum and grading system over which you have no control. Just how is a parent encouraged to get involved in this process?

You want parents to get involved? Give them a choice! Put the responsibility where it belongs—in their own hands. Let them be an integral part of their children's education! Let them compare the performance figures for government versus private schools. Let them trade notes with other parents about which schools offer better services, about where the best teachers and administrators are working.

When things could be so much better, why do we settle for our current fiasco? If you ask me, it's because most parents just don't know how much better things could be.

Many of you have enough years under your belt to remember

when AT&T had a virtual monopoly on your telephone service. Innovations were few and far between. In fact, I can remember only three significant innovations that occurred under the government-protected monopoly.

First, we got different colors for our phones.

Then came the amazing technological breakthrough known as the Princess phone!

Then, finally, there was touch-tone dialing.

Did you know that during this era it was actually illegal in many areas for a private citizen to purchase and use a telephone answering machine?

But then, at last, the monopoly ended. What happened? Call waiting, call forwarding, voice mail, speed-dialing, call-blocking. The list is long. Then came cell phones and all the advances that have been made in wireless communications.

Very little of this would have happened if the government-enforced monopoly had been left in place.

And so it would be with our schools.

Competition would bring innovations we can only dream about today. With school choice and school vouchers, an entire new industry would form around educating children. Fifteen years from now, parents would look back and wonder why they ever considered leaving the education of their child up to the government.

Are there arguments against school choice? Sure, but they're easily countered.

Opponents of school choice and vouchers are afraid that the best students would abandon their government schools, leaving the schools worse than they were to begin with, perhaps even forcing them to close and stand empty. And, yes, that's one possible outcome.

Do you think the fear of closing bad schools keeps me up at night?

The answer is obvious. If one government school gets closed because it can't compete, then that means there are other schools that are doing the job and attracting customers (in the form of students)! There will always be private operators out there who would be more than glad to purchase or lease the facilities of the now-closed government school and use them as the campus of another private educational venture.

Others complain that a voucher program would discourage wealthier families from sending their children to government schools, leaving them with only children from poor and broken families to educate.

Oh, yeah, that's a good argument. Why not just turn all housing over to the government while we're at it? After all, we don't want any children living in better homes than children from poor families, do we? *One size fits all* doesn't work in baseball hats, and it doesn't work in government.

The fact is, there are many private schools in virtually every community in America that do a better job of educating than the local government schools, and on less money per student.

Here's a surprise, folks: Poor parents want the best for their children, just like everyone else. In fact, poor parents may be *more* motivated than well-to-do parents, since they have every reason to make sure their children receive the educations they never got. These parents will create a demand for quality education that private entrepreneurs will be more than happy to address.

And don't forget: Under this plan, the government schools would be in there competing for those vouchers, along with everyone else. If the government wants to compete, they should compete. If all kinds of schools, public, private, and parochial, are fighting for the butts in those desks, it can only be healthy for the student body. And if the government schools win—well, hallelujah.

Because there's one way they can win: by offering a superior product.

Of course, that's hardly the attitude at play in many American schools today. I can just see all the teachers right now with their arms crossed, disapproving frowns on their faces. The last thing they want is competition.

Remember, folks, we're talking about government employees.

Teachers aren't any different in that regard than garbage collectors or airport security screeners. What they care about is job *security*, not job performance.

The late Albert Shanker, former president of the powerful American Federation of Teachers, certainly felt that way. "When schoolchildren start paying union dues," he said, "that's when I'll start representing the interests of schoolchildren."

This was one of the country's most respected educational leaders, people.

By the way, Shanker had toyed with Communism in his earlier years, but rejected it as impractical. "I knew that the Socialist Party was not going to elect a president of the United States," he said, "but you had a Democratic Party which was more liberal and stood for at least some of the things socialism stood for. So the thing to do was to operate within the Democratic Party."

Which only adds fuel to my next point.

There is one thing we could do, easily and inexpensively, to improve the quality of education in America almost immediately— and that is to reduce the power of the teachers unions.

These unions, which play an enormous role in the lives of our children, are dedicated to the concept that the government should be in charge of the education of the masses. If you doubt me, Google the words "American Federation of Teachers" or "National Association of Educators" and read up on their respective agendas.

A vast majority of the resolutions presented at the teachers union conventions concern opposing voucher programs and preventing private competition to the government school system.

Just look at what happened in Florida.

A few years ago, the state attempted to implement a voucher system. It was called the "A-Plus" school accountability program. As I said earlier, they started grading government schools. If a particular school received an "F" for two years in a row, the students from that school were offered vouchers they could use to find a better school, public or private. This meant that the teachers in the government schools had to perform. If they failed to perform they could lose students, and losing students could mean losing jobs.

But, as everyone knows, when you work for the government you're not supposed to have to compete with the private sector or fear losing your job. So the Florida teachers unions filed a lawsuit—and won. They successfully killed the Florida voucher system. The Florida Supreme Court shut the whole thing down in January 2006.

A teacher/activist named Ruth Holmes Cameron was one of the plaintiffs who rejoiced over the "victory." She gave newspapers one of the most inane, but telling, quotes I've ever read:

"To say that competition is going to improve education? It's just not gonna work," she said. "You know competition is not for children. It's not for human beings. It's not for public education. It never has been, it never will be."

Read that again. Then again.

We live and work in an economic system based on competitive free enterprise. Throughout our lives, each and every one of us has to compete. We compete for the best jobs. We compete for customers. We compete for clients. We compete for recognition. We even compete for mates. Then along comes this government school teacher to tell us that competition is "not for human beings."

This woman is teaching someone's children that nonsense!

Look, I know there are dedicated teachers out there, somewhere. I also know that they're vastly outnumbered. In Florida, four of the recent winners of teachers of the year awards praised the A-Plus accountability program. They knew that the program was working. Gains were being recorded in test scores. The percentages of students reading at or above grade level went up. The National Assessment of Educational Progress report showed gains in fourth grade math and reading in Florida . . . gains that put Florida above the national average!

Then the teachers unions stepped in and put a halt to the entire program.

Are you beginning to see why I consider these unions dangerous?

There have always been amazing teachers out there. I was lucky to have a few when I was floundering my way through government schools. In fact, I owe my broadcast career to a teacher at Pensacola High School named Roy Hyatt. Mr. Hyatt saw that I was completely bored with the whole process and sought to encourage me with some extracurricular activities. He talked the principal into allowing me to read the morning announcements over the PA system. That was my first experience with a microphone.

Fate.

But the exceptional teachers in our government schools are not the norm. (That's the meaning of "exceptional," after all.) Examples of teachers who can't even speak or write the English language are rampant. Just one of many is a report card sent to me by a listener, which contains a handwritten note from a teacher in one of the local government schools.

"Johnny are learning to read good," the teacher writes. "Johnny are getting along well with his pears."

Well, it's sure great to know Johnny are doing so well! I just hope Johnny are doing as well with his friends as he are with his fruit.

Just who are these numbskull teachers, anyway? Not a bright bunch of bulbs, it turns out. If you take a look at all the students who enroll in college to pursue a degree in education, you'll find that, as a group, their SAT scores were among the lowest in the country. Graduate school? The picture doesn't get any better. Check the academic record of college graduates who pursue a master's in education, and you'll find the same situation. As a group, they score in the lowest percentile on the GRE.

Sad but true: We're getting the dregs in our government schools.

Here's the funny thing. Government schools are the only schools in the country that require teachers to be certified. There's that professional licensing thing again.

A private school can hire anyone it wants to teach any subject. This means that you are far more likely to have someone teaching your child who has a solid knowledge base in the subject being taught.

Teacher certifications are merely another way to limit competition. You may have a retiree with a world of experience in any one of many different areas: business, science, medicine, math, communications, or government, for instance. Why should these people be turned away if they wanted to do a little teaching in their retirement years? Yet in many government school systems they can't even get in the door because they don't have that precious teacher's certificate.

What is our goal here: to educate our children, or to provide jobs for administrators and teachers?

Private schools generally do a better job at educating, and they don't usually require a teacher to be certified. They just want the teacher to have a little knowledge on the subject that they're teaching. Doesn't that sound like a more reasonable approach to you?

I care for this country, and for our future. But I see our potential slipping away. And the reason, in large part, is the abject stupidity of so much of the American public.

I believe the easiest and quickest way to turn this country around is to begin to educate its citizens, and the best way to do that is through an educational marketplace that stresses excellence brought on by free and open competition.

If some union school teachers lose their jobs along the way, so be it. The schools aren't there to provide them with permanent employment. They're there for our children. We need to take them back.

THINGS THAT SHOULD BE TAUGHT IN GOVERNMENT SCHOOLS

Fine, Boortz, you may be thinking. *We get the point. But if you think our government schools are doing such a bad job of teaching, why don't you tell us what you would teach?*

Say no more.

I know, I've already got government school teachers busy trying to learn the answers to the Neal Boortz Citizenship Test I offered earlier. But I'm eager to do more, so I've compiled a few things I think our children should learn before they escape to college or to their exciting careers in lawn maintenance.

Now, I'm not going to deal with the obvious here, items like basic math and reading. Instead, let's focus on a few ideas I suspect are being ignored, but which could certainly enhance anyone's educational experience.

1. We are not a democracy. Never were. Weren't *supposed* to be. And we shouldn't be. Explore the *Federalist Papers* with the children and explain to them why our Founding Fathers abhorred the idea of democracy. Ask them why the word "democracy" never appeared in a presidential state of the

union address until Woodrow Wilson, and today you'll hear the word no less than twenty times. Discuss the phenomenon of the lynch mob with the class and ask them to explain how such a mob might conduct itself differently under a system of pure majority rule as opposed to a system of the rule of law.

2. Tell the students that Exxon Mobil earned about $38 billion in profits in 2006. Then, to see if they're paying attention, ask one student what Exxon Mobil's profit margin was for 2006. If he says "$38 billion," you'll know that your students don't understand the difference between a profit and a profit margin. This means they will be easy prey for political demagoguery. Teach them the difference.

3. I know it's not that big an issue, but there is a big difference between a newspaper column and an editorial. The column is an expression of the opinions of the writer. The editorial is a statement of the official position of the newspaper. I don't know why it bothers me that people don't understand this difference, but it surely does. So teach them.

4. Explain to the students that the people who formed this country wanted most of the governing to be done as close to home as possible. Explain why a letter to a local politician will have far more effect than a letter sent to a congressman or senator in Washington. (Hint: Because Washington politicians are so isolated from interaction with the people they govern that they feel bulletproof—and complacency ensues.)

5. Teach the difference between "subjective" and "objective" writing and why a news reporter should practice one and not the other.

6. Teach them that it's absurd to believe that when the Bill of Rights was added to our Constitution, it was decided that

nine of the amendments should protect basic rights the people already held, while one amendment, the second, should *grant* rights to government.

7. Point out to them that the government of Uganda has official representation in Washington, D.C., but the government of Utah does not.

8. Explain the differences among the concepts of prejudice, bigotry, and racism. Explain to the students that there are racial problems in this country that need to be addressed, and that the first thing you must do when trying to address a problem is to make sure you have accurately identified just what that problem is.

9. Explain to the students that the part of the human brain that assesses risk is not fully formed until roughly the age of twenty-five. This means they'll probably be biologically incapable of evaluating the dangers of whatever dicey behavior they may be planning for this weekend.

10. Teach them that our Constitution sought to severely limit the powers of the federal government, and that these limitations are today being largely ignored. This is what happens when you consider the Constitution to be a "living document."

11. Teach them that teenagers are inherently cruel and that this will make their teenage years the toughest period of their lives. Tell them also that the word "popular" will cease to have any real meaning to them once they leave high school for college or work.

12. If there are any aspiring jocks in the class, teach them that the chances of them ever making a living as a professional athlete are far less than one out of a thousand, no matter how hard they apply themselves. But if they make the decision and dedicate themselves to the cause of becoming a successful busi-

nessman, doctor, or lawyer, it is nearly certain they will succeed.

13. Teach them that there are three keys to avoiding poverty: Stay
    in school, don't get pregnant, and take any job you can get
    and work hard at it until you can move to a better one. It's
    just that simple.

14. Teach them that government has one unique power that we,
    as mere citizens, do not have: the power to use deadly force to
    accomplish its goals. Teach them that this should make them
    suspicious of government at all times.

15. Teach them the miracle of compound interest. Teach them
    that if they were to take that money they're using to buy lot-
    tery tickets and invest it in a good mutual fund instead, they
    would be certain winners, instead of certain losers.

16. Teach them the difference between a credit card and a charge
    card. Explain to them that credit card debt will make their
    lives absolutely and completely miserable, and that this is one
    huge mistake they can decide to avoid today!

17. Explain to them that they're going to be absolutely amazed at
    how much their parents learn over the next five years.

18. And above all, teach them that despite the problems that exist
    both here and abroad, there is not now, nor has there ever
    been, any country that has done so much to foster the spirit
    of human freedom and to offer every person a chance, if he
    chooses, to use his talents and willingness to work hard to
    achieve great things.

MINIMUM WAGE

Now that we've finished with government schools . . . let's spend a few moments on the fate of those who decide that an education just isn't their thing.

Oh, I'm going to love writing this chapter. I'm going to love it because this is one of those true hot-button issues—that is, those searing, surface-of-the-sun hot-button issues that gets things going every time on my radio show. Every time I go on about the minimum wage, we get an avalanche of hate mail.

Nothing hurts like the truth.

I thought it might be fun to share some of that hate mail with you. As you read through this chapter I'll include a few e-mails. (No . . . they aren't *all* hateful. I did sneak in a few nice ones to boost my own ego.) Names are included where the sender had the courage to actually send one along with his message.

> I heard your commentary on minimum wage on the web.
> Though the comments were indeed stupid, I can't really say I
> hate you because the fact is, I never heard of you prior to your
> stupid commentary about the minimum wage. I listen to a lot
> of talk radio, but I must say your name is new to me (I don't
> live in NY obviously). You sound like some Bush-league (pun
> intended) Limbaugh wannabe. I bet you are on in my area at
> 3 or 4 am, right? Your commentary is unoriginal, fabricated,
> predictable and boring. The shtick that you, Limbaugh and

Hannity spew is getting tired and worn. You are all parrots, endlessly yammering the same talking points ad nauseum. Here's a new concept: Original thought. When is the last time you had one? If you did, it might piss off your neocon cronies, and I am sure that it may have an adverse affect on your next ratings book. Give it up, wimp. Though I shall try to phrase my thoughts in the most eloquent and stylized prose possible, I find that only two very simple words are needed to describe the pathetic sound byte that your draconian neocon crazed brain created. Short, simple and to the point: YOU SUCK.

So, what did I say to make this particular anonymous mailer so mad?

Simple. I told the insensitive, unpleasant truth.

Up until now my thoughts on the minimum wage, and the bulk of the people who earn just the minimum wage, have been expressed only on my radio show. So let's read them into the permanent record so there'll be no doubt whatsoever about where I stand.

Succinctly[1] put: If you're an adult between the ages of eighteen and sixty-five who has been in the workplace for longer than six months, and you still can't manage to earn more than the minimum wage . . .

YOU'RE A PATHETIC LOSER!

Mr. Boortz: Pause for a moment and just feel what it's like to be in your skin. That's "Loser." Michael H.

Now, some of my friends and family have urged me not to be quite that blunt about this. The fear, I guess, is that people who read this will have a hard time seeing me as the compassionate person I truly

---

[1] Just thought I'd throw in a word here to make the minimum wage crowd engage in a little head-scratching.

am. They'll wonder if I couldn't find a better way to make my point than to call someone a loser.

Well, maybe you can help me out. What's a better word for someone born into the most spectacular nation on earth, who somehow manages to completely ignore the educational and developmental opportunities it has to offer for years on end—and thus becomes yet another adult American without the skills necessary to earn a wage above the government-established minimum?

Did you think of another word? Fine. But please do me a favor: Don't change my language to read, "You're just one of the less fortunate." That phrase, a favorite of the left, will get what's coming to it elsewhere in this book. Having the job skills and work ethic necessary to earn more than the minimum wage is not a matter of good fortune. It's a matter of choices and effort.

I made minimum wage last when I was 13 years old washing dishes. I was given a raise before the end of my first summer.

I later took a job as a technician in a healthcare facility. They paid in full for my nursing education, which I completed in 1990. During Clinton's boom years, nurses were being laid off. I was promoted based on my work history with the company and my experience.

This year I'm going back to school and they will reimburse me 80%. This means I won't need financial aid or a student loan!

My husband went to a vocational school and became an electrician. He now runs his own business and employs others at better than minimum wage.

I guess we're the winners of life's lottery just by luck.

Maybe if you went to an interview without being pierced,
tattooed with red hair and ripped clothing, an employer might
think you had some value!!!!

Maybe if you had a job before you turned thirty and didn't
show up stoned you'd get a fair wage. Marsha

Every two years or so the Democrats in Congress put on their big
dog-and-pony act about raising the minimum wage. Campaigning
for an increase in the minimum wage is as much a staple of the
Democrat election diet as is telling voters that evil Republicans want
to make life miserable for the wizened citizens by stripping them of
their Social Security benefits.

The minimum wage earners are not the backbone of this
country, merely the backbone of the democratic voting base.
Flip F.

The Democrats, of course, would like you to believe that they want to
raise the minimum wage because they're full of caring and love for
humanity. Well, that sounds mighty warm and fuzzy, but here's something I bet you didn't know:

Only a very small percentage of the work force—about 0.33 percent (one-third of 1 percent)—actually earns no more than the minimum wage.

Let's face it, these job-market bottom-dwellers (there I go again)
are hardly going to make any huge contribution to the Democratic
vote totals on Election Day.

So why do Democrats push this issue election after election?

Unions, that's why.

Although this little factoid somehow doesn't seem to make it into
the mainstream media with any regularity, many union contracts are
tied to the prevailing minimum wage. These contracts call for the

lowest-paid worker in a given industry or business to be paid by some factor of the minimum wage. Such a contract might, for instance, call for the lowest union wage to be twice the prevailing minimum wage. So when the minimum wage goes up, so do those union wages. This makes union workers happy, and keeps union bosses in their cozy jobs.

Do the math. Minimum wage workers contribute very little to political campaigns, and they may well vote even less. Unions contribute heavily, both in terms of cash and labor. Follow the money.

> Neal, you are the prime example of how a person can be incompetent, stupid, and worthless, yet still be paid (note I didn't say "earn") far more than the minimum wage. What you have earned is a kick in the ass for being so insensitive to the plight of millions of Americans who have suffered horribly under the current Fascist-resembling Administration. Marvin S.

Democrats don't particularly like that 0.33 percent figure. They'll try to tell you that the percentage of American workers earning the minimum wage is more like 2.5 percent. What they won't tell you is that most of these people are in the hospitality and leisure industry, where their actual wages are kept low to offset a rather sizeable income from gratuities. These people may be paid at or below the minimum wage by their employer, but they're making far more.

> Mr. Boortz, your comments on minimum wage and the truth behind them, are astounding to read. You call us "losers" and "trash" but the simple fact of the matter is: we are. I am a well educated, somewhat financially capable, normal human male. I made a series, no, decade, of really bad decisions. None involved drugs or alcohol, just the idiotic brain of a useless 18–25 year old. I am now 28 and am finally able to provide for a son that is not mine. For a woman, who I love, that I have not married, with an hourly wage. How did I do this? I got a job that pays me way more than minimum wage. I am a server, you

call them waiters/ess, which is a profession. I am not quite
sure how noble, but . . . it pays the bills. I make 2.13 an hour,
plus tips. I also clear about 2000 dollars a month. I blame
myself for being a "well-educated" loser. I am. I take full
responsibility for it. You, Mr. Boortz, have an audience, a
forum, to espouse your beliefs. Please, for the love of God,
don't stop. You may be able to save one person from the runaway train that is irresponsibility. I don't blame the government, you, my parents, or society. I blame me. Respectfully
yours, Billy G.

Several years ago, I read a fascinating article concerning the top ten over-
paid professions in America. That list made for some fun talk radio.
Among those on the list were bond traders, wedding photographers,
and real estate agents selling high-end properties. (Radio talk show
hosts, you ask? Nope, didn't make the cut. There's a reason for that.)

Here was one of the surprises on the list: airport skycaps. In many
airports, skycaps are salaried at or below the minimum wage—yet
they can earn in excess of $100,000 a year. If you don't believe this,
then just stand at a busy curbside check-in on some Friday afternoon
and watch the five-dollar bills fly.[2]

Count these skycaps among those whom the Democrats want to
bless with an increase in the minimum wage.

You are a pathetic, worthless, incompetent, ignorant, stupid
human being and you earn more than the minimum wage!
Point made! Bob A.

There's still more that the Democrats don't want to tell you about the
minimum wage.

Another thing the Democrats won't tell you about minimum wage

---

[2] Skycaps, of course, are very careful to declare each and every dollar they receive in tips on
their income tax returns.

workers is that, according to Census Bureau and Labor Department statistics, most workers who enter the workforce at the minimum wage get wage increases within a year. For 40 percent of them, those raises come within four months.

> I agree with you completely on this subject. If they raise mini-mum wage then all that will do is raise what the consumer pays and increase the taxes that the companies pay. Minimum wage jobs were made up for part timer, and people starting in the work place, after school job. I believe a quote Ronald Reagan once said, "To sit back hoping that someday, someway, someone will make things right is to go on feeding the croco-dile, hoping he will eat you last—but eat you he will." You want to make more money make your value go up to the com-pany you work for, or sell your self to another company and show them what you can bring to the company, not what the company can do for you. Shannon F.

The philosophical argument against minimum wage laws is an easy one to make.

When government passes a minimum wage law, it is effectively telling private sector employers that they must pay some of their employees more than those employees are worth. Does that seem like an appropriate function of government in a free society?

When the government forces you to pay your workers more than the value of their work, the difference between what you have to pay them and what they are worth to you must be made up elsewhere. Basically, there are two ways to make up the difference:

1. Fire workers or slow down future hiring to cover the increase in your labor budget. You can accomplish this through automation, or by expanding the workload of those to whom you are forced to give unearned raises.

2. Increase the price of the goods your workers produce. This, of course, results in an increase in overall consumer prices; an

increase that can all but wipe out the minimum wage
increases for lower-income workers.

Enough cutting-edge economic theory. The bottom line (to coin a
phrase) is that you have to clear a very low hurdle to pull yourself out
of minimum-wage status in today's economy.

> Obviously, one doesn't have to earn minimum wage to be stu-
> pid, incompetent and pathetic—after all, look at you. If there
> is EVER a more pathetically "stupid" being in this current
> wage debate, it is you and the Republican leadership that con-
> demns those earners to live in poverty. What, exactly is your
> point in keeping the wages down? What is your agenda to
> keeping the least amongst us, wage-wise, under these kinds of
> conditions? You make the world sick. You and your politics are
> despicable. Shame on you. Kimberly M.

During their biannual minimum wage push; Democrats and other
OCCD[3] sufferers love to point out that it's all but impossible to raise
a family on the minimum wage in the United States.

Well, guess what? It's all but impossible to own and maintain a
150-foot yacht on a middle-class salary in today's economy. The
maintenance on the engines will cost more than you make, and you
haven't even put fuel in the tanks. So what's the answer?

Don't buy a yacht if you can't produce the income to support it.

DON'T HAVE A FAMILY IF YOU CAN'T AFFORD DIA-
PERS.

Now what part of that do you find difficult to understand?

> . . . why don't you actually do some research before you blast
> hard-working Americans (most of whom on the minimum wage
> would put in many more hours a week than you do). Some of

---

[3] Obsessive Compulsive Compassion Disorder

the most dangerous people in the US right now are people like you—rich, narrow-minded blowhards who can't see beyond their own backyard. Get out of your booth—indeed, get out of Atlanta (have you ever traveled outside the US?)—and find out what the world is really like. Your ignorance is breathtaking. . . . Cyndi T.

Research? You want research?

The U.S. Department of Agriculture estimates that if your child was born in 2000 you can expect to spend about $165,630 to feed, shelter, and provide basic necessities for that child until he is eighteen. Adjust that figure for inflation, and you're starting to crowd one quarter of a million dollars.

Note, please, that these figures presume that you kick the kid to the curb when he's eighteen—so college tuition isn't even factored in. If you want to foot the bill for higher education, you'll soon be breathing some high-altitude $300,000 air.

Question: If your job skills are such that you can only earn the minimum wage, what in the hell are you doing with children?

At $5.15 per hour, and with two weeks off per year, you're going to be able to parlay your incredibly pathetic job skills and work ethic into a whopping $185,400 during those first eighteen years of your child's life. With inflation in the picture you're going to come up about $50,000 short of what you need to just raise your child . . . with no extras!

There you are, fifty grand short, and you haven't even purchased a carton of cigarettes and a case of beer yet![4] Yet you're going to begat a child?

What in the world are you thinking?

---

[4] Cheap shot? I think not. A person who can earn only the minimum wage is far more likely to be a smoker than someone who is worth far more in the jobs marketplace. The smarter you are, the more you can earn. The dumber you are, the more likely it is that you will be a smoker. Sorry, but the truth hurts. So does ignorance.

> Families earning minimum wage tend to have more children
> because sex is their version of "Disneyland." It is about the
> only entertainment they can afford. It is not realistic for you to
> expect them to actually consider the problems of having chil-
> dren when they don't earn enough to support them. It is kind
> of like expecting flotsam to have a desired direction. Gail H.

Oh, wait. Forget I asked. I already know what you're thinking, and it's no wonder. You've been conditioned by decades of the welfare and dependency mentality in this country to believe that all you have to do is just upload, gestate, and download, and the government is there to take care of the rest.

You don't have to be responsible for the cost of childbirth, because your employer has provided you with a health insurance policy . . . or there's always Medicaid.

You don't have to worry about feeding your child in the early years because of the government's WIC[5] program.

You won't have to worry about being able to afford someone to look after your child while you work, because the government has an income redistribution program—called the child care tax credit—to take care of that.

You won't have to worry about educating your child. After all, there are always all those incredible government schools.

So what the hell? You have no job skills to speak of. You've ignored and squandered the educational opportunities brought before you, and the government is poised to transfer tens of thousands of dollars to you from other people who do actually have skills, and who actu-ally did apply themselves to get a good job.

So . . . have the child! It's not like you're going to have to give up your new car, your cell phone, or cable television, is it? The govern-ment will force the burden of raising your child onto other, more

---

[5] Woman, Infants and Children. A federal welfare program designed to feed the children of people who couldn't afford to have babies.

responsible Americans through taxes, and on your employer through an increase in the minimum wage.

> I use to listen to your show all the time, but after your comments I can NO LONGER LISTEN. I am just beside myself to think you could want to say people who have min. wage jobs with kids are stupid! First and foremost I have a niece that has a College ed. and can't find a job. . . and she has NO KIDS! I have to ask why would you want to kick someone for trying? Your statements from the show were RUDE!! Why don't you try working a 5 dollar an hour job and see if it don't land you on the streets!!! I hope and pray that GOD has some mercy on YOU. Shawnna

Before we move on, I want to make it clear that I understand that some people encounter physical or mental disasters that either limit or eliminate their earning power. These people are worthy of our compassion and deserving of our help. Those aren't the people I'm addressing in this particular rant.

Have you ever heard of an "enabler"?

Merriam-Webster's Medical Dictionary defines an "enabler" as "one that enables another to achieve an end; *especially:* one who enables another to persist in self-destructive behavior by providing excuses or by helping that individual avoid the consequences of such behavior."

The failure to develop a marketable job skill or work ethic is the very definition of self-destructive behavior. Those who constantly drone on about minimum wage increases or "living wage" ordinances are their enablers. In every sense they help unskilled individuals avoid the consequences of their self-destructive behavior. This isn't evidence of love or compassion. More often than not, it's evidence of either a complete ignorance of the consequences of your action, or of political gamesmanship.

> Having worked for minimum wage for a number of years, and
> being college educated, I really am tired of hearing rethugli-
> cans put down those who are stuck in jobs that the rethugli-
> cans have made by sending jobs to other countries and
> rewarding the corporations with welfare. Deborah B.

Someone once said that ignorance should be painful. People will
work awfully hard to avoid pain.

Our federal minimum wage laws are not only an unwarranted
government intrusion into the free-market relationship between
employer and employee; these laws also form a system that rewards
behavior our society could well do without.

The easier you make it for people to fail in their primary responsibility to develop some marketable value in our business world, the
more of that self-destructive behavior you will see.

Punish that behavior—or allow the jobs marketplace to mete out
its own punishment—and these negative behavior patterns will fade.

Wouldn't we go a lot further in prompting those with no earning
power to change things if we didn't work so hard to shield them from
the pain of their own actions?

Those who favor the protection of laziness and bad behavior
through the ill-gotten rewards of the minimum wage are doing a dis-
service to the very people they profess to be helping. The idea behind
raising the minimum wage—or having a government-mandated minimum wage at all, for that matter—is simply to increase and solidify
the power of the political class by creating and maintaining a class of
workers more dependent on government largesse for their daily bread
than on their own hard work.

One more point.

Didn't I ever work for the minimum wage? Sure, I did. Once.

During my senior year in high school, I bagged groceries at the
A&P on Ninth Avenue in Pensacola, Florida. I was paid minimum
wage—$1.00 an hour—but the tips from women admiring my

hunky physique as I carried their groceries to their cars took me well above the minimum.

The manager's name was Brown. I'll never forget him. He was the first of many bosses to fire me. When the minimum wage went to $1.25, they had to let a bag boy go. Last hired, Boortz fired.

I told Mr. Brown I was perfectly willing to continue to work for the $1.00 an hour. He said I couldn't. The government wouldn't let me. I think that was my first experience with government intervention in what I considered to be my personal life.

Little did I know . . .

SORRY, NOT INTERESTED

One of the things that really illustrates the dangerous level of ignorance in the American population is the statement, "I'm not interested in politics."

This statement astounds me. Do you really understand what you're saying? How in the world can any aware person interested in one's family and one's future *not* be interested in politics?

To be sure, the talk radio business has plenty of consultants who hammer into our heads the idea that listeners don't want to talk about politics. And, of course, we're told constantly that a good way to become a social outcast is to try to discuss politics or religion with your friends.

Well, religion I can see. I seem to have a penchant for getting in trouble for discussing religion on the air. I should know better.

But politics? Sorry. That's one subject I cannot ignore.

Look at what we average Americans go through as we work our way through our daily existence. We're looking for jobs, working, planning for the future, educating children, making house payments, buying groceries, fueling up cars, planning family vacations, worrying about our health, paying down our debt, and watching *Desperate Housewives.*

If you think politics doesn't influence each and every one of these pursuits, you're tragically mistaken. No matter what you do, from tying your shoes to tying the knot to tying one on, politics is lurking in there somewhere, making things better or worse.

Perhaps the biggest impact politics will have on your daily life will be in the area of taxes.

Are you trying to save money for a house right now? Well, how much money do you have left over after taxes, Social Security, and Medicare are taken out of your check?

If you're part of a typical two-parent American household, both of you are out there working; your children are probably in day care, being taken care of by relatives, at school, or just running wild.

Do the math.

No, really, do the math. Write down the take-home pay of each parent, and then look at the total tax burden your family pays each year.

In determining that tax burden, remember to include not just federal income taxes, Social Security taxes, and Medicare taxes, but also state income taxes, automobile license fees, property taxes, school taxes, sales taxes—and don't forget the embedded taxes in the cost of every item you buy.

It's tough, but try to come to some sort of a figure. What is your family's total tax burden?

Once you have a figure, take a look at the take-home pay for the spouse who earns less money—usually the wife—and if I'm not mistaken, you'll come to a rather shocking realization:

She's working for one purpose and one purpose only—to pay your family's tax burden.

How's that for a wake-up call?

Before the middle of the last century, the average federal tax burden on an American family amounted to about 5 percent of that family's total income. Now it amounts to well over 30 percent, and for many families the number is over 40 percent.

Turn back the clock about half a century, to 1955 or so, and you'll find that the breadwinner in an average American family had to work until sometime around the first week in February to pay all of that family's taxes for the year. Fifty years later, not only are both parents breadwinners, but they both have to work well into late May, and sometimes even early June, before those taxes are paid in full.

If you come in at 8:30, work until 10, take a half-hour break, work until noon, take an hour for lunch, and finally work until 5:30 in the afternoon—you don't earn the first dollar for yourself until you're back from lunch. The entire morning is dedicated to earning money to support government.

This, my friends, is where politics intersects with your life—by picking your pocket. Those politicians you see on TV aren't just making obscure laws and fighting over foreign policy. They're out there seizing your money and spending it on vote-buying programs that help them maintain their positions of power and prestige—while you and your spouse labor every day to cover the tab.

Want to buy a new car? The price of a new car is going up every year, due to government action. Now the government requires cars to have air pressure monitoring systems on all tires. Next year it will be some other alleged safety improvement. Soon you'll have to settle for a used car, thanks to those price increases. That's politics.

Want to build a house on a nice little lot you've found? You might want to build 2,100 square feet, but the local building code says it has to be 2,800 square feet. You can't afford a house that big, so you look elsewhere. That's politics.

Want to send your child to a private school in your neighborhood? Fine, but after paying your property taxes, there's not much left over. It'd be nice if the county issued you a voucher you could use to send your child to school where you want instead of spending it on taxes. Oh, whoops, the teachers unions killed that deal. That's politics.

Hoping your husband will get that promotion he's been angling for at work? He comes home with the long face and explains to you that the company's diversity committee has decided that the job needs to go to a minority. That's politics.

Enjoy that nice view out behind your house? Sorry—turns out that property has been seized by local government to make way for a private developer to build a water park. Don't want a water park in your back yard? That's politics.

Maybe all this helps explain why I'd like to tell all those talk radio consultants to take their "don't talk about politics" nonsense and try to sell it to my competition.

Respectfully, of course.

Like it or not, we live in a society where almost every action we take is regulated or controlled in one way or another by government, and our government is controlled by politicians.

I'm not here to talk about how to rewire your toaster or clip your dog's toenails. I'm here to engage people by talking with them about things that will actually have an impact, sometimes profound, sometimes not, on their lives. That means I talk about politics. If I can pull that off in an entertaining manner, then I need to go ahead and retire right now . . . before Hillary gets sworn in.

And as for you listeners who are part of the "I'm not interested in politics" chorus: Politics is what's going on all around you while you're grabbing for the sports page in the morning, jogging with your iPod in the afternoon, or programming your Tivo in the evening to record *Entertainment Tonight.*

"I'm not interested in politics" is an affirmation that you're not interested in the actions of people who control your bank account, your personal freedom, and your very life.

This republic cannot survive the continued neglect of its people.

REASONS NOT TO
VOTE FOR . . .

As this book is published, we're a bit less than two years away from a presidential election. Though we can't be sure of every last issue that will be on the front burner for this election, I think it's safe to say that the primary players will be Democrats, Republicans, and Libertarians.

And so, instead of listing all the reasons you should support a political party, in the great tradition of negative advertising and campaigning I give you the reasons why *not*.

WHY YOU SHOULDN'T VOTE REPUBLICAN

Republicans have absolutely no fiscal discipline whatsoever. No Congress has ever blown money on vote-buying programs quite like the newly departed Republican Congress did.

There are far too many Republicans who want to take their personal religious blueprints for behavior and make them law.

Republicans seem unwilling to press the legislative advantage when it's theirs to press.

They're prudes.

They pay more attention to K Street lobbyists than they do to the American workers and businessmen carrying the load.

They can't even protect America's borders.

If they had their way, Terri Schiavo's soul would still not be at rest.
Stem cell research.
Donald Wildmon.
The McCain-Feingold Campaign Reform Act.
The Medicare Prescription Drug benefit for the Gimme Genera-
tion
Do you want your kids to come home from a government school
and tell you that the Earth is only six thousand years old?

WHY YOU SHOULDN'T VOTE DEMOCRAT

Democrats clearly have no intention of defending America from
Islamic fascism—not now, not next month, not until the price of that
defense is catastrophic.
They think terrorism is a law enforcement problem.
They think it's odd that the jails are so full while our crime rate is
going down.
They think America is great because of its government.
They have this strange idea that income is distributed, not earned.
They promote class warfare.
They love the concept of mob rule.
They have almost single-handedly destroyed black family culture
in America.
They're joined at the hip with the teachers unions.
They never met a tax they didn't raise.
Hillary Clinton.
The leftist-inspired and Democrat-supported war against individ-
ualism.
They fully intend to destroy talk radio.
They fully intend to turn illegal aliens into Democrat voters.
Like the Republicans, they refuse to protect America's borders.

WHY YOU SHOULDN'T VOTE LIBERTARIAN

Even though more than 50 percent of the American people harbor strong libertarian feelings, the Libertarians have never managed to mount a viable third-party campaign. How would they manage to govern?

Not only will they not defend America's borders, they don't really think the borders need defending.

Though they're right about it, they've never accepted that their "legalize drugs" agenda isn't exactly a winner with the American people.

Though it *would* be a winner with the American people, they've never jumped on eminent domain abuse as a party agenda. When they think their property rights are being threatened, the people will react. But the Libertarians have never taken up the cause.

Oh, and have you seen the way some of the people at their convention dress?

THE DEMOCRATS' (SECRET) PLAN FOR AMERICA

If I haven't given you sufficient reason not to vote for Democrats, Republicans, and Libertarians, I don't know who could. On the other hand, if you were to actually take my advice (a pretty uncommon strategy, I'll admit) and refuse to vote for any of those party's candidates, you'd be left with little choice but to vote for some moonbats from, say, the Green Party or some such gathering of political oddballs.

If you vote at all, the smart money says, you'll probably vote for either a Republican or a Democrat.

You would lose that bet on me.

I've voted for the Libertarian Party candidate for president in five out of the last seven presidential elections. I also vote heavily for Libertarian candidates in local races. People are constantly scolding me about this; when I vote Libertarian, they say, my vote is "wasted."

Somehow, however, I have a tough time accepting the premise that a principled vote is a wasted vote. And goodness knows, the two mainstream parties haven't exactly offered return on investment.

The free-spending behavior of the Republican Party during the first six years of the George W. Bush presidency validated my votes thoroughly.[1]

During most election seasons, one group of researchers or another will generate a voter questionnaire highlighting planks from the Republican, Democrat, and Libertarian election platforms. Using excerpts from the party platforms, these pamphlets propose to present three alternative ways to address specific issues—without identifying which plank comes from which party. The people taking the survey merely have to choose the positions that most clearly mirror their own.

Interestingly enough, the majority of those taking this blind test tend to favor positions taken from the Libertarian platform over those from the Democrats or Republicans.

Does that tell you something?

What it tells me, I already knew. My years of conversations with talk radio callers have left me with the unshakeable feeling that most of the people in this country—at least, most of those people who take the time to call talk radio shows—have views that are basically libertarian. The Cato Institute, a respected Washington think tank, is a little more conservative (in both senses), but even they put the number at around 21 percent.

But there's one problem: Libertarians have yet to show the ability to attract these people to their candidates or party when election time rolls around. Result? My vote enjoys the status of being part of the lost 3 percent.

To those of you who are with me in that slender slice of electoral pie, I salute you. For the rest of you, who will likely vote either Democrat or Republican in the coming election, let me share with

---

[1] In light of the war against Islamic fascism, I must say that I'm glad my vote didn't tip the scales in any of these races. As I said in the previous chapter, the Libertarians seem to have a bit of a problem with the concept of defending America from enemies abroad . . . at least not until they come storming across our borders.

you a list of some of the little surprises the Democrat Party [2] might have in store for you if they retain control of Congress and seize the White House again.

Every time a general election rolls around, the Democrats pull out the same tried-and-true playbook. This plan calls for Democrats to spend their time (and election war chests) trying to frighten the wrinkles right off our senior citizens with a carefully honed litany of scare tactics.

The Republicans want you all to die, they suggest. *The GOP will see to it that you never get another Social Security check as long as you live.*

And another: *The Republicans want you all to be sick! They're going to destroy Medicare! Oh, and they want your children to starve to death, too.*

Of course, there's nothing in the Republican platform aimed at destroying Social Security and Medicare. So how do the Democrats explain that? They just tell the voters that the Republicans' plans are "secret," not to be revealed until the election is over.

Well, since the Democrats are so eager to talk about "secret" plans, I thought I'd spend a few fascinating pages discussing the secret plans of the Democrats.

Just what legislative agenda does the Democrat Party plan to pursue if and when they gain control of the government?

Your friendly author has been watching these socialists for years, and taking notes. I present you now with just some of the goodies the Social Democrat Party has in store for the people of America.

If you think I'm just making this stuff up, then go run to the polls in the next election and give the Social Democrat Party even more power.

Nobody loves a good "I told you so" more than me.

All right—clear your mind, grab your ankles, and kiss your buns goodbye. Here is the Democrat Party's Secret Plan for America.

---

[2] I read recently that Democrats get their thongs in a wad when their party is referred to as the "Democrat Party." If you find any stray "ic" after the word "Democrat" anywhere in this book, please get out your handy correction fluid and white them out. It's the least you can do. (Hey . . . give me a break here. At least I stopped calling Hillary "Hitlary.")

MAKE THE (EVIL) RICH COVER THE TAB

Priority one: Remove a majority of voters from responsibility for paying any federal income taxes. The Democrats have been working on this plan for decades—with no small amount of help from the Republicans. The idea is simple. Using "refundable" tax credits and deductions and ideas like the fraudulent Earned Income Tax Credit to free the bottom 50 percent of income earners from their federal tax burden, they're well on their way to shifting the entire burden for the payment of federal income taxes onto a minority of U.S. taxpayers.

Let's think about this for a moment. It's election time. You're a Democrat running for office. You know that the majority of the voters in your district pay no federal income taxes at all. And you know that very close to a majority of these voters get various tax credits and welfare payments that more than pay back any Social Security or Medicare taxes they may pay. Most are getting a free ride. Many are coming out ahead!

You're the candidate. What do you tell these people? It's obvious, isn't it?

If those Republicans win, they're going to make you pay income taxes, Social Security taxes, and Medicare taxes!

Money talks. That's a sure winner.

So how are the Democrats doing with their grand plan to shift the entire federal tax burden onto a minority of voters? Not bad at all—thanks for asking.

Right now the top 50 percent of taxpayers pay almost 96 percent of the taxes. The top income earners—the evil top 1 percent—earn about 16.5 percent of the income and pay almost 33.7 percent of the income taxes. This is what Democrats call "not paying your fair share."

The Democrats are close to their goal. When the majority of voters have no federal income tax liability, it'll be almost impossible to pass any meaningful tax cuts—and further tax increases will be a piece of cake, especially if the taxes only affect those classified as "rich."

This is how the Democrats plan to create a defeat-proof socialist Congress.

SHIFT SOCIAL SECURITY AND MEDICARE TAXES TO THE "RICH"

It's crucial to understand the depth of the Democrats' dedication to the idea of totally eliminating all elements of the federal tax burden from their core voters.

Lifting the income tax burden from the majority of voters isn't really all that difficult. The argument that the rich need to pay "their fair share" plays well with the dumb masses, as does the consistent Democrat whining about "tax cuts for the rich."

Social Security and Medicare taxes, however, present a tougher challenge. To solve the problem, hard-core Democrat Robert Reich, Clinton's secretary of labor, floated an idea on Fox News Channel's *Hannity & Colmes* a while back. His idea? "Lift the tax burden off the poor" by eliminating payroll taxes on the first $15,000 of income.

This plan, my friends, is absolutely brilliant—a surefire cinch to broaden the loyalty of the Democrat voter base, and keep spreading it until Social Security finally collapses under its own weight.

Here's how it's done: The Democrats pass a law that says nobody has to pay any payroll taxes on the first $15,000 of their income. So wage earners making $30,000 a year will have their Social Security payroll tax bills cut in half! Bingo—a huge segment of our low earners are now on the very brink of getting a completely free ride.

What a windfall! If that won't make you a lifelong, dedicated Democrat voter, I don't know what will.

But hold on a minute here! Wouldn't Reich's idea cost the government a bunch of money? After all, these people are still going to get their full Social Security and Medicare benefits when the time comes. So just who *is* paying their Social Security taxes?

You're not serious. You don't know?

You, you sap! The difference will be made up by that minority of productive Americans who are still paying the taxes. All they have to do is raise the earnings limit on the evil, hideous, stanky rich to cover the cost!

Now, at first blush, you might think they would just take that $15,000 off the bottom and add it to the top. That would bring the Social Security earnings cap up to the neighborhood of $110,000. But hold on here. There are many, many more people who earn that first $15,000 than there are people who earn $110,000. The truth, then, is that they'd actually have to raise the earnings limit by much more than $15,000 to cover the lost tax revenue. Try $20,000 or $25,000. So the lower-income ranks will get a free ride for a good portion of their future Social Security benefits . . . a free ride paid for by the wicked rich.

Wait. We're not through here. Now I want you to think about what the Democrats would do with each new federal election after they manage to create this $15,000 exemption. Can't you just hear Joe Democrat's campaign ad right now?

Cast your vote for me, Joe Democrat, and I'll work to raise your exemption on Social Security payroll taxes to your first $18,000 in wages!

Well, what myrmidon isn't going to go for that? Vote for Joe and get another tax cut! What a deal!

For many voters who earn less than the Social Security earnings limit, this will be the defining issue of the election. They won't give one second's thought to the high achievers in the upper income levels whose taxes will be increased; nor will they care that the tax increases on those evil rich bastards will exceed the tax cut they're getting from Joe Democrat. Joe and his fellow Democrats have already wiped out any federal income tax liability they might have had with a laundry list of exceptions, deductions, and tax credits . . . now they see the Democrats working hard to get rid of their payroll taxes!

Keep voting for Joe Democrat and that free ride is on its way!

It's a classic case of taking away from the upper income earners to give to the lower income earners—and since there are more lower income earners than higher, it's an automatic vote-getter!

Charlie Rangel, the new head of the House Ways and Means Committee, knows the opportunities that await here, and as the Democrats look toward 2008, he's prepared to move.

Think that's too harsh a scenario? Ignore me at your peril. I've got plenty of *I told you so*s ready and waiting.

END THE HOME MORTGAGE INTEREST DEDUCTION

Democrats have been gunning for the home mortgage interest deduction for decades.

You're probably working under the impression that virtually everyone who has a mortgage on their home deducts the mortgage interest on their income taxes.

Not so.

The fact is that around 37 percent of people who owe money on their homes don't even bother to itemize deductions on their income tax returns, and thus lose out on the deduction all together. That 37 percent, by the way, are in the lower and middle income brackets; they're the same people the Democrats want to relieve of any responsibility for paying taxes in the first place.

So attacking the home mortgage interest deduction doesn't really constitute an attack on the Democrat voter base.

Democrats aren't at all fond of this particular tax break. They like to refer to it as a tax "subsidy." Now, the more intelligent among us clearly understand that allowing people to keep more of their income can hardly be called a "subsidy." People likely to vote Democrat, on the other hand, are happy to accept that characterization.

Unless you have a fairly sizeable mortgage you aren't aware of it, but this home mortgage interest deduction is already being whittled away. Right now, a taxpayer can deduct the interest on only the first million dollars of principal.

The Democrats want to reduce that . . . steadily . . . until the deduction is pretty much gone.

As soon as the Democrats have completed their seizure of the federal government, then, you can bet they'll make their move to start hacking away at the mortgage interest deduction. They know there'll be little adverse political fallout. It's not *their* voter base that's going to take it in the chin. After all, the mortgage interest deduction is valuable only to people who actually pay income taxes *and* who itemize their deductions. The Democrats have already succeeded in removing most of their core constituency from the income tax rolls.

So, you see, they have tax revenue to gain, and nothing to lose!

Besides, they get the added bonus of telling their core constituency that they've made the evil rich pay even more of their ill-gotten booty in taxes! People who vote Democrat just love hearing stuff like that.

So you can get ready to kiss that mortgage interest deduction— and a lot more of your money—goodbye. Just don't whine about it when it happens. After all, the Democrats will tell you, there can only be two reasons you have a home of your own in the first place: Either you got lucky and somebody gave you the money, or you exploited some of the poor, poor pitiful victims of our evil capitalist system to get it.

SOCIALIZED MEDICINE

Our Democrat friends already tried this with Hillary Care.

It failed.

But when it comes to growing the size and intrusiveness of government, Democrats aren't discouraged by setbacks. Give them the chance, and they'll try again . . . and again . . . and again . . . until they finally get you to swallow the poison pill.

There are two basic reasons the Democrats are working so hard for complete government control of this huge segment of our economy. One, of course, is power. Health care comprises no less than 15 percent of our national economy. If the government can seize control of a booby prize this large, we'll have taken a giant step toward a socialist economy.

The second reason is control—the type of control that leads to loyal voters. Think about it: If you control a person's access to health care, you effectively control that person. Tug on the leash and they'll follow you wherever you go . . . and that includes right into the voting booth.

For years, the Democrats have had to put their plans for socialized medicine on hold. Those insipid Republicans in the Congress and the White House made things tough. Until they got control, the Democrats had to be satisfied just sitting up there in the Beltway blocking any efforts to introduce competition into the medical marketplace.

Why? Because Democrats live in abject fear of free market competition. Private sector solutions to any health care crisis must be fought at all costs.

Here's how the Democrats play their hand:

Early in George W. Bush's first term, he introduced an economic stimulus plan that had a little too much of that free-market elixir to please big-government Democrats.

There was much weeping and hand-wringing in the media about the plight of workers who'd been laid off their jobs. How were they going to afford health insurance?

The Bush idea was to allow these laid-off workers to go into the marketplace to purchase individual health insurance policies. The plan was to allow these people a tax credit to cover their health insurance premiums.

The Democrats would have none of it. Allowing American workers to go into the private marketplace to find health insurance was simply out of the question. Why, what if these people found they could shop for a plan that suited their families, get reimbursed through a tax credit, and never have to worry about that insurance going away when they change jobs? What's worse, what if they found a better health policy than was available through their employer?

Well, the Democrats saw the problem with all that: A person who's taken control of his own health care is a person who has begun to wean himself from dependence on the Washington political class.

So that was the end of that.

The Democrats knew they had to propose an alternative. Their idea was to make federal funds available to employers who extended the health insurance benefits of laid-off workers.

You do see the magic in this plan, don't you? The Democrat plan would have left employers in charge of an individual's health insurance policy—thus preserving the timeworn leftist tenet that every American citizen should entrust his health care to someone other than himself (such as his employer or the government).

Alas, this argument is purely academic at this point. With the Democrats back in control, the age of socialized medicine—complete with three-month waits for elective surgery, inefficient clinics and hospitals, and impersonal service—will be upon us.

There's one way you can avoid the health care chaos the left has planned for us:

Stay healthy.

THE MAGIC OF IMPUTED INCOME

Imputed? What does "imputed" mean? Let's ask the dictionary:

Im-put-ed [*im-pyoo-tid*] — *adjective*

estimated to have a certain cash value, although no money has been received or credited.[3]

---

[3] From dictionary.com. Based on the *Random House Unabridged Dictionary*. © Random House, Inc., 2006.

That seems innocuous enough, doesn't it?

Actually, it doesn't.

Tie the word "imputed" to the word "income," and the picture starts to become rather unnerving.

Let's see: The government taxes your income. Okay.

And "imputed" refers to a cash value where no cash has been received.

So you do the math: "Imputed income" can only mean "adding cash value to your taxable income . . . without actually putting any cash into your pocket"!

Here's something you need to know: The left wants to milk America's high achievers for as much money as they possibly can. And there are really only three ways the Democrats can get more income taxes out of any of us: They can raise the tax rates, eliminate more deductions, or somehow change the definition of income.

Raise taxes? That's a given. Eliminate deductions? They're already doing it. Still, this isn't enough to slay the Democrats' thirst for your money.

The Democrats may not understand principles like "liberty" or "fairness," but even the ones who went to government schools can do a little simple math. They know they can get more money out of you if the "taxable income" line on your 1040 can somehow be increased. After all, 40 percent of $120,000 is more than 40 percent of $90,000. But how in the world do you boost taxable income for someone who hasn't actually increased his taxable income?

Simple! You impute more income to that taxpayer! Up goes the taxable income, and up goes the "tax due."

This is an idea the Democrats have been kicking around since the early days of the Clinton administration, back before the voter revolution of 1994. The Clintonistas wanted to impute extra income to people who own their own homes. There were two motives behind their plan. First, they wanted to push more people into the higher income brackets, where Clinton's tax increases could reach them. Second, they wanted to increase the amount of taxes actually collected from these people.

Here's how their version of the imputed income scheme would have worked:

Let's say you've owned your home for about twenty years. During that time, your home has been appreciating in value . . . big time. But your original purchase price—and thus the terms of your loan—were set two decades ago, so your monthly payments on that home are much, much lower than they would be if you bought the house today.

Let's say those payments are about $550 a month. There isn't much of a home mortgage tax deduction left at this point, since you almost have the home paid off, and the bulk of your payments go to principal instead of interest.

The very fact that you're living in such a nice home, and paying so little for it, attracts the interest of Democrats. They know there are a lot of people in your neighborhood who paid more for their homes than you did, and their mortgage payments are a lot higher. Not only that, but the people who rent in your neighborhood are paying *much* more than you do every month. It's obvious that your longtime homeownership, and your foresight, have rewarded you.

Well, where there's an economic benefit, there's a Democrat waiting to tax it!

As one of America's "rich" homeowners, you're about to get a little visit from the imputed income fairy. The Democrats want to squeeze a little more money from you, to spend on those poor renters and people who aren't as "fortunate" as you are (in exchange for their votes, of course). So under the imputed income plan, they would figure out how much your home would rent for every month. To do this they would use every new piece of census data that supports their views, plus any information that they can develop on current sale and rental prices up and down your street.

Let's say the government—the IRS, if you will—determines that your home would rent for $3,250 a month. That would add up to $39,000 a year. But the IRS discovers that you're only paying $550 a month—the equivalent of $6,600 a year if you were paying rent. Well, in their way of thinking, that's one advantage you're enjoying by virtue of your long-term homeownership. The economic benefit of your home ownership, in their view, is the difference between the $39,000 you should be paying to live there and the $6,600 you're actually paying.

You see? By their ingenious logic, you're "getting away with" $32,400 every year in untaxed economic benefits!

How would the Democrats right this wild injustice? Simple. They'd take that $32,400 and add it to your taxable income on your next tax return. That would give you the privilege of paying income taxes on the economic benefit you derive from your long-term home-ownership. The IRS has "leveled the playing field" in your neighbor-hood, so to speak. Just as your neighbors have to pay taxes on the full $39,000 they're paying to rent that house down the street, you'd have to do the same. It's only fair, right?

After all, you're *rich,* remember? You've got a little extra money, you should take a little extra punishment—all in the interest of gov-ernment programs for the "less fortunate."

As noted, this imputed income notion first gained some traction in the Clinton years. But it went underground only because the Republicans got the upper hand in Congress. The Democrats have kept on introducing imputed income bills on the Hill. Several years ago, for example, they introduced a similar imputed income bill—this one pertaining to unpaid child support, not home mortgages. Under this law, deadbeat dads who owed back child support would have been required to add the amount of their arrears to their taxable income and pay taxes on it. Remember, this is income that's already been taxed once. The bill would have been a simple double dip, forc-ing the deadbeats to pay tax on their income a second time—a strat-egy designed to punish the dads, but which would only punish their suffering children, by swiping money from the deadbeats' pockets and making it less likely than ever that they'd send a few pennies to the kids.

Today, child support. Tomorrow, renter support—money you could be keeping if you only rented your home instead of owning it.

A SNATCH-AND-RUN ON YOUR PENSION FUNDS

Do you have any idea how much money is sitting in private pension and 401K plans belonging to American taxpayers?

Not millions, not billions—trillions. Trillions of dollars sitting out there in various investment accounts, pension funds, and 401K plans, earning interest and growing in value . . . and the government can't touch it!

Imagine how frustrating this must be for your average tax-spend-elect politician. All that money out there, hard at work in the private capital marketplace, completely out of their reach! Just think of the votes that could be bought with this money! Think of the millions of Americans who could be made more dependent on government through the programs that could be established and funded with this cash!

The Democrats and their economic advisors have also got a plan to raid those pension plans. They've been sitting on it since the Clinton years, and I just know they're itching to bring it back.

Their justification is simple (simple-minded, you might say). Pension plans are for the rich, right? Only those evil rich people have those fat pension plans to fall back on when they retire. It's just not fair that they should be able to set aside all that extra dough while "working" families have to scrape just to get by.

So all they have to do is start yammering about "leveling the playing field" and "helping out the less fortunate" and the way is cleared for their grand plan.

The key was to make everyone report to the government exactly how much they have in their pension or 401K plan—and take some of it away from them.

In its original, Clinton-era form, the plan called for a one-time 15 percent tax on the outstanding balance of all private pension and 401K retirement plans. This money would have been paid into the federal government's general fund, and used to fund various social vote-buying programs for low- and middle-income earners.

You can see why this plan would have been a real winner for Democrats. It would have taken money chiefly from those who earn enough to pay income taxes and contribute to pension plans in the first place. Remember, these aren't exactly the core of the Democrats' voting bloc.

If you just lean back, close your eyes, and pretend you're listening to *Meet the Press,* you can almost hear Nancy Pelosi pushing this idea right now:

> *These people with the pension plans are the fortunate. They've been able to set aside money for their retirement while the working class has had to live from paycheck to paycheck, always earning just enough money to survive, never enough money to save. It's time that America play fair with the working class. The rich, with their fat pension plans, have benefited from the labors of the poor. Now it's time for them to contribute their fair share so that the working class can nurture their dreams of retirement along with the rich.*

Damn! I almost convinced myself for a minute there! Guess my natural compassion genie got out of the bottle for a moment.

It's easy to be compassionate with someone else's money, isn't it?

So when the Democrats return to claim their birthright—complete control of our federal government—get ready to kiss a good portion of your retirement funds a fond farewell.

But hey . . . think of all the good your money will do in someone else's pocket!

LET'S TAX YOUR PENSION CONTRIBUTIONS, TOO!

Surely you don't think the Democrats are going to pat themselves on the back and slither off after they've pulled this raid on your pension plans, do you? Come on—that would be way too easy. All they had to do was cook up a little of their class warfare casserole and the table was set!

So how about dessert?

After the Democrats revive their plan to tax the outstanding balance of all pension and 401K plans, they're bound to follow up with a similar tax on all future contributions to these plans.

Once again, the argument will be simple:

"Look. It's not as if we're asking the rich to pay the full income tax rate on the money they contribute to their pension plans. We're just asking them to contribute their fair share to the retirement dreams of the working class."

Different tax, same theory: the so-called "rich" shouldn't be allowed to invest their money tax-free when "poor" people don't have that opportunity.

Sounds ludicrous? Sure. But it's bound to resonate with their voters.

ECONOMICALLY TARGETED INVESTMENTS— CONTROLLING YOUR PENSION FUND

By this point, the Democrats will be feeling their oats. Having nailed the filthy rich[4] by confiscating part of their pension funds (15 percent? More? Who knows what they'll get away with?), now they'll have to pay another 15 percent on their future contributions to those funds. Surely there must be something the left is missing!

As a matter of fact, there is. There's another step in their seizure of

---

[4] Can you imagine what would happen to someone who used "filthy poor"? Maybe I'll try it on the air.

your personal freedoms: The politicians will start telling you where you can and can't invest your pension funds!

No joke, my friends. This idea has been around for a while, under the name of Economically Targeted Investments (ETIs). Simply put, it's a tool that allows Democrats to take the money that's left in your pension plan after their tax raid and use that money to buy even more votes!

Here's how ETIs work:

The government grants various tax breaks to these retirement plans. As you know, these tax breaks are usually granted to force individuals or corporations to conduct business in a way that's favorable to government, or to prevent them from acting in a way that gives politicians ulcers. The Democrats' (not-so)-secret plan is to change the rules on the tax deductibility of donations to pension and 401K accounts.

Instead of just investing these funds in the stocks, bonds, and other investment vehicles of their choosing, fund managers and individuals will be required to invest these funds in specific investments, following guidelines dictated by politicians.

How could they possibly enforce this? Easy: Stray from those guidelines, and they'll take your tax breaks away!

This, folks, is a sickeningly brilliant scheme. It allows politicians to fund some of their favorite spending schemes—without using a dollar of government funds.

Here's how:

The politicians would simply create regulations requiring fund managers and individuals to invest their pension or 401K funds in businesses doing things the politicians like—building low-income housing, for instance, or investing in alternative energy research. Another favorite might be corporations that take extra steps to hire workers off welfare rolls.

The politicians would regulate this new investment protocol by giving these corporations a politically inspired grade on their dedication to diversity, the environment, charitable contributions, and employee benefits. Rest assured that companies that don't provide their employees with full health coverage would see their investments dwindle almost immediately.

And there are so many other ways to play! Let's not forget so-called "affirmative action" programs for systematized racial discrimination in the workplace. That would serve nicely the Democrats' traditional fealty to one key voting bloc—minority voters. Another such bloc—our old friends the unions—would have its wheels greased the same way: You can bet your next born that the pressure would be on to forbid pension fund investments in nonunionized corporations.

You get the picture here: The Democrats' secret plan would be one big discount store for their long-treasured special interests.

The genius of all this is that Democrats would be able to claim credit for increasing funding for some of their favorite programs— without actually increasing the traditional tax rates. All they have to do instead is pass these soft controls on our pension money. Make no mistake—the end result would inevitably be lower returns on pension fund investments, and lower pension benefits to retirees.

But that won't bother the Democrats. The less money you have to retire on, the more dependent on government you will be.

AND WHILE WE'RE ON THE SUBJECT OF UNIONS . . .

Anyone with the mental power to grow a fingernail has got to know that the Democrats will be moving fast to throw some bones to their union friends now that they're on their way to complete control of the reins of power in Washington. Steering ETIs to union companies is just a first step. The next will be making it easier for workers to unionize!

As things stand now, union organizers have a pesky little hurdle to overcome in the process of unionizing a workplace—a vicious little thing called the secret ballot. Goonions don't like secret ballots, at least not when workers are voting on whether or not to unionize. It's easy enough to apply pressure at the right points to get workers to sign a petition calling for an election; after all, it's easy to tell who has signed up and who has not. Actual elections are something else. A worker can bow to pressure (or something worse) and sign a petition, but when the ballots are cast he's free to express his true feelings.

There must be a way around this problem. Hmmmmmmmm-mmmm.

Wait! I've got it! We'll just eliminate the secret ballot.

And that, my friends, is precisely what the goonion bosses have in mind as soon as the Democrats are fully installed. After years of union "volunteers" helping in election campaigns for Democrats, of union contributions to Democrat campaign war chests, payback time is right around the corner!

Here's how they'll do it: Democrats will amend the labor relations act to allow for unionization of a particular workforce solely through the petition process, with no actual vote. Once the majority of eligible employees sign the petition to unionize, it's done. This means that every worker who doesn't want to see his workplace unionized will have to face the music by refusing to sign the petition—or will have to go along to get along.

What a fine choice. The Democrat choice. Mob rule.

And who wants to go against the mob?

FORCE EMPLOYERS TO PAY FOR "FAMILY LEAVE"

Right now the Family Leave Act requires employers to give employees about twelve weeks of unpaid "family leave" to tend to certain family events and emergencies—having a baby, recovering from an illness, coping with a death in the family or a persistent hangnail or any number of other situations.

The insensitive truth about businesses, however, is that they hire people to produce, not *re*produce. Employers have jobs they need to fill. Having the right people in those jobs is essential to the overall health of the employer's business and to the job security of everyone else working there.

The decision to grant an employee an extended leave, whether paid or unpaid, should be left up to the employer, not to some political hack trying to scam votes. If an employee is worth the sacrifice, the company should give him or her the time off. If not, their pregnancy or other family emergency should be a golden opportunity to say goodbye. If your employer finds you valuable and believes you'd be difficult to replace, then he may well agree to an extended leave when the situation warrants.

Bottom line: It should be up to you to make yourself valuable enough that your employer wants to accommodate and keep you.

Of course, this is a challenge many don't want to face. Those who don't bring extraordinary skills or a superb work ethic to the job should hardly expect their employers to go to the trouble of hiring a temporary worker to replace them until they return. It would make far more business sense to get rid of you and hire someone else. Who knows? Your replacement might be a better, more motivated worker![5]

The only reason this whole "family leave" scam has gotten anywhere is that the leave is *unpaid*. It only prevents employers from replacing employees while they're gone. For the Democrats, though—and for the marginal workers who make up so much of their base—this situation is hardly satisfactory. They want the employers to keep paying employees who take these little extended vacations.

As the Dems crawl back to power, you can bet they've got this near the top of their agenda.

The Democrats' "secret" plan will start off slowly—with legislation that requires the employer to cover, say, a third of the employee's

---

[5] And let's not hear any of that "I want my job back" whining. Here's a hint: It's not "your" job. The job belongs to the employer, not to the employee. The employee is merely hired to do the job that the employer has created.

salary. This would give future Democrat candidates the opportunity to campaign on promises to increase that percentage—a lousy idea made worse, but a sure vote-getter nonetheless.

Paying people for not working—Democrats love this stuff.

REQUIRE EMPLOYERS TO PAY FOR SICK DAYS

This proposal is already on the table in the 110th Democrat-controlled Congress, courtesy of the illustrious and "honorable" Ted Kennedy.[6] The idea here is to force employers with more than fifteen full-time employees to give each of them six paid sick days every year.

Studies have shown that most American workers take sick days even when they're not really ill. You'd be amazed at how many people phone in sick on the first day of hunting season, for example. Getting paid to fish—now, that's a concept only a Democrat could love.

What we have here is the government forcing a business to give up its claim to any rights under the basic relationship between employer and employee. The employment relationship is one in which the employee trades his intellectual and physical capital to the employer for money. If the employee gives his intellectual and physical capital to the employer and is not paid for it, then he's been cheated. Likewise, if the employer gives money to the employee and receives nothing valuable in return, the employer is being cheated.

Perfect! the Democrats say. They've always been a "something for nothing" crowd.

SEIZING THE PROPERTY OF THOSE WHO FLEE DEMOCRATIC TAX TYRANNY

As Democrats work diligently to increase our taxes, to exercise more state control over our economy, and to increase the pace of income

---

[6] Come on now. How can anyone refer to Ted Kennedy as "The Honorable . . ." without busting a gut? If this guy is honorable, than Mark Foley is in line for sainthood.

and wealth redistribution, many high-achieving Americans are making escape plans. Working to build your own wealth is one thing. Working to build the wealth of those who have never managed to wean themselves from government is quite another.

The greater the confiscation of wealth becomes, the more people start looking for other places to invest their money and base their businesses—and if that means going out of the country, more and more of them are saying, *So be it.*

In 2006, the best estimates were that there were about $11 trillion in dollar-denominated deposits in overseas investment and banking accounts, where those dollars could work and earn while being protected from our confiscatory tax structure. Just why do you think you run into so many banks when you step off that cruise ship onto Grand Cayman Island? It's not because the Cayman Islanders have a fondness for banks. The dollars in these banks are refugees—from a punishing tax system that rewards indolence.

Not only are our American dollars fleeing overseas, but American businesses are moving offshore as well. Democrats like to call these businesses "Corporate Benedict Arnolds."

Why, though, do these corporations flee America?

I'll keep the explanation brief and as simple as I can. For verification and clarification, feel free to consult your friendly, though probably dull, local corporate accountant.

American-based businesses, of course, are required to pay corporate income taxes to the U.S. government on profits earned by its operations both at home and abroad.

Most European countries, on the other hand, require their native corporations to pay taxes only on profits earned *in that country.* A European-based business would generally not pay taxes at home on profits earned from its American operation.

This means that when a business relocates its base of operations from the United States to Europe or some other foreign venue, it's very likely to see an overall reduction in its tax burden. This is generally good for the employees and stockholders—but it doesn't tend to do much for politicians, who believe that all profits belong to them anyway.

Once more, the Democrats have a very straightforward plan to redress this imbalance: They would impose confiscatory taxes on those who seek to relocate their business headquarters to another country, or who seek to move large amounts of capital out of the United States to work in foreign (less taxed) capital markets.

There is a tax reform plan that would address these issues quite nicely. It's called the Fair Tax, and the adoption of this plan would make America the world's number-one tax haven.[7]

If you're interested in knowing more about it, I've got a book to sell you.[8]

GOVERNMENT-PAID CHILD CARE
FOR THE MAJORITY OF VOTERS

The very last thing a good liberal Democrat would ever want to do is suggest that anyone shouldn't have a baby they can't afford to raise.

God forbid that people should be able to afford their own children.

Democrats know that children are the most important things in the lives of millions of Americans. Our love for our children affords the left with boundless opportunities to expand the reach and cost of government. After all, anyone who tries to oppose Democrat efforts to redistribute wealth and grow government on behalf of "the children," as they say, is open to charges of hating kids, of wanting to duct-tape them to the toilet until they're old enough to head out on their own.

An alarming number of children in America today are raised in single-parent households. And when you actually do stumble across a

---

[7] I think someone wrote a book about this plan, called *The Fair Tax Book.* Perhaps you can find a copy somewhere.

[8] It's called *The Fair Tax Book,* written by someone named Neal Boortz and Congressman John Linder.

two-parent household, more often than not you'll find both of them working.

The Democrats *know* you both have to work. They know child care is expensive. And they know they can get away with almost any expansion of the welfare state—as long as people believe that they're doing it for "the children."

So once the Democrats retake control, stand by for an explosion of programs designed to relieve parents of the burden of having to care for their own children. There will be new day care tax credits, new and expensive grants. Slowly but surely, our nation will succumb to the idea that child care is the responsibility of the government, not of the parents.

You can almost hear the Democrat campaign ads now: "Elect those Republicans again, and you'll end up having to pay for your own child's day care!"

Think I'm exaggerating? Think again. No matter what sorts of international and domestic crises might face our nation, all you need to do is tell parents that they might not be getting much more help in raising their child, and that will be the one thing on their minds the next time they vote.

While we're at it, here's something else to worry about: How soon will it be before pressure mounts to put all of these day care centers under government control? The sooner the politicians can get their hands on them, the quicker the indoctrination begins.

For more on that, I'll refer you back to my earlier chapter on the scourge of government schools.

GOVERNMENT-IMPOSED LIMITS ON EXECUTIVE INCOME

This one is really going to have to wait until Democrats have got a firm grip on the federal machine.

As soon as they do, the Social Democrat Party will move to institute limits on executive compensation. The idea is to impose confiscatory corporate income taxes on companies who pay their top executives more than a certain multiple of the compensation paid to the lowest-paid employees. After all, the free market simply can't be trusted to set wages at those delicate extremes of the wage scale. That's clearly a job for politicians.

Limits on executive compensation will, as you can imagine, be a huge hit with the unions and the so-called "working class."

And what of the highly paid executives? Well, they'll simply take their skills overseas to a business marketplace with more economic liberty, or they'll retire!

Let the local union steward figure out how to save the company from economic ruin.

REPEALING THE SECOND AMENDMENT

Haven't you ever thought it a little odd that leftists and Democrats are generally opposed to the concept of the private ownership of firearms, while conservatives and libertarians favor the idea?

Well, there's a reason.

Those who value and celebrate the worth of the individual, and of individual freedom, generally believe that individuals should be allowed to own and bear arms. Those who put the power of government over and above the power of the individual would just as soon see individuals unarmed.

Democrats are no friends to the Second Amendment. Remember, when guns are outlawed, only that government will have guns. If you're comfortable with that thought . . . well, let's just say you might want to think a little harder.

Armed individuals are, of course, a threat to state control. Coincidence?

Or just another instance of the "secret" plan at work?

OUR ABSURD WAR ON DRUGS

It was around 7:00 in the evening of November 21, 2006. Thanksgiving was two days away, and eighty-eight-year-old Kathryn Johnson of Atlanta was no doubt looking forward to a Thanksgiving dinner with her children, nieces, and nephews. She was also worried. It was dark now in her crime-ridden neighborhood, and even the burglar bars on all of her doors and windows didn't make her feel truly secure. A few days before, she had heard, a seventy-five-year-old woman down the street had been raped.

Kathryn never allowed strangers into her home; she even turned neighbors and friends away. From time to time, people would bring her food from the grocery store; she just asked them to leave it on the front porch, and waited until the coast was clear before retrieving it.

As Kathryn was settling in for another night of caution and worry, an Atlanta Police Department drug task force team was on the way to her modest home. The police had gone before a judge with the story that someone in Kathryn's home had sold drugs to a police informant earlier in the day, and they were going back with a no-knock warrant to look for drugs and perhaps arrest the dealer.

Kathryn Johnson must have heard the racket as the police ripped the burglar bars off her front door. She was ready with her rusted revolver when they came through the old wooden door. Kathryn, it appears, fired first. Though there is a dispute as to how many shots she fired, all three police officers were hit, none fatally. The police did just what you would expect: They returned fire.

Kathryn Johnson was hit several times and died on the scene.

This tragic incident was followed by a chaotic war of words:

- At first, the police claimed that one of their own undercover officers had bought drugs from some male in Johnson's home earlier that day. Later they conceded that it was not a policeman at all, but a paid police informant who'd reported the drug buy.

- As publicity grew, the informant started telling reporters that the police told him to say he had bought drugs at Johnson's home.

- The police initially reported that they had found narcotics inside the home. Later they admitted that all they found was a small amount of marijuana.

- Initial reports were that three police officers were hit by bullets from Johnson's gun. Yet later ballistics tests would show that only one officer was shot; the other two had been hit by shrapnel.

Of course, before the smoke had cleared the local race pimps and civil rights warlords were on the case. Though the real victim here was an eighty-eight-year-old woman shot dead by the police in her home, that never stopped the grandstanders and glory-seekers from exploiting a situation to launch a reputation or strengthen a power base.

- One Atlanta "civil rights activist" announced that he was heading to Washington, D.C., to demand an investigation, saying that the police officers were guilty of "shooting first and asking questions later." Never mind that Kathryn Johnson fired the first shot—as everyone agrees.

• Another "activist" led demonstrations outside Johnson's home, waving signs saying "Don't call 911, the police will kill you."

• Other demonstrators expressed outrage that the police officers involved were suspended with pay pending an investigation. "Shoot an innocent person," their protest signs read, "get a paid vacation."

Why the police blotter, Neal? Why all this detail on a local case?

Because nobody gets it, that's why.

Kathryn Johnson was a victim. So were the police. So are we all— in this idiotic, expensive, and unwinnable war on drugs we're waging in this country.

Sure, I'm a libertarian, and libertarians have been decrying our nation's foolish drug policy for years. But we're certainly not alone. Less than two weeks after Kathryn Johnson's death, Cynthia Tucker, the editorial page editor of the *Atlanta Journal-Constitution,* wrote: "The investigation may reveal police incompetence, and it may reveal police malfeasance. Unfortunately, however, it is unlikely to point to the root cause of this tragedy—a foolish, decades-long effort to curb illegal drug use through arrests and incarceration." Tucker then proceeded to veer from the broader issue by making race the focal point of the rest of her column, but at least she got that part right.

Perhaps one of the dominant factors that prevents the Libertarian Party from becoming a viable third-party threat in local and federal elections is the party's stance on drugs. When I introduce myself as a card-carrying Libertarian, more often than not I get the same old response: "Oh, you're the people who want to legalize drugs."

Well, not exactly. We're the people who understand that American taxpayers are paying absurd amounts of money to accomplish goals that could be met at a fraction of the cost. We're the people who think it's ridiculous that the majority of the growth in our prison populations in this country is due to slamming people in jail just because they were caught using drugs. We're the ones who understand that so much of the crime on the streets of our country is drug-related—crime that would largely disappear if the massive profits brought on by drug criminalization were eliminated. We're the party that understands that you can reduce drug usage more efficiently, and at a lower cost, through treatment than through law enforcement.

There's plenty of data out there to show that our war on drugs is not working, and cannot work; and that the real way to reduce illicit drug usage in this country is through treatment programs. The problem is that these data are excruciatingly boring, and rarely reviewed by anyone outside of academia or our drug control agencies.

In the 1990s, the Rand Corporation[1] conducted a study on cocaine use in the United States and various control strategies to reduce that usage.[2] One of the objects of the study was to consider the cost of reducing cocaine usage by 1 percent in this country through various different control programs. The four control programs studied were defined in the Rand report as:

1. *Source country control:* Eradicating coca leaves and seizing coca base, cocaine paste, and the final product in the source countries (primarily Peru, Bolivia, and Colombia).

2. *Interdiction:* Using the U.S. Customs Service, Coast Guard, Army, and Immigration and Naturalization Service to seize cocaine and drug-related assets before the contraband enters the United States.

3. *Domestic enforcement:* Assigning federal, state, and local law enforcement agencies to seize cocaine and related assets within our borders, and arresting, convicting, and imprisoning the responsible drug dealers and their agents.

---

[1] Described in its website as a corporation that "helps improve policy and decision making through research and analysis." I thought that was what talk-radio hosts did.

[2] "Controlling Cocaine: Supply vs. Demand programs," C. Peter Rydell and Susan S. Everingham. MR-331-ONDCP/A/Dprc, 1994. Order @Rand.org. Wow. An actual useful footnote.

4. *Treatment of heavy users:* Solving the demand side of the problem through outpatient and residential programs.

The results? The Rand researchers found that Option 4—the treatment option—was seven times as cost-effective as Option 3, the
domestic enforcement option.

Dollar figures? You want dollar figures? Here they are, in early
1990s dollars:

• To reduce cocaine usage by 1 percent through treatment
  programs would cost about $34 million.

• The domestic enforcement method would accomplish the same
  goal for about $238 million.

• The interdiction option would cost around $360 million.

• The source country control option's tab would be nearly $800
  million.

So just what is our primary goal here? Is it to reduce illicit drug usage
in this country—or is it to exact some measure of revenge against
these poor, weak, and pathetic souls who have abandoned themselves
to drugs and gotten their addicted rear ends slammed in jail?

Consider the case of Richard Paey from the Florida Gulf Coast.
After a horrible automobile accident, Paey endured painful, and
unsuccessful, back surgery. He's now confined to a wheelchair,
wracked by constant, excruciating pain.

Anxious for relief, Paey tampered with some prescriptions;
over the course of about five weeks, he managed to get about 700
oxycodone pills and a stash of other pain relief medication. When the
authorities found out, Paey was arrested.

Richard Paey wasn't getting these medications to sell or share. He
was taking desperate measures to alleviate the hideous pain that was

destroying his life. But it didn't matter. Convicted under a law designed to deal with drug lords, he received the mandatory minimum sentence. Paey is now propelling his wheelchair around a prison for the next twenty-five years with no chance of parole.

I sincerely hope that not one person reading this approves of such an atrocity.

A December 10, 2006, editorial on the *St. Petersburg Times* website quoted Associate Judge James Seals of the 2nd District Court of Appeals in the case *Paey vs. Florida:*

> I suggest that it is unusual, illogical and unjust that Mr. Paey could conceivably go to prison for a longer stretch for peacefully but unlawfully purchasing 100 oxycodone pills from a pharmacist than had he robbed the pharmacist at knife point, stolen 50 oxycodone pills which he intended to sell to children waiting outside, and then stabbed the pharmacist.

Unfortunately, Judge Seals was writing in the dissent. Paey's appeal was denied. Later he wrote to me asking for help in getting this travesty corrected. "What makes America great is not that injustice doesn't happen. No. It's that when injustice does happen we're not afraid to fix it."

Okay, now tell me again how proud you are of our war on drugs. Tell me again how well it's actually working. You were smart enough to pick up this book in the first place; you can't be dumb enough to think that all the money we're spending—including the millions we're spending to feed and care for those we've railroaded off to jail—is actually making a difference.

In the 1990s, the drug of choice was cocaine. The current rage is methamphetamine—so much so that even stopping by your local drugstore to pick up some cold medicine can arouse suspicions that you've got a meth lab in your kitchen. In a few years maybe we'll take up licking toads.[3] (No kidding: One esteemed member of the Georgia legislature once warned of the "extreme danger of cane-toad licking becoming the designer drug of choice.")

The point is, those who feel they need chemicals to feel good about themselves and to enjoy life are always going to find what they're looking for—and if we continue chasing them around with SWAT teams and no-knock warrants, innocent people like Kathryn Johnson are going to die, and tens of thousands of other innocents are going to be victimized. Not to mention the billions of dollars we'll be spending that should have remained in the pockets of those who earned them.

We Americans seem to derive a great deal of pleasure out of punishing those who fail to measure up to our standards of morality and conduct—regardless of whether or not their conduct has any affect on our personal rights to life, liberty, and property. In Alabama it's even illegal to own a vibrator! What the hell is that all about?

We need to get off our puritanical high horses and deal with our drug problems as rational human beings, not vengeful bluenoses bent on punishing behavior we don't like, even though it doesn't directly affect us. The streets will be safer, the drug dealers will be out of business, and the next Kathryn Johnson will be able to celebrate Thanksgiving with her family.

---

[3] *Bufo alvarius,* if you're looking for a species. Bufotoxins if you're looking for the substance. Makes your mouth water, doesn't it?

CHASING CATS

Whew. All this talk about Democrats and drugs has me eager for a break.

Breaks are a good thing. I truly don't think I would have made it to thirty-six-plus years in talk radio if I didn't allow myself, every so often, to take a serious show and turn it into a good time. Sure, everything these power-hungry wombats inside the Beltway are trying to do to us and to our country deserves constant attention. But if we don't have fun once in a while, we're just going to go nuts.

So here it comes.

Remember when I promised I'd never intentionally lie to you?

You didn't really believe that, did you?

The truth is, from time to time, I do lie on the air—usually for a good reason. Like, say, to keep people listening to the show.

Hey, at least I'm *honest* about the fact that I lie. But I usually do it just for the entertainment value.

A couple of times a week, I tell my listeners, in almost these exact words, "Do not believe everything you hear on this radio program. In fact, do not believe *any*thing you hear on this radio program, either from the callers or me, unless it is consistent with what you already know to be true, or you have taken the time to research that issue for yourself. Because I'll flat-out lie to you to make the show interesting."

You see, people often make the mistake of assuming that just because I'm a talk-show host, I have a firm position on every issue of public or political importance—and that's just not the case. Issues come up all the time that I haven't yet investigated enough to form a strong opinion one way or the other.

When that happens, I start dancing on both sides of the issue—pushing the callers and listening to the responses.

First of all, I know that my listeners may well help shape my opinion, or lead me to a conclusion I might not have come up with on my own.

Second, and more important, it enhances my show's entertainment value.

Does that mean I play a little devil's advocate just to make people mad enough to pick up the phone and call? You bet![1]

After all, conflict is at the heart of what I do. The entertainment value in hearing a bunch of listeners agree with a talk show host is minimal. Listeners want confrontation. So, yes, sometimes, I push the envelope: adjust the knobs, tweak the little whisker on the crystal—whatever it takes to create a sense of confrontation.

In other words, I lie to get a rise out of the audience. And sure, it's fun.

So much fun, in fact, that sometimes I lie about matters of no importance whatsoever, just to see what happens.

Once, on the air, I encouraged female listeners to turn their television sets upside down. "Ladies, try this," I said. "I've just discovered that any TV set with a screen under nineteen inches, by federal law, has a little switch inside, and if you turn it upside down, in a couple of minutes, the picture will flip over and right itself."

---

[1] The math here may be a bit crude, but let's try to figure out how many phone calls I've taken on the air. We'll go with an average of three hours per weekday, 49 weeks per year (I do take vacations) for 37 years. That works out to 27,195 hours of taking phone calls. We'll subtract the time we spent carrying the Watergate hearings live in the 1970s, and the time I've spent rambling on about general aviation (my passion), and put the number at 27,000 hours. I would say that a good average for phone calls is around seven per hour. Now, even though I did go to government schools, I can multiply 27,000 by seven, and I come up with 189,000 phone calls. Can we agree that I should be accorded expert status on what people in this country like to talk about, and what they're likely (or unlikely) to say on a rather extensive list of topics?

Did anyone actually do it? Oh, yeah.

Before long, bewildered husbands were calling the show. "I got home and my wife was sitting there watching the TV upside down, and she said you told her that the picture would right itself. What are you thinking?"

I'm thinking those women would make great Democrat campaign volunteers.

I've also had a great deal of fun toying with listeners about an incident I witnessed on a Delta Airlines flight from Denver, Colorado, to Atlanta.

We were experiencing extremely strong tailwinds on that trip, somewhere in the neighborhood of 100 knots. The Delta 757 was flying so close to the speed of sound that the extra 100 knots brought the speed up to something like 99.9 percent of the speed of sound.

Well, wouldn't you know it? There was a bratty little kid on that flight; back around row 25. After kicking the seat in front of him for fifty minutes, the little demon thought it would be fun to do some wind sprints up and down the aisle. As luck would have it, the aircraft was getting perilously close to the speed of sound, thanks to the tailwind, when the kid initiated a sprint into first class.

Passenger interviews suggest that the brat broke the sound barrier somewhere around row 11 in coach. The ensuing sonic boom broke all the wineglasses in first class and burned most of the hair off the brat's head.

I haven't followed the lawsuit, so I can't tell you how it turned out.

Trust me. You can get people to believe anything. That's why we're so dangerous.

You'd expect some people to know better, though. Like, say, newspaper reporters. That's why it's so hard to believe that, back in 1989, the venerable[2] *Los Angeles Times* published an article in its Sunday

---

[2] "Venerable" is a word reporters often use as a modifier before the title of the *Los Angeles Times,* the *New York Times,* or the *Washington Post* and other newspapers they themselves admire and/or are employed by. It's journalistspeak for "very, very liberal."

magazine under the headline "Even for a Nation of Sports Nuts, Competition is Getting Nuttier and Nuttier." The first-person piece by a semifamous humorist named Margo Kaufman was apparently based on one of her conversations with a colleague:

> "Trash sports," exclaims John Cherwa, associate sports editor at *The Times*. "That's our official name for them. Because they're not traditional and, in many cases, they're not real. Supposedly, in Atlanta they have a thing called cat chasing."
>
> What?
>
> "They throw a cat out of an airplane and then different parachutists try to chase and catch the cat. I don't know if it's true, but I've heard it."
>
> For the life of me, I can't figure out why anyone in his right mind would do such a thing. Of course, I also can't fathom what draws a person to competitive cheerleading, curling or the granddaddy of dubious sports—synchronized swimming. Some sports are glamorous. Some sports are exciting. Some sports are good for your heart. Some sports are good for making money. But some sports are good for nothing.[3]

Woodward and Bernstein would have been so proud of Margo.[4] I can say with confidence that there's no such thing as cat chasing. Never was. How do I know? I made the whole thing up.

Well, technically, that's a lie, too. I didn't come up with the original idea. Some skydivers in Arizona made the whole thing up—didn't *do* it, you understand, just made up the idea. Those wiseasses printed a very short item about cat chasing in their newsletter, and somehow

---

[3] *Los Angeles Times Magazine,* November 12, 1989.

[4] I can say whatever I want to about Margo Kaufman because, as a lawyer, I know she can't sue me. How can I be so sure? Because she died in 2000. I checked. Oh, and by the way, she wrote a book called *1-800-Am-I-Nuts*. It's out of print, but I don't need to read it to know the answer.

their little joke made its way to my desk. It was just a single paragraph, as I recall.

Of course, I'd never heard of cat chasing—and neither had anyone else, for that matter, although the concept is fairly simple in concept (if rather difficult in execution). As Margo explained to her L.A. readers, all you need to do is take a cat up in a plane, toss it out, wait a few seconds, and then signal half a dozen skydivers to jump out and give chase. The one who lands with the cat is declared the winner.

It was a spoof, obviously. At least I *think* it was. Honestly, I don't know. Nor do I really care, since I'm not exactly what you would call a cat person. They really *do* suck the breath out of sleeping babies, you know. And they defecate in houseplants.

No matter. All I knew was that this was a chance to have a little fun—not fun with cats, which are notoriously arrogant and unfriendly, but fun with stupid people.

So one day on my show I revealed to the audience that I had some inside information about a rather bizarre competition that was going to take place right here in our own back yard. The Georgia Cat Chasing Championships, I declared, would be under way in just a few weeks. The most talented and daring skydivers in the area would be competing for the title of state cat chasing champion; the winner would represent Georgia in the National Cat Chasing Championship, to be held in Phoenix later in the year.

What's more, we were going to be covering this exciting event live.

"You know, I've jumped, ladies and gentlemen," I told listeners, "and I think this is going to be a lot of fun."

I promoted this happy fraud relentlessly—not in every single broadcast, mind you, but fairly often. "We here at *The Neal Boortz Show* have arranged to do a remote broadcast from the airport to bring this amazing event to you as it happens!"

I'd let it go. Then, a couple of days later, I'd mention it again.

Needless to say, a few callers started to get agitated.

"Where's it gonna be?" one asked.

"Well, I've been asked not to say," I answered, "but it's an airport somewhere in South Georgia."

As the date of the 1988 Georgia Cat Chasing Championships approached, I started inviting guests into the studio to discuss the skills involved in cat chasing—actual skydivers, by the way, who were in on the joke.

"Well, do you have to hold onto the cat all the way to the ground?" I asked one.

"Oh, no," he said, "No, no. You just take that cat and stick it to your chest. Those claws are going to dig in, and that cat will hold on right up until the point you land."

"What happens if you don't catch the cat?"

"Well, I mean, that's very rare, but they do land on their feet."

"What about skydivers? Ever lost one of them?"

"Just one."

"What happened?"

"Well, it happened in Australia. Some poor bloke caught the cat and somehow the cat latched on and dug into his parachute pack. When he pulled the rip cord, the cat kept the 'chute from deploying. He was too close to the ground to deploy his reserve. The cat walked away."

"Sad."

"Yeah. Bloody cat."

In the meantime, with help from our production crew, we were building a rather sizeable library of sound effects—everything from airplane noises and the murmur of a large crowd to (please don't ask why) chain saws and trees falling. Naturally, we also collected every kind of cat sound imaginable—purring, meows expressing every emotion from mystification to distress, hisses, and the inevitable screech.

"We're probably going to lose three or four cats," I told my listeners. "I'm told that's the average. We don't really know what happens to them. Hopefully they've found good homes."

Contrary to popular belief among mainstream media, not everyone who listens to talk radio is a moron. So, yes, quite a few listeners suspected a hoax and called in to quiz me about it. I assured them that I'd been a little skeptical in the beginning, but that I'd done some investigating on my own, and had satisfied myself that this group of enthusiasts was indeed planning to toss little kitties out of airplanes. I was so convincing that even the skeptics had to wonder.

And the cat lovers? Lord help us. They wanted my head on a platter. They called for the FCC to yank the radio station's license. And, of course, like poor Margot—who would later catch wind of the Georgia Cat Chasing Championships all the way out in L.A.—they believed every word.

All the while, we were working on our sound effects. The sound of a cat hitting the ground after being thrown out of an airplane is a little tricky, but we finally achieved a very satisfying *splat* by taking an entire roll of paper towels, soaking them in water, placing a microphone on the floor, then climbing a stepladder and dropping the wet glob right onto the microphone.

Yes, I do realize I'm probably squandering whatever touchy-feely goodwill I may have amassed with my sappy little Schenectady chapter at the beginning of this book. But let's face it, I don't get paid to do warm and fuzzy. Besides, cats are an arrogant breed of beast. And God knows we've got enough of them.

Cat lovers, it turns out, are another breed entirely. They're *crazy.* I think some psychologist could make a name for himself by studying them.

As championship day approached, the vitriol of the cat lovers intensified. I must say, I was enjoying every minute of their anguish. I do confess, though, that I dramatically underestimated just how much controversy would be stirred up by my little fiction.

My eyes started to open, however, on the morning of the contest, when I arrived at the studio to find the sheriff of Fulton County waiting in the parking lot.

"Neal," he implored, "you gotta help me."

"What's the matter?"

"I've got every sheriff in South Georgia calling me about this cat thing that you're doing today. You've got to tell me where it is. We've got to stop this."

I said, "Sheriff, I'm sorry. I cannot. I cannot reveal that."

That wasn't what he wanted to hear. "I'm going to arrest you," he said.

"For what? Just what are you going to charge me with?"[5]

"Come on, Boortz. Some of these guys are up for reelection, and if this cat drop thing happens in their county they're gonna lose!"

"Sorry, Sheriff," I said, and walked into the studio. That was one unhappy Southern sheriff.

Inside, the entire cast of characters was assembled. We had a loose script, but most of our "coverage" was ad-libbed.

Cue the sound effects.

For the next hour, as promised, we provided exclusive live coverage of the Georgia Cat Championships. Wind roared, cats screamed, tree branches splintered, and crowds wildly cheered the winners. I even went up with one group of jumpers to try to corral a particularly nasty cat. Our Doppler effect got a great workout as the jumper with the howling cat roared by me as I peacefully floated to the ground.

Apparently, while the show was in progress, outraged listeners were calling the Home Depot and all our other advertisers en masse. (Incidentally, I have it on good authority that many of the people who swamped our switchboard with complaints have since been found dead in houses filled with the stench of urine and feces, houses with a hundred cats or more preening indifferently around the body.)

Only in the last thirty seconds of the broadcast, as I was signing off, did I finally give in. "Folks, I'm in the studios in Atlanta! This has all been a fake and you've been had!" By then, Home Depot and sev-

---

[5] You'd be surprised how often that "being a lawyer" thing comes in handy.

eral other major advertisers had already called to cancel their advertising contracts with the station for the rest of the year. In retrospect, it's amazing I survived.

Now don't get me wrong—most listeners loved it. And I still had one more card to play.

We immediately took the entire show and placed it on cassette tapes. (CDs would have been nice indeed, but nobody had seen a CD yet, so the logistics would have been overwhelming.) We put those cassettes of the Great Georgia Cat Chasing Championship on sale—and raised thousands of dollars for Cleveland Amory's Fund for Animals.

The detractors raised hell with the station. We raised money for helpless animals. Ain't life grand?[6]

A few months later, Margot Kaufman heard about the stunt. But somehow she missed the word "fake," and consequently a generation of *Los Angeles Times* readers no doubt believe that we Georgians are all albino, inbred, banjo-playing skydivers who throw cats out of airplanes between slugs of white lightning.

So much for believing everything you read in the newspaper.

At least with me, I tell you I'm going to lie.

Somebody's gotta say it.

---

[6] Apologies to Widespread Panic. What a great instrumental!

FREEDOM-LOVING?
I THINK NOT

While the image of cat-chasing skydivers is still fresh in our minds, this might be a good time for something Stupid.

After thirty-six years on the air, I'm used to being called everything but a child of God. Offensive? Sure. Insensitive? You bet! Guilty as charged. Life is insensitive; so is the truth. I don't hide from either.

Well, this chapter ought to certainly stir the puddin'.

Allow me to make an observation that most of you will probably find both offensive *and* insensitive. I really don't expect to make any friends here, but maybe I'll get you thinking.

One day, a long time ago, I asked my listeners to call and tell me what they thought was the most important thing they'd learned listening to talk radio. Then, at one point during the show, a caller turned the tables. He asked me to share the most important thing *I* had learned hosting a talk show.

My self-editing mechanisms were on the blink that day—not an unusual situation—so I immediately blurted out the first thing that came to mind. I told the caller that the most amazing thing I had learned was how truly ignorant the American people are. Actually, I think I said "stupid" instead of "ignorant." I've since learned that you can't fix stupid, so "ignorant" is probably the better word. (Even better: I should have said "obtuse." That way the truly ignorant ones wouldn't have understood, and I might have hung on to a few more listeners.)

Well, sad to say, things haven't improved much in the many years since that broadcast. The bulk of talk radio listeners may be better informed than they used to be, but I'm afraid the rest of the American public is as ignorant as ever.

The majority of Americans can't tell you who the vice president is. Not two out of ten could name one of their two U.S. senators and their congressman. Most Americans still think the United States is supposed to be a democracy.

New Mexico, by the way, *is* a state.

My opinion was reinforced by a Fox News Opinion Dynamics poll conducted in the fall of 2006, which found that a huge majority of Americans think that our economy is growing worse.

What have they been smoking? At the time of this poll, our economy had just registered a growth rate of 4.4 percent, and these people thought it was in the tank. Employment numbers were up. Manufacturing was up. Government revenue was up. Incomes were up. Home sales were up. Home ownership was at record levels. Poverty was down.

The truth is that our economy is doing amazingly well . . . and poised to do even better. Yet the majority of Americans don't realize this. The forecast for economic growth for the last quarter of 2006 was 4.5 to 5 percent. With these numbers, how could anyone say our economy was doing poorly? You could stick what the average American knows about economic matters down an ant's throat and it would rattle around like a BB in a boxcar.

This is what happens when more Americans get their news from *Entertainment Tonight* than from any other source.

I've come to the reluctant but inescapable conclusion that roughly 50 percent of the adults in this country are simply too ignorant and functionally incompetent to be living in a free society.

You might think I'm off base, but every day around half the people in this country go out of their way to prove me right.

Here's the depressing twist to this story: Not only are many Americans unequipped to live in a free society, they actually don't *want* to live in a free society.

The so-called "love of freedom" we hear about in our patriotic songs and stories is a myth. Americans don't really want to be free. They have enthusiastically abandoned their sovereignty to the lure of the welfare state. They have no working concept of the responsibilities of individuals who would live free of government tyranny or mob rule. Their ignorance renders them incapable of coping with the responsibilities of liberty.

Many years ago I stopped doing a radio show on July Fourth. I had to stop because I found I was completely incapable of being civil with my listeners. All their flag-waving and independence-celebrating was grating on me, and more often than not I would erupt into an hour-long tirade about what a bunch of hypocrites these flag-wavers were, lining the streets for the parade and waiting for the fireworks.

Freedom? These people want true freedom about as much as they want a poke in the eye with a sharp stick.

Let me just run a few questions by you:

Would you like to bear the entire responsibility for your own retirement? What if we were to eliminate the Social Security program so that you could use that money to invest as you see fit for your retirement years?

No! The vast majority of Americans shrieks in reply.

We got a real taste of our so-called "love of freedom" when President Bush proposed some basic Social Security reforms after the 2004 election.

Bush's proposal was designed to fix a fundamental flaw in our system: When you include the phony employers' matching contribution, every American sees about 14 percent of his earnings confiscated for Social Security. The government takes the Social Security taxes it collects and uses the funds to cover Social Security benefits for current retirees. The rest of the money—every penny of it—is then spent. Not one penny is saved. Not one penny is invested. Our politicians simply take the money and hand the Social Security Administration an IOU.

The Social Security trust fund you hear so much about? Doesn't exist. There is no trust fund. There's nothing but a stack of IOUs sitting in a gray filing cabinet somewhere in West Virginia. (Not only that, but there's no law on the books that guarantees that you'll get back one single penny of the money you paid into Social Security. But I digress . . .)

Bush's proposal was simple. Of that 14 percent of your salary the government seizes for Social Security, you would be allowed to take 2 percent and put it into a private account. This account would be yours. You would receive that money no matter what happens to you. The government couldn't take it away. Die early, and it would go to your heirs. You would invest it for your retirement, and you would choose who gets it if you don't live long enough to spend it all.

Did "freedom-loving" Americans everywhere rush to embrace this idea?

Hardly.

It was overwhelmingly rejected by the American people. They were simply unwilling to take responsibility for investing even a minuscule 2 percent of their earnings for their own retirement.

I remember watching one thirtysomething woman on the streets of New York being interviewed on the subject by a network news reporter. When asked what she thought about Bush's partial Social Security privatization plan, she said no thanks. She didn't want to have to choose where that money would be invested. She said she just wanted the government to take care of it for her.

Music to the politician's ears!

If Americans truly loved freedom they would not only be embracing the privatization of Social Security, they would be demanding it.

Which brings up all kinds of questions.

Do you like being free to negotiate your own wages? Or would you prefer to have the government or a union handle that for you, too? For far too many Americans, the answer is "No. I don't want to have to go to my employer and negotiate my own wage. I want the government to set my pay scale, or my union."

How about health insurance? Do you want your employer to provide you with a health insurance plan, or would you rather just take the money your employer is spending and shop for your own plan in the marketplace? Then again, perhaps you think your health care is the government's responsibility in the first place. Good luck with that.

Speaking of health care, do you want to be free to choose the doctors who provide you with health care? Or do you want the government to give you a list of people you can choose from, using private sector accreditation agencies if you wish?

Yeah. Just as I suspected. You don't want to be bothered with researching the credentials of your health care provider yourself. You'll give up that freedom if the government will just do it for you, right?

You'd probably feel pretty much the same way about choosing an attorney, right?

What about television? Do you want to accept responsibility for choosing what you're allowed to watch on broadcast TV? Oh, I know. You're afraid for the children. My God, what if they should see a breast?! I guess you want the government to set the standards there too, right? As long as you still get to watch your sleazy soap opera.

Not that you would need one, but in Alabama and many other states you can't buy sex toys. You can buy toy guns—and real ones—but not sex toys. Are you okay with that? If you are, what does that say for your love of freedom?

Blue laws. In many states you can't buy beer or wine from your grocery store on Sunday. Why not? Because someone just might be in a church at the very time you're popping that top on a cold one. Just whose decision should this be—yours or the government's?

If you approve of blue laws, don't talk to me about your love of freedom.

Should your neighbor be able to call up a bookie and place a bet on this Sunday's Falcons game? If not, why not? How would that hurt you? In fact, what business is it of yours? It's not your money; it's his. Why should you have any say in the matter at all?

And—here we go—what about prostitution? A woman, or a man for that matter, can sell her skills in the marketplace, so long as those skills aren't sexual. Why in the world should prostitution be illegal? Just because you don't approve? How do you reconcile that with your alleged love of freedom?

Let's just make this easy. I'm in favor of a Constitutional amendment that would read something like this:

> Neither the federal government, nor any state or local government shall make any activity a crime unless said activity violates another person's right to life, liberty, or property, either through force or fraud.

Could you live with that? Could you live with the thought that anyone in your community could do pretty much what they wish, so long as it doesn't interfere with anyone else? Now there's a definition of freedom—and it's something I suspect most of you just couldn't go along with.

So spare me your Fourth of July celebrations and fireworks. It's all so empty. To so many Americans, the love of freedom means nothing more than the love of the thought that other people are doing just what you believe they should be doing, and nothing more.

Freedom means the freedom to succeed, and the freedom to fail. Freedom means the freedom to make bad choices and suffer the consequences, and the freedom to make good choices and enjoy the rewards.

When you want the government to use its police power to protect you from failure and shield you from the consequences of bad choices, then what you really want isn't freedom at all. Instead of going out and crowing about freedom on the Fourth, maybe you should try staying at home this year and thinking about what you really value.

This country is populated by far too many people who cannot exist at anything other than a basic level without someone else stepping forward to take care of them. They're adult children. They look upon the government as their mommy and daddy, there to kiss whatever hurts and make sure food is always on the table.[1] These people yearn, and deserve, to live in a dictatorship where their fealty to the government is rewarded by lives absent of uncertainty and choice.

Would that dictatorship be a benevolent one? Depends on who seizes power.

All of this causes me to get a bit antsy before any major election.

Why? Because the modern American election is an open invitation for people who haven't had a working relationship with a clue since their first driver's test to step up and participate in a decision-making process that will have profound implications for my life and the life of my family long after I've been tucked in for the eternal, celestial dirt nap.

Frankly, it scares me to death.

I think it's safe to say that a good portion of the voters who manage to find their way to a polling place in November do so with one thought in mind: *Which one of the people on this ballot can I count on to take the most money away from people I don't particularly like, and spend that money on me—or give it to me outright?*

These people want to escape from the chaos and uncertainty of freedom to a land where the biggest choices they ever have to make are what TV show to Tivo, what to have for dinner, and whether tonight's entertainment should be a six-pack of Bud or a bottle of Mad Dog.

These are the people I would like to see locked in their homes on Election Day.

For years, I have been a firm advocate of developing a system to

---

[1] During the 1992 presidential campaign, one college student actually addressed Bill Clinton at a campaign forum with the astonishing revelation that "We will look upon you as our father."

limit the people who can vote in this country. These people need to be kept away from ballot boxes before they screw everything up for the rest of us. If we don't weed out the chaff, soon it'll be too late.

Why? Among other things, because the rest of us are constantly suffering encroachments on our own freedoms to provide for the survival of the ignorant.

We're forced to invest (if that's the word) 15 percent of our paychecks into a disability insurance and retirement plan that would constitute criminal activity in every one of the fifty states if it weren't run by the government. We must do this, we're told, because there are just too many people out there who aren't bright enough to do it on their own.

Moreover, we're facing the inevitability of socialized medicine. As soon as the Social Democratic party gets its way, with no small amount of help from the Republicans, Americans will be waiting months—if not years—for basic elective surgery. Private citizens will be sent to jail for trying to find a private doctor to treat their ills, outside of the approved and official government plan.

Our freedoms are being lost in the flurry of political pandering to the clueless.

Oh, come on, Neal. Take away our right to vote? You can't be serious.

You bet your sweet jeans I am. You heard what I said about the so-called "right to vote" earlier. I would like nothing more than to see about half of the registered voters out there have their voter registration cards yanked out of their pockets and burned in front of their eyes.

(And surely by now you know better than to cry "democracy" with me.)

Solutions? You want solutions?

Look, I just came here to grumble. I'm tired of seeing rampant widespread stupidity tear down the greatest attempt at self-government in the history of world civilization. But you're right—it's nice to think somebody could do something about this mess.

Surely one improvement would be to build a wall between government and education. Another would be to force prospective voters to prove they have a clue—or even to prove they can *play* a game of Clue. There's certainly nothing in our Constitution prohibiting that.

One thing's for sure: As the ranks of the clueless increase, as more and more Americans opt for security over freedom, as more people surrender their individuality for the ease of running with the mob, the erosion of the liberties, social and economic, that made this country great will proceed apace.

Maybe it's just time for a good escape plan.

TERRORIZING
THE MAILROOM

Around the mid-1990s, the Atlanta police apparently decided that the best way to improve the quality of life in Atlanta was to seize as many rusted old unusable guns as possible—and to get vibrators off the streets.

Now, I've done my due diligence, but for the life of me I was never able to track down those statistics on vibrator-related crimes during the years in question. But it must have been substantial indeed, because one night we were treated to news of police raids on several so-called "adult shops" in Atlanta, where boxloads of vibrators were seized.

Can't you just imagine how well Atlanta slept the next night without the threat of all those vibrators lurking around in the dark, ready to pounce on any unsuspecting citizen who might happen by? The buzzing alone was affecting the sleep of so many in the affected neighborhoods.

Being a community-minded talk show host, and recognizing the threat posed to the health and safety of my fellow Atlantans by the Great Vibrator Epidemic, I decided that I should be part of the solution . . . since I certainly wasn't part of the problem.

Those rusty old guns I mentioned? Well, around the time of the crackdown on vibrators, various groups around town were also trying to address the issue of crimes committed with handguns through gun buyback programs. Gun buyback programs have to rank at the top of the list of mindless feel-good attempts to address a serious problem in the history of our republic. I once had a statistician from Georgia Tech study these much-hyped programs to determine their effectiveness in reducing murders committed with handguns. To reach a statistical certainty of saving one human life, he found, you would have to buy back about 65,000 handguns. That means that Atlanta's gun buyback programs have not yet saved a single human life. And yet you'll find no shortage of antigun nuts arguing that a life is saved for virtually every gun turned in.

My statistician, alas, was stymied by a lack of data on vibrator-related crime. So I decided to take matters into my own hands. After all, if the vibrator problem was so serious that the police were spending precious time rounding those suckers up and impounding them, then certainly it was serious enough to warrant my attention and assistance. We needed to get those vibrators off the streets.

I didn't have a cash fund, like the cops running the handgun buy-back program, but I did have some baseball tickets. So, without alerting anybody in advance,[1] I took to the airwaves and announced the Neal Boortz Vibrator Buyback Program.

I told my listeners that the first ten women (I don't know why I said *women;* that kind of discrimination just isn't in my nature) who came to WSB to turn in their vibrators would receive a pair of tickets to that night's baseball game.

I guess I just didn't fully think this thing through.

At that time, any listener coming to WSB to claim a prize would be directed to our mailroom. The mailroom was under the charge of a pleasant but somewhat straitlaced gentleman who shall remain nameless. This man had worked at WSB through the decades of "Music for Quilting," and just wasn't ready for the type of chaos an errant talk show host can generate. He was sitting there quietly, sort-

---

[1] It is, indeed, easier to ask forgiveness than it is to ask permission. This is doubly true if you happen to be number one in the ratings.

ing the mail, when he heard a growing clamor down the hall and around the corner. Suddenly he was confronted by a wall of not-all-that-pleasant women, waving vibrators in his face and demanding baseball tickets.

Remember, this poor man had the odds stacked against him.

1. He had no idea we were running a contest.

2. He didn't have any baseball tickets.

3. He'd probably never seen a vibrator before.

And now he was faced with a mad rush of baseball-loving women, waving their sex toys in the air and demanding satisfaction.

He didn't stand a chance.

A few weeks later, Mail Guy retired. We haven't heard from him since.

That'll teach me to get involved with community outreach.

SMOKERS

I pull this stunt every spring on my show, and every spring I get outraged responses from clueless parents.

Toward the end of the show, I'll make this little announcement:

"Ladies and gentlemen . . . especially you fathers of teenage girls. Before we go, I just wanted to give you a little reminder. Something you really need to know.

"Does your daughter smoke? Does she have a date for the prom this weekend? Well, if your teenage daughter smokes, I just want you to know that when she comes home from the prom on Friday night and gets into bed smelling like an ashtray . . . it'll be the second time that night that her prom dress has come off."

There's the harsh truth for you, Dad. If your daughter smokes, she's having sex. So you might as well stop by the CVS on the way home and get her a box of condoms or some birth control pills.

Insensitive? You bet. But flip back to the title of this book. You might as well know what every boy at your daughter's school knows: If you want sex, date the girls who smoke.

The sociologists would have an easy time explaining this one: Any girl who shows a willingness, or even eagerness, to engage in one type of risky behavior is all the more likely to broaden her horizons into other risky behaviors—like sex.

But no male in high school needs a sociologist to explain it. He already knows.

Girls who smoke are a sure thing.

And if boys know that, why are parents always surprised—sometimes even shocked, and occasionally outraged—when I say that on the air?

Over the course of a career like mine, you develop a feeling for where the hot buttons are.

Smoking is one of the hottest.

Hey, we radio hosts have slow days just like everyone else. It's not every day that a president of the United States enjoys a good cigar (there's that smoking thing again) with a chubby intern while his wife and daughter are upstairs getting ready for church. In fact, it's been a long time since anything *nearly* that interesting happened in the West Wing.

When a slow day hits, you go to your relief hitters in the hot-topic bullpen.

Number one on the list is smoking.

There are *so* many ways to get people wound up on this topic. For starters, you can state your opinion that smoking is an act of self-hatred, which it most definitely is. The people most likely to disagree with you, as you might suspect, are smokers.

As the denials start flowing, ask your friends how, with today's wealth of knowledge on the dangers of tobacco, anyone who truly loves and respects himself would ever systematically poison himself that way?

I am a business traveler. I am on the road 3 to 4 days a week. I listen to talk radio morning and afternoon. I have listened to a couple of your rants about smokers. I am a pipe smoker (32 years) just so you will know (I am sure you don't care) but I thought I would throw that in. You sit there and blast people who smoke, call them losers and sad. These are the people who pay your salary and put food on your table. I wanted to let you know that there will be one less smoker listening to you from now on. When you went on the first rant a few months ago, I just brushed it off and kept on tuning you in. Not this

time. I just don't have to listen to someone use their place on
the airways to bite the hand that feeds them, in such a vile
and hateful manner. So I guess you won't miss me but I will
say goodbye with a last few words of advice, you need to move
to Air America.

Troy

Ah, the old "I'm never going to listen to you again" threat. Some
adults have no idea how childish they sound. *Awwww, poor wittle
Troy. Did that mean old talk show host say something that made you
feel bad?*

Once you're done acquainting your friends with their own self-
hatred, move on.

Try this: Tell them that if you ever own a business, you're going to
make sure you don't hire smokers. Remind them that smokers are
generally less productive than nonsmokers, they take more breaks,
they're out of work with illness more often, and they just generally
stink up the workplace. Not to mention the way they hike up the cost
of your health insurance.

Sure, there are exceptions—but the general rule prevails. Why
play the odds when you can just hire people who don't smoke? If a
person has so little pride in himself that he would destroy his health
with tobacco, what makes you think that he's going to treat his work
with any real pride?

Subject: Neal - your wrong about the smoking thing
Name: tom reynolds

Smoking is a choice, albeit unhealthy. There are many
things that are unhealthy for a pregnant woman (McDonalds,
Alchohol, Potato Chips, Soda, etc). I think you're drifting to
the right of libertarian when you say there should be rules

regarding smoking. It should be up to the owner of the land, car, child, etc.

Just my opionion.

Rules regarding smoking? Hey, all I said was that employers should be free to turn away job applicants who smoke. Since you've mentioned rules, however, I will say that I believe that pregnant women who have decided to carry their pregnancies to term should be prevented by law from smoking. There is no doubt that a smoking mother will harm her fetus. Low birthweights and reduced lung capacity are just two of the problems. Smoking while pregnant is child endangerment.

I would never miss the chance to embarrass a smoking pregnant woman I might encounter in a public venue. After all, I'm doing it for the children.

Subject: Boortz you boob

You say on the air that if a pregnant woman smokes it will harm the child. I would like to know what study you are refer-ring to that says it is a fact that every woman that smokes harms their child. You look at one source, if it agrees with you it must be true. I agree with you that smoking is very bad for you but it is not a definite that every woman that smokes harms their child. So to go along with your argument, driving a car while pregnant should be illegal also, and anyone who rides a motorcycle is a fool.

Robert

Well, Robert, there is one stark difference between riding a car or a motorcycle and smoking while pregnant. Driving and riding may hurt your unborn baby . . . if you have a wreck. Smoking *will* hurt the fetus. No ifs about it.

In 2005, the journal *Environmental Health Perspectives* published a study showing that children exposed to secondhand smoke have lower test scores than children who don't smoke and aren't exposed to smoke. The research, which involved nearly 4,400 school kids, confirmed earlier studies showing that tobacco exposure is harmful to intellectual development.

It was old news to me. Consider this sampling of headlines from over the years:

- "Smoking Mothers More Likely to Have Hyperactive (ADHD) Children." *Canadian Psychiatric Association Journal,* Vol. 20:183–187, 1975.

- "Child Test Scores Lower When Mothers Smoke." *British Medical Journal,* 4:573–575, 1973.

- "Math, Language & Behavior Problems Elevated in Children of Smoking Parents." *Neurotoxicology and Teratology,* Vol. 13, 1991.

- "Severe Child Behavior Problems Linked to Mother's Smoking." Associated Press, September 4, 1992.

- "Auditory Processing Reduced in School Age Children Exposed to Cigarette Smoke." *Neurotoxicology and Teratology,* Vol. 16(3), 1994.

- "Nicotine Damages Brain Cell Quality." *Neurotoxicology and Teratology,* 16(4), 1994.

- "Smoking During Pregnancy Increases Conduct Disorders." *Archives of General Psychiatry,* 54:670–676, July 1997.

- "Children Age 14 Still Show Harmful Effects if Mothers Smoked During Pregnancy." Department of Public Health, University of Oulu, Finland.

Sorry, Robert.

There are some other startling facts that I've gleaned in my years of irritating smokers. For instance, smokers are more likely to vote Democrat.[1] And smokers generally score lower on basic intelligence tests than nonsmokers.

No lie.

This affords another huge advantage to employers in the hiring mode. If an applicant smokes, you can expect two things: first, he or she will pester fellow workers incessantly with mindless drivel about Democrats this and Democrats that and Democrats are for the working man and Democrats want to take care of us, yakkity yakkity.

Second, they may very well not be bright enough to get the job done anyway.

Still not persuaded? Try this:

Eye care trade journals are reporting a strong link between smoking and development of an extremely serious eye disease called age-related macular degeneration. Macular degeneration is a leading cause of blindness. So, if you're a smoker, you'd better turn these pages faster—your time may be running out.

Macular degeneration isn't the only eye disease associated with smoking, either. Smoking damages the eye in a number of ways, including its effects upon capillaries—the tiny blood vessels that help carry oxygen and nutrients to the retina, lens, and optic nerve in the back of the eye.

Why do I care? Well, I don't really. Not unless you're indulging your filthy, loathsome habit in my presence.

If there is any chance that secondhand smoke can cause me health problems, you ought to have the decency to put the cigarettes away. I'm not interested in losing my eyesight just so you can get a fix. And that's not even getting into the fact that your smoke makes me cough, hurts my eyes, and just plain stinks.

Besides . . . I certainly don't want to smell like you.

---

[1] It goes with that self-hatred thing.

I'd like to find something positive to say about smokers. I suppose I could point out that they're quite possibly responsible for thousands of public sector jobs out there. I'm sure it takes an army of people to pick up all those cigarette butts smokers like to toss out of car windows. Is there a rule somewhere that butts aren't litter?

Hold on. I have a great story for you.

When I was practicing law, my office looked directly out into a parking lot. I owned the building, so I was somewhat concerned with how people treated my property.

One afternoon, a woman pulled into a parking lot directly in front of my window. She couldn't see me watching her through the one-way tinting.

As I sat there watching, she took an ashtray full of cigarette butts and dumped them on the ground. Then she went into the building for an appointment in some other office.

It was time for action.

I went into my junk drawer and retrieved a tube of Super Glue. I then went outside and proceeded to glue each and every one of those butts to her windshield.

I'm telling you, I was enjoying every minute of it.

I then went back inside, poured myself a cup of coffee, and waited.

After about forty minutes, that weed fiend came out and discovered the work of art I had produced. She stood there and literally shrieked at the top of her lungs for about three minutes. People started coming out of their offices, thinking some kind of assault was in progress. Finally, she started ripping the butts off her windshield and throwing them on the ground. Each butt left a little bit of paper firmly glued to the glass.

As she screeched out of the parking lot, her windshield wipers were going full tilt as she sprayed the car with cleaner.

I'm telling you, it was damn near orgasmic.

For sheer entertainment value, it's hard to beat the smoker's aquariums at Atlanta's Hartsfield International Airport. These are glass-enclosed rooms on each concourse where these hopeless drug addicts go to satisfy their cravings.

I love standing outside the glass to gawk at these people. There they sit, in their cloud of smoke, gulping in every last bit of nicotine they can before they have to get on their flights.

Do you want another illustration of just how pathetic smokers can be?

Of course you do.

Many moons ago, when airlines were just starting to get on the no-smoking bandwagon, smoking was banned on domestic flights only. On a flight from Atlanta to Los Angeles, you couldn't smoke. On a flight from Atlanta to Mexico City, you could.

These pathetic drug addicts would actually book flights from Atlanta to Los Angeles through Mexico so that they could have their precious cigarette fixes on route.

I have enjoyed listening to your radio show for some time. Today's broadcast will be the last. How dare you characterize tobacco smokers in such disparaging and hateful words? I respect your right to be so very mean-spirited, but such words place you solidly with the ultra liberal left, who use such tactics to "enlighten" those of us who disagree. "Vile," "despicable," "losers" . . . perhaps you should just round them all up and force them to spend the rest of their days in the "pleasant" confines of the Atlanta's airport smoker's lounge. Even better, just line them up against a wall and shoot 'em all!

Stephen

Come on, Stephen. You think I want to shoot smokers? Talk about a wasted effort. You're killing yourself with those cigarettes, Stephen. Why waste a bullet on you?

For three decades I've been ranting about smoking like this, and for three decades I've been taking the heat for it. But the wake of hurt feelings, angry listeners, and outraged parents is more than offset by the literally hundreds of letters I've received from people who told me they quit just so they wouldn't have to hide under the bed when I went on my next tirade. Teenage girls included.

So I may be hurting feelings, but I'm also saving lives.

Sounds like a good tradeoff to me.

THE PRESENCE EVER FELT

When I was about eight years old, I spent the summer on my grandfather's farm in Thrall, Texas. One evening my cousin Cindy, always a bit precocious, came to me with a forbidden secret to share with me and me alone.

She opened a book and there it was—a label, torn from the underside of a mattress. I was horrified. She was using the DO NOT REMOVE UNDER PENALTY OF LAW label as a bookmark! This was a sure sign, in my young mind, that Cindy had crossed the line into juvenile delinquency. I fully expected the sheriff to arrive at any moment.

To ensure my silence on the matter, Cindy told me I would have to join her in a criminal conspiracy by removing a similar label from one of Grandma's mattresses. I did, and didn't sleep for three nights.[1]

This small childhood trauma was the start of a lifelong crusade against warning labels.

Now, I don't have much of a problem with a simple skull and crossbones on some caustic cleaning fluid. But our culture has been on a prohibiting jag for decades, and it's gone a bit too far.

None of us particularly likes having the authorities looking over

---

[1] In later years, when I was attending Texas A&M and would sometimes go back to Thrall for weekends, Cindy would set me up with dates. She was not cut out to be in the matchmaking business. I can, however, say that those Texas farm girls grow up rather quickly.

our shoulders. I was that way with my parents and siblings, I'm that way with co-workers and even my wife,[2] and I feel particularly strongly about it when it comes to our Imperial Federal Government.

For some reason—and remember, much of what gets stuck in my brain doesn't necessarily make all that much sense—I especially remember an incident that occurred many years after I was married and I'd finally stopped worrying about the consequences of my petty crime spree with Cindy.

Donna and I have been taking vacations to Walt Disney World for more than three decades. Unlike most Orlando visitors, we don't actually enter the Magic Kingdom and spend our days standing in lines, riding the Pirates of the Caribbean for the gazillionth time, and eating hot dogs. We just drive our motor home down from Atlanta and find a nice space at the Fort Wilderness campground to chill for a week. If we decide we want to go to Epcot to watch the fireworks, or to Blizzard Beach to act like children on the waterslides, we catch one of the Disney buses.

A vacation is supposed to be an escape, right? So there I was, far away from the confines of the radio booth, relaxing in the Central Florida sun and trying to forget all the things that yank my chain.

Until I stepped onto one of those Disney buses, and noticed a sign up front:

FEDERAL LAW PROHIBITS OPERATION
WITH ANYONE STANDING IN FRONT OF WHITE LINE

Just damn.

There I was, trying to get away from the kinds of things that upset me—like, say, government intrusiveness—and there was a big fat sign

---

[2] Stop reading now. Go to the auto parts store and get one of those little convex stick-on mirrors. About an inch in diameter will do. Stick it on your computer monitor. Remember, the spouse in the mirror is *much* closer than he or she appears.

telling us (for our own good, of course) how to ride a bus. If one of those buses were ever to operate with some miscreant standing in front of that all-important white line, I have no doubt that Disney would have to put up a makeshift morgue to handle the carnage that would surely have resulted.[3]

Somewhere in Washington, D.C., you see, there must have been some faceless gargoyle who spent the better part of a year (and who knows how many hundreds of thousands of taxpayer dollars) conducting extensive tests and studies to determine just where that white line ought to be. One inch over the line, and the highway would be strewn with teeth, hair, and eyeballs.[4]

I can just see him now, our Assistant to the Deputy to the Assistant Transportation Secretary in Charge of Line Painting, proudly boarding a bus at Disney World with his family and friends in tow. "See that line?" he says, beaming. "I'm the one who did that! I'm the one who figured out where that line ought to be, and then I wrote the rule that said that the driver had to park the bus if anyone stood in front of that line! See that sign? I wrote that!" His family's eyes would bulge with joy and amazement, and the spectacle would fill the hearts of those lucky enough to be in the presence of someone who has had such a profound impact on the lives of so many Americans, and the hero who had doubtless saved hundreds of lives.

Now, here's where this book becomes unexpectedly helpful. My friends, what I'm about to tell you will make every penny you paid for this book worthwhile, even though this chapter wasn't part of the original outline.[5]

It's brought to you by a substance called "Goof-Off."

Not too long ago, you see, I bought a new car. It was my first brand-spanking-new car since that Chrysler Cordova in 1977. That's

---

[3] I also have no doubt that "It's a Small World" would continue to play relentlessly in the background.

[4] Thank you, Brother Dave.

[5] A trait this chapter shares with many others between these covers.

not to say I hadn't *driven* plenty of new cars since then, but they always belonged to someone else—sponsors, for instance.[6]

Immediately upon getting into one of these cars, I would rip those air bag warning notices off the sun visors. Hey, I'd read them once; that was enough for me.

Well, apparently the government feels otherwise. In case you haven't purchased a new car in the past few years, you need to know that those obnoxious air bag warning stickers won't come off anymore. They've made them permanent.

It's the same bureaucrat, I'm sure of it. That pencil-necked geek sitting in his windowless office somewhere in the massive Department of Transportation building decided he'd been resting on his white-line laurels far too long; it was time for another blaze of glory. So the DOT's answer to Dr. Stephen Hawking decided that guys like me should no longer be allowed to remove those air bag warning labels.

In his brilliant vision of the future, those labels would stay in place day after day, mile after mile, a constant nagging reminder that no matter where you go, no matter what you do, the government is there. The huge, text-filled eyeballs of Big Brother, one on each visor, staring at you. (And in case you hadn't noticed, many of them are actually subtitled in French! I guess that adds to the snob appeal.)

Look, I know. Airbags can hurt babies. But I'm not Britney Spears; there are no babies in my front seat. Enough already!

Now, here's where that little can of Goof-Off comes in.

Next time you buy a new car, stop by your friendly neighborhood hardware man and buy a can of the stuff. Then go out to your car and dab said Goof-Off on the labels with a small washcloth. Wait a few minutes, dab on a little more, then start peeling the label off the visor. As soon as the label is gone, wash the visor down with a sponge and some warm soapy water.

There! You've washed the federal government right out of your car.

(With luck, the next time you take your car in for service some

---

[6] I never said the job didn't have its perks.

eagle-eyed technician won't report you to the federal sticker police—or, worse, replace them.)

This may sound trivial, folks, but this kind of government supervision can turn into death by a thousand cuts.

I don't know if you've ever been inside the cockpit of a general aviation airplane, but the newer ones are covered with stickers. The FAA has mandated stickers for this, stickers for that, stickers for everything else in between. If something isn't working, you have to put a sticker on it yourself, saying it's not working.

Now, what do you want the pilot paying attention to—the altimeter or a bunch of stickers?

The DOT, thank goodness, is still running behind the FAA. But they're suffering badly from an advanced case of sticker envy. Give them a few years and the dashboard of your new car will look like an urban graffiti wall.

How absurd can the government's label mania get?

Many years ago there was a dairy in Atlanta, Georgia, named Mathis Dairies. Mathis was proud of the fact that they would deliver raw milk to the consumer's door. "Raw" meant straight from the cow. This milk was so fresh the cow hadn't even missed it yet.

Pasteurization and homogenization are only needed for milk that's going to go through a lengthy shipping and retailing cycle. This Mathis stuff was headed down the gullet almost as soon as it was out of old Elsie.

Well, needless to say, the Food and Drug Administration didn't like that situation. So, one day, Mathis was ordered to put a label on their milk—a label to warn unsuspecting families this wasn't exactly the type of milk you would get from the grocery store. And just what did the label say?

ARTIFICIAL MILK

I kid you not. Because Mathis Dairies hadn't done what the federal government thought human beings ought to do with a pure, natural substance like milk, they were required to give it a label that distinguished it from their usual product. Only milk that was run through various mechanical processes, and injected with the usual Vitamin D goodies, could be called "genuine."

I guess the only alternative left was to call the raw stuff "artificial."

And milk isn't the only thing that's been subjected to this artificial-versus-real battle in recent years. Around the same time, the FDA started requiring producers of organic foods to put an "artificial" label on *their* products. I even came across a bag of "artificial" pasta at a health food store. A cashier explained that the government required said label because the spaghetti hadn't been processed with chemicals and other additives.

Think these examples are isolated? Think again. And yours truly isn't the only one who has noticed.

The flood of ridiculous warning labels on American consumer products has unleashed a number of searches to find and highlight ridiculous examples. The results of one such search are posted on the website Common Good,[7] founded by New York attorney Philip K. Howard, author of the outstanding 1995 bestseller *The Death of Common Sense: How Law Is Suffocating America.*

Howard's favorite warning label appears on a baby stroller: CAUTION: REMOVE BABY BEFORE FOLDING STROLLER.

Another favorite is printed on one of those fake fireplace logs you find near the checkout stand of your grocery store: CAUTION: RISK OF FIRE.

In fairness to Big Brother, Howard points out that some of the most inane labels aren't exactly federally mandated. Rather, they're made necessary by a legal system that generously rewards a woman who scalds her crotch with piping-hot coffee while driving away from a McDonald's with the cup between her legs, or the ignoranus[8] who

---

[7] http://www.cgood.org/society-45.html.

[8] OK . . . I got this word from a *Washington Post* article on neologisms and from urbandictionary.com. "Ignoranus: A person who is not only ignorant, but is also an ——hole." I'm certain you will join the author in clearing the way for a broader acceptance of this word throughout our social discourse.

decides to trim his shrubbery by picking up a running lawn mower with his bare hands.

Want more? Howard has plenty.

FITS ONE HEAD. That's the warning on a hotel shower cap.

MAY CAUSE DROWINESS. From a bottle of Nytol Nightime Sleep-Aid.

MAY IRRITATE EYES. On a can of pepper spray.

THIS CAPE DOES NOT GIVE THE WEARER THE ABILITY TO FLY. Yep, a Batman Halloween costume.

REMEMBER OBJECTS IN THE MIRROR ARE ACTUALLY BEHIND YOU. On a bicycle helmet-mounted mirror.

DO NOT USE ORALLY AFTER USING RECTALLY. A thermometer. Sorry, folks, I couldn't resist.

DO NOT USE ORALLY. Another one, this time on a toilet brush.

Having fun? There's more where these came from.

You can actually buy irons today that have a label warning you not to iron clothes while you're wearing them. Some Christmas lights carry the label "for indoor or outdoor use only." In case you were thinking of using them underwater, I guess.

Have you taken a flight on American Airlines recently? Their little packages of peanuts come complete with instructions. "Open bag, eat nuts."

Here's the sorry truth: Every one of these gems—and there are *thousands* more—came from one of those lawsuits where individuals do incredibly stupid things and juries decide to reward them for their idiocy . . . or from some government mandate created by bureaucrats who believe we would all surely perish without the constant supervision of our superiors in government.

Is there anyplace in this wonderful country of ours where a fellow can go and not feel the presence of some government employee or agency watching his every move?

Bedroom? No.

Bathroom? Nope. (Don't forget those one-liter flush toilets.)

Closet? Sorry, strict regulations on lighting and doors. (Besides, there are too many congressmen in there with you.)

We have smoke-free workplaces. We have drug-free school zones. I say let's start establishing government-free oases, where we can be free to step over the white line, leave our seat belts unbuckled, and peel the labels off anything we choose.

TRIGGER WORDS

There are a few words and phrases out there that were designed to send me on a lengthy tirade, guaranteed to leave hapless passersby stunned and offended by my insensitivity and lack of compassion.

Imagine my concern.

We've touched on a few of these points already. But I think you'll agree that the sheer impact of collecting them all in one place is staggering.

THE LESS FORTUNATE

You've probably heard that phrase literally hundreds of thousands of times without ever giving it a second's thought. Well, that changes now. There's a purpose behind this "less fortunate" nonsense, and that purpose is to manipulate your emotions.

You're being suckered, and the time has come for it to stop.

The term "less fortunate" is usually applied to the so-called "poor." My dictionary defines "fortunate" as "having unexpected good fortune" or "bringing something good and unforeseen." The idea behind tagging the poor as "less fortunate" is to convey the idea that they're merely victims of circumstance. Their lack of resources, to this way of thinking, is entirely unexpected, unforeseen, and unavoidable.

Nonsense.

The poor keep getting poorer because they keep doing whatever it was that made them poor in the first place. Ditto for the rich.

There is nothing at all unexpected or unforeseen about the behavior that's responsible for most of the poverty in this country. If you ignore your education, fail to develop a work ethic, do drugs, get pregnant before you're out of high school or before you can afford to raise a child, become a petty criminal, join a gang, hang with what you obviously know to be the wrong crowd, become a drinker, or generally comport yourself like a self-loathing slob, guess what? You're probably not going to make one hell of a lot of money! You're going to end up poor, with nothing to do but work at that occasional minimum-wage job you may find while spending the rest of your time complaining that the government isn't doing enough for you.

Politicians and those suffering from HCCD (hypercompulsive compassion disorder) will call you the "less fortunate."

They're wrong.

Your situation has nothing to do with luck or fortune. You did this to yourself. You're suffering the obvious and easily predictable result of your own failures and laziness. And things aren't going to get any better until you stop clinging to that idea that you're "less fortunate" and start looking in the mirror for the source of your problems.

There's another aspect to this "less fortunate" nonsense that we need to cover.

If those who have screwed up their lives and their futures are the "less fortunate," then that suggests that those who *have* made the proper choices, and who have succeeded as a result, are the "fortunate."

Is this how things are supposed to work in our society? If you study hard, work hard, delay gratification, save, plan, invest, and make every effort to use your decision-making powers wisely, you're probably in fairly good shape right now. You have a good job, a decent income, a nice home, an investment program, and a retirement plan. You were certain that you got here through hard work and good living.

And yet the left keeps implying that you're merely "fortunate," that your good job and comfortable lifestyle are all derived from "unexpected sources."

Well, that's a fine way to dismiss your years of hard work and determination, isn't it?

There is a solid strategic reason why the leftist big-government types favor this fortunate/less-fortunate idea. It's an invaluable tool in their scheme to build the size and power of government through income redistribution.

Their first order of business is to convince everyday people that the wealthy enjoy their status in life primarily through good luck (that is, "fortune"). Then they must convince the myrmidons that the poor are living in their misery because of bad luck. Once this becomes the conventional wisdom, it'll be easy to promote income redistribution. After all, they're merely trying to even out the odds a bit, right?

This fortunate/less-fortunate idiocy reached a new height during the 2000 presidential primary season, when Democratic contender and House Minority Honcho Richard Gephardt referred to the high achievers in America as those who "won life's lottery."

Now there's a pretty good slap in the face from the left! You bust your royal hindquarters for years on end to achieve some measure of success, and this politician comes along and tells you that you achieved all of this through the luck of the draw.

Let me tell you something. You win life's lottery when you're born—especially if you're born in the United States, hands down the best place in the world to begin and live your life. You're an American, the envy of people around the globe. From that point on everything else is gravy—and it's all up to you.

If you think you have what you have because you were lucky, then maybe you *deserve* to have the government take it from you. Those who recognize the hard work that went into their success might feel otherwise.

INCOME REDISTRIBUTION

So what is this "income redistribution," anyway?

This idea of redistributing income is really quite sexy to the left. Just imagine how much power the political class will wield when they manage to amass not just the power, but the consent of the people, to seize your hard-earned income and reapportion it out among the rest of the country!

This is such a favorite of liberals. The very idea of taking income from those who don't support them politically, and redistributing that income to those who do . . . what political paradise!

There's just one little bitty problem with the phrase "income redistribution," though.

Income, you see, isn't *distributed* in the first place. It's *earned.*

Before income can be traded for votes, it first has to be seized. From whom do you seize it? From the poor sap who actually earned it, of course! This whole "seize and redistribute" process works so much more smoothly, though, if you can somehow mask what's truly going on.

The idea of income redistribution is also very popular with those who analyze and comment on government income and poverty statistics. If they can convince us that there is something inherently wrong with the way income is being distributed among Americans, we're far more likely to accept the idea of redistribution at the hands of our compassionate and eminently fair political class.

GOVERNMENT DOLLARS

Don't you just love it when you read that "government dollars" are being spent on the latest boondoggle or pork project? That phrase was designed to make you feel better about these government projects; after all, if it's only *government* money, that's no skin off our collective nose—right?

Tell me, just what did our wonderful Imperial Federal Government do to *earn* those dollars? Did they have a bake sale somewhere that I missed? Does government manufacture some great and wonderful consumer item and sell it on the open market for a profit? Is this the profits from the marvelously efficient United States Postal Service?

No. Those "government dollars" they're talking about are dollars that were seized from us! They're dollars taken from the people who actually worked for them. They're "taxpayer dollars," not "government dollars."

Newspaper editors, take note. Every time you allow that phrase to be set in type, you're not a part of the solution, you're a part of the Great Big Propaganda Problem.

WORKING PEOPLE

You'll usually see the phrase "working people" used to differentiate those who earn their money working with their muscle from those who earn their incomes (usually somewhat higher) working with their brains.

Pro athletes aside, statistics show that brain power is a more valuable commodity in the jobs marketplace than muscle power. This is why people who hang out in the college library are likely to earn more later on than those who hang out in the gym.

It's that pesky little law of supply and demand at work again. Since it's easier to work with your muscles than it is to work with your head, you find a larger supply of people who earn their pay through largely physical effort than those who earn by thinking and reasoning.

Now, don't start slobbering with rage all over these pages again. I understand that even the most menial of tasks requires some mental effort, and that the world's smartest lawyer has to lift a law book every once in a while. Still, the more tools you bring to your job, the more you're going to make.

But here's the rub: The left has tried to co-opt the term "working people" to sell the idea that if you work with your brain instead of with your brawn, somehow you're not really working. You're not one of the "working people."

It's a simple class warfare tactic: Lead those who make less into resenting those who make more, because those nasty rich people aren't really working for their money. They're not part of the "working class." And since they aren't working for their money, it's really not a bad thing to hike up the tax rates on them a bit. That way the government can spend that money on the true working people—us!

FILTHY RICH

This isn't the first time you've heard that phrase, is it? For some reason, somewhere along the way, "rich" became a half-word. It just didn't sound complete until you added "filthy" to the front.

The purpose, of course, is to demonize the rich. When you successfully manage to connect the word "filthy" to the idea of wealth, you've succeeded in denigrating the hard work that goes into the accumulation of that wealth. You've also given the green light to open class warfare. Why *shouldn't* we revile the rich? Why shouldn't their money be taken away from them and used to pave the way for people who really need it? What right do they have to keep it? After all, they're just filthy rich people, aren't they?

The use of the phrase "filthy rich" does offer some degree of emotional comfort to the poor, poor pitiful poor. Climb into the head of a poor person, and you might find that their thought processes go something like this:

Look at that rich bastard over there with his big-shot BMW. I'll bet he lives in a big fancy house somewhere. He probably flies around the country on private jets too. I know how he got all that money. He's a crook, or he has a crooked lawyer. He probably cheated someone out of that money, or he has a bunch of people doing all the hard work for him, and doesn't pay them squat. He thinks he's better than me, with that fancy car and that Rolex watch and everything. But he's not. I'd be rich, too, if I was willing to cheat and steal like he does. I'd be rich, too, if I had a crooked lawyer like he does. I'm honest, though. I'm a working man. That's why I'll never have all those things—because people like him have to keep me down. I'll never be that rich, 'cause I don't cheat and steal.

That line of thinking, the demonization of the filthy rich, allows our hero to believe that the only reason in the world he doesn't have the nice things he'd like to have is that he's an honest guy; while the guys with all the toys and the flat-belly at his elbow is nothing but a lazy crook. It helps him forget that he's never done anything to put away some money, so that he could afford to buy a few toys himself; that he doesn't conduct himself in a way that radiates success; that the class divides in America today are entirely self-selected.

THE POOR

Give me a break. There are very few people in this country who fit any sort of a realistic definition of being poor. The average so-called "poor" person in this country has a higher standard of living than the average European. Now, do you consider the average European to be poor?

Those defined as living in poverty in this country usually own at least one color television, a microwave oven, an automobile, and a cell phone. Not too long ago, every one of these items was considered a luxury. Today you'd be hard pressed to find a poor person without them.

Let me tell you something about the pitiful poor—something I've said on the radio show countless times, and that gets people angry every single time I do it. The truth hurts, and this truth seems to hurt more than most. Know this: Barring some sort of mental or physical disaster, the people living in what we describe as poverty in this country are there because of the sum total of the decision and choices they made during their lives up to this point. Poverty is something you do to yourself, not something that's done to you. Poverty isn't a condition; it's a behavioral disorder at best, and a mental disease at worst.

It's important to understand the genesis of the method we use for measuring poverty in this country. The poverty scale, and the methodology behind it, was designed during Lyndon Johnson's "Great Society," and it was created specifically to exaggerate the need for funding anti-poverty programs. The more poverty the government could show, the more money they could spend. The more government spends, the more powerful government becomes. The more powerful government becomes, the weaker *we* become.

The poverty statistics were a sham then, and they're a sham now— a sham with a purpose. Strengthen government, weaken the people.

Just how meaningless are those poverty stats? Just try to wrap your mind around this concept:

You could have $15 million in your checking account, a paid-for $23 million dollar home, a different private jet for every day of the week, color-coordinated BMWs for every suit you own, and $1 million of walking-around money in your pocket—and still be classified by our government as living in poverty.

Why? Because you don't have any income! You're rich; you don't have to work! You're just living off your assets, and doing it rather well, I'd say. To the simple-minded government bean-counters, though, what makes a person poor is a lack of *income,* not a lack of wealth. Sign up for your benefits right here!

Are there people in need in this country? Sure. Could they use a little help? You bet. Do they usually put themselves in this position? Absolutely.

And that brings me to the following totally insensitive observation:

One of the undisputable facts of life is that you will always get more of the behavior you reward, and less than the behavior you punish. So if poverty is a behavioral disorder, as I believe to be the case, why are we rewarding it? Why do we reward laziness in this country, and punish hard work?

Doesn't common sense tell you that we would have less poverty in this nation if we were to *punish* the poor? And wouldn't we have more in the higher income brackets if we *rewarded* their behavior rather than punishing it?

Punish the poor? How?

I dunno. Maybe a public spanking. Take away their TVs and cell phones. Make them pick up cigarette butts from the roadways. We'll think of something.

OBSCENE PROFITS

Here's a phrase that's used by the left to demonize successful businesses and soften them up for the kill. (By "kill," I mean higher taxes. Perhaps even a so-called "windfall profits tax.")

As I've said, if you were to walk into your local shopping mall and ask the first one hundred people you met to tell you the difference between a profit and a profit margin, you wouldn't find two who could give you a correct answer. To most people, the only figure that means anything is gross profit. Leave that margin nonsense to the bean counters.

This ignorance really came into play when Exxon Mobil announced record profits—around $38 billion—for their 2005 fiscal year. The media and the political class went nuts! Here was an ideal opportunity to exploit the ignorance of the public to further the leftist agenda.

The most important point, of course, wasn't the size of Exxon Mobil's gross profits that year, but the size of their profit margin during that year of record profits. In other words, how much profit did Exxon Mobil earn on every dollar of sales?

Before you answer that, let me ask you to tell me what you think a *fair* profit margin would be. Out of every dollar of business a company does, how much would it be fair for them to keep as earnings? Most people would answer around 20 percent. When you tell them that this far, far exceeds the normal profit margin for an American business, they can't believe it.

Back to Exxon Mobil. During the year of the great $39 billion gross profit, Exxon Mobil earned about a dime on every dollar of revenue. That's right, around 10 percent. And a huge portion of that 10 percent was plowed right back into research and exploration for new sources of energy.

Here's your economics lesson. Perhaps after reading this you'll be willing to challenge the next clown you hear complaining about the "obscene profits" those evil corporations make.

Let's say you sell widgets. It costs you $90 to make a widget, and you sell each one for $100. Your needs are small, so you only make and sell a hundred widgets a year.

Do you need your calculators for this?

So you spend $9,000 making a hundred widgets, and you collect $10,000 in sales revenue. Your profit is $1000. Your profit margin is 10 percent. You've earned one dime on every dollar of sales.

Now let's say that the price of raw materials you need to make your widgets suddenly skyrocket. The next year, it costs you $180 to make the same widget that used to cost $90. You want to earn the same percentage on every dollar of sales, so you hike the price of your widgets to $200 and quickly sell all one hundred of them. (Widgets, it seems, are a necessity.)

Now you've spent $18,000 making the widgets, and you sold them all for $20,000. Your profit margin is still only 10 percent. You're still only making ten cents on every dollar of sales. But look— your profit has doubled! You sold the same amount of widgets, but you made $2,000 in profit!

Quick! Someone pass a windfall profits tax!

Our politicians would really be crippled if the people of this country had even the most rudimentary understanding of economics.

PRICE GOUGING

Now here's a favorite of the political class. Politicians just love anti–price gouging laws because they leave the impression that they're there to protect the poor consumer in times of urgent need. The truth is, they hurt the situation more than they help it.

Florida is a hotbed of anti–price gouging demagoguery. Every time a hurricane approaches the Florida coastline, the governor rushes to sign a proclamation declaring a state of emergency. As soon as the proclamation is signed, the anti–price gouging laws go into effect. Shortages on essential items soon follow.

Anti–price gouging laws may make politicians look good to government-educated economic illiterates, but that's about all they do. The fact is, the laws actually *decrease* the available supply of the very goods and services that people in hurricane-damaged areas desperately need.

Let's take hotel rooms. When those anti–price gouging laws go into effect, a hotel operator can be severely fined—I think the penalties include having one limb amputated—if he dares to increase the price of his limited resource in the face of increased demand.

Let's say you have a family of five evacuating a coastal area—Mom and Dad, the two rug rats, and the mother-in-law. They arrive at the Comfort Inn near Ocala to find that rooms are running at their usual rate . . . say, about $79 a night.

What luck! Now you can afford to get three rooms! Mom and Dad can have a room of their own for a little motel nookie. The kids can have another room, and the mother-in-law can have a third room so she can smoke to her heart's content.

Then, an hour or two later, along comes another family looking for shelter. The Comfort Inn has no more rooms. Why? Because most of the people who arrived earlier took advantage of the low prices and got multiple rooms.

Now, if the motel operator had increased the price of these hotel rooms in response to the increased demand—say, to $200 a night—our evacuees wouldn't be so eager to rent three rooms. Perhaps one would have sufficed, and the old bag would just have to sleep on the pull-out couch and smoke her butts outside. Then there would still be rooms available, although at higher prices, for that second family driving in.

The anti–price gouging laws hurt consumers in almost all other areas. Generators, for instance. When the electricity goes out, and stays out, people want generators. Once the local Home Depot and hardware store run out, the supply is pretty much exhausted.

When the price is kept artificially low in the face of increased demand and limited supply, people suffer. Just as with the hotel rooms, you will get some eager buyers who will walk out with two or maybe three generators! Not only do they want to power the essential equipment in their kitchen, and maybe the downstairs air conditioning unit, they want another generator as a standby unit, or to power extra equipment.

Now . . . allow the price of generators to rise with the increased demand and the situation changes. Fewer people buy multiple units. You will also have entrepreneurs buying generators in other markets, loading them on trucks, and driving to Florida to sell them. When some people did this after Hurricane Charlie they were arrested and their goods confiscated.

So—you want to call these entrepreneurs greedy? They're profiteering? They're making money off the misery of others? Oh, I get it. In your world a person is only allowed to make a profit selling something or providing a service that people don't really need, right? How brilliant is that?

So, congratulations to the politicians who push these anti–price gouging laws. They're not stupid. They know what the true economic impact of their action is. It's about pandering—pandering to the economic ignorance of the common man, even if the common man suffers as a result. Votes are everything. Leadership is nothing.

HATE SPEECH

Talk about an over-used term. You'll be hard-pressed to read any article dealing with talk radio without running across the "hate speech" phrase at least once.

It's easy to understand what's going on here. Liberals increasingly find themselves unable to effectively counter some of the ideas presented on libertarian and conservative talk radio shows. They know the facts aren't on their side ("there was no Al Qaeda in Iraq") and they're unprepared to argue the point on any logical basis. The "hate speech" line is their escape valve.

"I don't have to respond to your arguments; I don't have to even talk to you because you are full of hate. I prefer to spend my time discussing things like this with people who are not so full of hate. So take your hate speech and go away."

To many liberals the very definition of "hate speech" is "any utterance made by a conservative that I disagree with."

NEO-CON

Excuse me, but just what in the hell is a "neo-con"? I'm sure there's a definition of that term out there somewhere, but it's my experience that most of the people who bandy the "neo-con" line about can't tell you what that definition is.

Basically, I believe that "neo-con" is simply intended to be a derogatory epithet used to define anyone-not-liberal.

I can say this: Since the word "neo-con" came into our vocabulary I have not received one single on-air phone call, e-mail or letter from anyone who had any ability to use the phrase in any manner that sounded even marginally intelligent.

There's more, but there are only so many pages between the covers of this book. The only way to cram more in here would be to reduce the size of the typeface. Studies show that liberals don't like to read smaller type. Since we don't want to deny them the privilege of reading this book, we'll just move on.

THE INSIPID
UNITED NATIONS

Well, that pretty much kills the suspense, doesn't it?

No, I don't think a lot of the United Nations. Never have. I am two hundred days older than the UN, and not nearly one-tenth as corrupt.

One big difference between the United Nations and me is that I've loved America since the very day I came to understand what America stood for, while the UN has not. Since the day I came to my senses (sometime around my senior year at Texas A&M), I have been dedicated to the cause of individualism, human freedom, and economic liberty. The UN hasn't yet come within shouting distance of those challenging concepts.

It shouldn't take any time at all to set even the most ardent UN supporter on the road to doubt. All it should take is a little refresher course on how the United Nations was originally set up.

First, let's take a look at the UN General Assembly.

How many votes do you think every member nation should get in the General Assembly? One? Sounds reasonable to me. One country—one vote.

And that's—*almost*—the way the United Nations was set up. Every single member of the United Nations does have one, and only one, vote.

Every member, that is, save one. Guesses, anyone?

Now, remember, the UN was established in 1945. Who was out there, shaping up as a source of problems and concerns for the U.S. government in 1945?

Right: the Soviet Union. The race for world military and political domination was under way as soon as Japan and Germany folded their tents, and the UN started playing against U.S. interests the moment the starter's gun sounded.

The Soviets' first advantage? The United Nations charter singled them out for an outrageous advantage in the General Assembly. The United States got one vote in the Assembly. Likewise, every other member of the newly formed UN got one solitary vote.

The Soviet Union received three. How the hell did that happen? The Russians exploited a technicality. The UN decided to give each of the Soviet "republics"—Russia, Byelorussia,[1] and the Ukraine—its own vote, notwithstanding the fact that these were all indivisible parts of the Soviet empire. It was roughly like extending sovereign nation status to Texas and California.[2]

A similar disparity existed in the United Nations World Court. No member country, including the United States, was allowed to have more than one judge sitting on the World Court at any one time—except, that is, for the Soviet Union, which was allowed to seat three.

Now, you can sing the praises of the United Nations and the good intentions of its founders all you want. But when the original charter stacks the deck in favor of the Soviet Union over every other nation in the world—by a factor of three—there's got to be a charter rat hiding somewhere.

For most of its history, the UN has been preoccupied with what it calls "peacekeeping missions." Oh, yeah, what a success story. The truth is that UN peacekeepers are more likely to be *involved in* the

---

[1] Today you know Byelorussia as Belarus. Translation: White Russia.

[2] Yeah, I know, not exactly. That's why I said "roughly."

rape and plunder of the nations they're supposed to be stabilizing than trying to combat those who would disrupt the peace.

Let's tick off some of the places where the UN has "kept the peace," shall we?

Rwanda.

Somalia.

Darfur.

Triumph after triumph.

And lest we forget, there's the UN's infamous oil for food program in Iraq. How many millionaires did that one create?

The failures are easy to chronicle. What about the genuine successes?

Fairness compels me to admit that the United Nations, largely with the financial assistance of U.S. taxpayers, has done a rather good job of monitoring and addressing potential health crises in various parts of the Third World.

That's about it. That's how they escape being labeled a 100 percent pure, unadulterated failure.

In the meantime, they're busy on the East River, busying themselves with plots to take over the Internet, or trying to figure out how they can drag U.S. citizens before a World Kangaroo Court to answer for purported crimes against humanity.

But wait, some of you may be thinking. *What about all the grand things the UN has done in the name of human rights?*

All right, let's play ball. You go ahead and start your list of everything you think you know about the UN's grand and glorious record of human rights accomplishment. While you're thinking, I'll tell you a few things you may *not* know.

For starters, let's take a quick look at the United Nations Convention on the Prevention and Punishment of the Crime of Genocide, commonly known as the "Genocide Treaty."

The UN General Assembly adopted this travesty at the end of 1948. The purpose was admirable: Following the revelations of the

Holocaust, the fledgling UN wanted to make genocide a crime under international law.

So far, so good.

The problem comes when you start trying to define genocide. Article II of the Genocide Treaty defines genocide as:

> . . . any of the following acts committed with intent to destroy, in whole or in part, a national, ethnical, racial or religious group, as such:
>
> (a) killing members of the group;
>
> (b) causing serious bodily or mental harm to members of the group;
>
> (c) deliberately inflicting on the group conditions of life calculated to bring about its physical destruction in whole or in part;
>
> (d) imposing measures intended to prevent births within the group;
>
> (e) forcibly transferring children of the group to another group.

Now maybe it's just the lawyer in me, but did I just read that causing *mental harm* to members of a national, ethnical, racial, or religious group is considered genocide? Just thinking about that causes *me* mental harm. Does that mean that if I say something on the air that's deemed offensive by, say, some Hispanics who are trying to enter our country illegally, I might have committed the crime of genocide? Sorry, but I'm not particularly anxious to be dragged off to some world court to be tried for genocide because I had a rough day on the air. I'll take my chances right here at home with my nifty little Constitutional protections, thank you very much.

And there's more. Let's see: "Imposing measures intended to prevent births within the group." Does this mean that a birth control program in an impoverished region of Africa could get someone charged with genocide? I know Catholics consider birth control a sin, but that's a pretty stiff penance.

Which brings us to the very cornerstone of the UN's human rights agenda: the United Nations Universal Declaration of Human Rights.

The United Nations was barely three years old when this document was crafted. It was adopted by the General Assembly on December 10, 1948. Fifty years later, it had become such a hallowed charter that our then-president, Bill Clinton, presided over an event at the White House for its fiftieth anniversary, celebrating it in these glowing words: [3]

> *This Declaration is one of the most important documents of the twentieth century, indeed of human history, for it represents the first time men and women sought to articulate the core aspirations of all the world's people. The authors of the Universal Declaration struggled to understand and harmonize their differing cultural traditions and convictions during a three-year debate that culminated in a set of rights recognized by all as transcending national, social, and cultural boundaries. The eighteen delegates who met under the wise, compassionate leadership of Eleanor Roosevelt and framed the Universal Declaration did not refer simply to men, or to the privileged, or to any specific race or religion. The language of the document clearly states: All human beings are born free and equal.*

Strong stuff, isn't it? "One of the most important documents . . . of human history." That would put it in the company of such trivialities as the Magna Carta, the Declaration of Independence, and the Constitution of the United States.

---

[3] If you can't detect sarcasm at this point in this book then you need to work a bit on your reading skills.

So is Clinton's cherished Universal Declaration of Human Rights really all that?

Hardly.

The Universal Declaration is a Universal Disaster. It's nothing less than a blueprint for tyranny. A shallow and poorly crafted document, it could only appeal to three groups:

1. Those who love government

2. Those who love tyrants

3. Those educated in government schools

During his eight years in the White House, Bill Clinton managed to utter some incredibly ignorant statements about our country, our Constitution, and our heritage.[4] The prize for mindless bloviations, though, must go to Clinton's fatuous endorsement of this human rights declaration.

Now, I know that most of you probably haven't taken time away from your busy schedules washing the minivan, reinflating the soccer ball, listening to the iPod, and keeping track of Lindsay Lohan to actually read this United Nations human rights declaration. But if there's a president of the United States running around calling it one of the most important documents in the history of freedom, perhaps you won't mind giving it a bit of attention.

If you wish, you can just read the entire document on the Internet. (Don't do this while driving, talking on the cell, with a mouthful of hot coffee, or after a greasy meal.)

Or you can let me do the hard work for you.

The declaration starts off well enough, admittedly. Here's the opening paragraph of the Preamble:

---

[4] Bill Clinton believes, for instance, that the U.S. Constitution gave us our rights. Those of you who didn't go to government schools might have a different view. If this book is really worth the price you paid, you will find that I have covered this elsewhere.

Whereas recognition of the inherent dignity and of the equal and inalienable rights of all members of the human family is the foundation of freedom, justice and peace in the world;

Not bad, right? Equal rights, freedom, justice—all important concepts. Of course, there's no *definition* of peace or justice; still, it's a good start.[5]

So what other wonderful rights does the United Nations declare that we citizens of the world are entitled to? Some of the enumerated rights sound like they came right out of our own Constitution:

- Human rights should be protected by the rule of law.

- The right to life, liberty and security of person.

- The right not to be held in slavery.

- The right to protection from torture or cruel, inhuman, or degrading punishment.

- The right to a presumption of innocence.

- The right to privacy.

- The right to freedom of movement within the borders of your own state.

- The right to own property.

---

[5] To many, peace is simply the absence of conflict. The Soviets would describe "peace" as an absence of opposition to world Communism. For my part, peace is worthless without liberty. As for a definition of the word "justice," that one is easy. Justice is when someone gets what he or she deserves.

- The right to freedom of opinion and expression.

- The right to peacefully assemble.

But there are also quite a few rights in the human rights declaration that seem a little more problematic:

- The right to marry.

- The right to social security.

- The right to work.

- The right to protection against unemployment.

- The right to equal pay for equal work.

- The right to rest and leisure.

- The right to a paid vacation.

- The right to an adequate standard of living.

- The right to enjoy the arts. (No . . . I'm serious. It's there.)

- The right to an education.

We could spend the next hundred pages trying to figure out just how a government might address someone's right to rest and leisure—or debating any number of these other eye-opening provisions. (There's a universal right to *paid vacations?*) But in the context of the United Nations human rights declaration, it would be a complete waste of time.

Why?

Because every single one of the rights I've listed above is nothing but vapor. They're all invalidated by an escape clause so outrageous it should be considered its own crime against humanity. Skip down to Article 29(3) of the Universal Declaration of Human Rights, and you'll find the following paragraph. It may look innocuous at first . . . but you need to read it. Digest it. It captures the very essence of the United Nations—that wonderful world body we hope will someday solve all of mankind's problems—and its ulterior motives.

ARTICLE 29(3) OF THE UNITED NATIONS UNIVERSAL DECLARATION OF HUMAN RIGHTS:

"These rights and freedoms may in no case be exercised contrary to the purposes and principles of the United Nations."

Forget about the rest of the declarations in the Declaration (most of that stuff was self-evident anyway, except for the parts that are self-evidently ludicrous). Article 29(3) is the most important sentence in the entire declaration. It may well be the most important sentence in *any* United Nations document, including the UN charter itself.

For the effect of this sentence is simple: After setting forth all of the glorious human rights to which every human being on this earth is entitled, in one twenty-word sentence *it takes all those rights away.*

That's your wonderful United Nations at work.

Think about it. There you were, merrily rolling along, enjoying your rights to freedom of expression, to freedom of movement, to own property, to be presumed innocent before a court of law. Maybe even exercising your wonderful God-given right to enjoy the arts!

What happens if suddenly the United Nations comes up with some "goal or purpose" that would be inconvenienced by your exercise of these rights?

They're gone!

Read 29(3) again. Apparently, if the UN decides that your right to free speech, or to own and remain in your home, stands in the way of some kind of UN goal (say, seizing your home), you're out of luck.

Are you getting the picture? Good. That puts you ahead of Bill Clinton.

Here's the sobering truth: If the United Nations comes up with some grand scheme that would require seizing you and placing you into slavery, the Universal Declaration of Human Rights offers you *no protection whatsoever.* In fact, it positively affirms that the UN's own rights trump your own.

Hello, ball and chain!

Under our Constitution the federal government derives its powers from the consent of the governed. That means the government gets its powers from us.

The United Nations sees things a different way. Under their hideous human rights declaration, the people derive their rights—their power—from the United Nations. And when the United Nations adopts some goal or purpose that's inconsistent with our exercise of these rights, the rights go right into the toilet.

As someone once said, *The people be damned.*

UNICEF

Several years ago we had a protestor outside my flagship radio station in Atlanta, NewsTalk 750 WSB. This fellow used to put a huge sign in the windshield of his car—"Shame on WSB," I think it said—and park it on the street outside the station.

Protestors are nothing new at WSB. Every once in a while, a group of local Muslims will march up and down the street to protest my insensitivity to the wonderful peace-loving religion of Islam. The last time they held such a protest, I ordered about a dozen pizzas (just cheese, veggies, and ground beef) and had them delivered to the marching Muslims. They ate heartily and left. Haven't seen them since.

The man with the "Shame on WSB" sign in his car wasn't a Muslim, and he wasn't looking for a free pizza. He was upset over some comments I made on the air about the United Nations Children's Fund—UNICEF.

I'm sure that UNICEF does some good work for children. My problem with UNICEF has nothing to do with what they do or don't do with those dollars that are collected by our little trick-or-treaters on Halloween.

My problem with UNICEF is that, whatever good works they do manage to pull off, they do so in the name of the United Nations— burnishing its reputation when it ought to be tarnished instead.

When you donate money to UNICEF—through Halloween collections, gift card sales, Ted Turner's United Nations Foundation, or any other charitable group—the money stands a good chance of helping children around the world. That's good. Still, in the politically correct world of the twenty-first century, the United States needs all the friends we can get. Why, then, should we spend our American charity dollars through the United Nations, an entity not at all friendly toward our country, and allow them to take all the credit for our kindness as Americans?

There are many U.S.-based charitable organizations that do absolutely wonderful things for children all over the world. When those children receive food, clothing, or medical supplies from these agencies, they and their parents are told that the items came from the United States. Americans donate the funds, Americans get credit for the good deed—and the rest of the world learns a little bit more about how generous we are as a nation and a people.

Not so with UNICEF. When the UN's charity relief organization pays to help children overseas, much of the funding comes from American citizens. Yet when the children and parents involved feel like giving thanks, they're told that the United Nations deserves the credit.

Why does all this matter? Not because we care about credit for credit's sake. That would be nice, but complaining about it would be petty. Charity shouldn't be conditioned on a pat on the back.

It matters because the rest of the world has spent too much time running down the American people—claiming that we're nothing but shameless exploiters, exporters of trash and looters of treasure, spreading violence in underdeveloped countries—while throwing roses at the United Nations and its irresponsible, profiteering ways.

For an organization that goes around crowing about justice, that doesn't sound very just to me.

THE TERRIBLE TRUTH
ABOUT TALK RADIO

I'm a talk jock. A radio talk show host. If you're a bed-wetting left-winger, the current vernacular of liberalism would require that you call me a preacher of hate. If you like what I do, it's talk radio. If you don't, it's hate radio.

I'm also a lawyer. I started running my mouth on the radio in 1970. Four years later I decided to fill my off-air hours with law school. Three more years and I had passed the bar and was having those "attorney at law" cards printed.

The plan was just to cruise along with both careers, practicing law and talk radio, until one overpowered the other either in my heart or my wallet. That happened in 1992, when I bade farewell to clients and devoted myself to listeners.

Heart . . . not wallet.

No disrespect intended to the legal profession, but I still walk into my radio studio every single day with the words "beats the hell out of practicing law" on my lips. And believe me, it does. Every lawyer learns that his worst enemy out there is his client. A talk jock's worst enemy is a slow news day. There are far more clients than slow news days. I made the right choice. Besides, I don't have to bill listeners to pay the mortgage.

Life is good.

Now, I'm not trying to slam the legal profession. I know many fine and dedicated lawyers. I also know some that should be doing front-end work at the local tire shop. One thing I know is true, though: I don't have a lot of talk-show hosts telling me how much they'd love to practice law, but I do have a lot of lawyers telling me how much they'd love to hang up the shingle and run their mouths on the radio for three hours a day.

Well, get in line.

Now, let me tell you about my job. Some of you seem to think that my purpose in doing the show is to present and win converts to a certain political ideology. Or maybe you think my assignment is to garner support for some particular candidate or proposition.

Wrong.

My job description is simple. I'm supposed to be interesting and compelling enough for about four eight-and-one-half-minute segments out of every hour to attract listeners from certain predefined demographic groups, and then keep them listening long enough for the radio stations to play some commercials for them. The longer they listen, the more commercials they hear. The more commercials they hear, or the more people who hear the commercials, the more money the radio stations make . . . and the more of that money that will end up in my pocket.

That's it. That's my job.

That is the essential truth of talk radio.

I'm not there to change the world. I'm not there to create social upheaval. I'm not there to get one politician elected or another defeated. Like anyone else on the radio, I'm there to keep you, the listener, interested enough to stay tuned until the time comes for us to play the next block of commercials. Some jocks do it with music; I'm one of those who do it with ideas. With luck, if I've done my job, you'll even be interested enough to sit through that commercial break while I catch my breath, then listen to me for another few minutes, so I can then play even more commercials.

I've never heard another talk-radio host admit any of this to his audience, nor do I expect to. Perhaps it's more fun, or more fulfilling, to believe that you're part of—dare I say the leader of—some great crusade for God, motherhood, and Krystal Hamburgers than to consider yourself highly paid filler inserted between commercials.

I'm happy doing what I do. And judging from the number of people who approach me in public, I gather a few of you would like to take over when I retire.

"I'm hoping to get in the business. I want to be a radio talk show host!" they say.[1] "What can you tell me?"

My best piece of advice is to move to a small radio market and get a job doing anything they'll let you do at the local talk station. Sooner or later you can weasel yourself into a weekend slot, then maybe a daily show. Keep plugging away at it. And whatever you do, never get to the point where you start believing that your listeners are your followers. Once you've bought that idea, it's a slide back to obscurity. They're not your followers. They're your listeners. You're there to entertain them, not to lead them. I've never forgotten that. Maybe that's why I've lasted.

Once you've snagged that talk show spot on some station in the number-185 radio market . . . stick with it. You won't make any money. You'll probably have to work an extra job. But you'll soon develop the ability to put odd twists on obscure news stories, present them to the audience, and play with their reactions.

If you're hoping for a long career, be honest with your listeners. If you say something, mean it. Nobody has a good enough memory to be a successful liar.

I titled this chapter "The Terrible Truth About Talk Radio" for several reasons. First, I wanted to 'fess up about what we're supposed to do. Second, I wanted to explain just why it is that conservatives and libertarians seem to be so much more successful at this than liberals.

---

[1] It usually happens at some very inappropriate moment, such as when I'm having dinner at a nice restaurant with my family. Someone inevitably will recognize me, come over to the table, pull up a chair, and start talking as if he or she knows me. Please do not do this.

People who listen to talk radio have some of the most finely tuned bullshit detectors you'll find anywhere. They can smell a phony right through the radio dial, and that's exactly where they head when they detect one. Talk radio listeners will accept and tolerate any position on any issue if it's presented with rationality and a modicum of logic. They'll also tolerate irrational and illogical banter if it's presented with a good dose of humor.

This means that liberals are pretty much screwed when it comes to success in talk radio. They have the facts working against them, and they can't carry forth an argument using logic or reason. And as far as a sense of humor is concerned . . . well, let me know how your search for a truly funny liberal turns out.

Liberals are very successful in the printed media. They're also successful in what is commonly, though erroneously, referred to as TV journalism. There's a reason for this.

Let's consider two hypothetical liberals: one a columnist, the other a talk show host. And let's take an issue of great importance on which they share opinions—say, gun control.

The liberal columnist and talk show host get together and write a quick essay on the need for more stringent gun control measures. The columnist has his piece published in one hundred newspapers. The talk show host offers the very same words as his opinion at the beginning of his talk show, heard on one hundred radio stations.

So what happens after the liberal columnist and talk show host have each had their say? Thousands of liberals who read the column agreed with every word they read. Thousands of left-wingers who listen to the talk show host's statements agree with every word they heard. Thousands of readers and listeners, of course, are of the considered opinion that they haven't heard or read such a load of dog squeeze in years. Agreement and disagreement; fans and detractors.

So where does it go from here?

The columnist retreats into his office, sits down in his leather recliner, pulls out a Cuban, and has a few nice puffs. His e-mail in box fills up with expressions of outrage over his column. Readers are sending him letters with copies of articles relating statistics that prove convincingly that the columnist's position on the gun control matter is startlingly wrong. He never reads the e-mails, nor does he see the letters. They are all carefully screened by some intern or assistant who is careful to feed his ego with reader accolades rather than criticism. If one discouraging word should get through, the columnist can chose to either consider or ignore it. No matter what course he chooses, nobody else is the wiser—especially not the readers.

Contrast the easy life of the columnist to that of the liberal talk show host. The liberal talk jock purveys the same views as the writer, perhaps in the very same words, making the same case expertly and convincingly. Thousands of listeners agree; thousands don't. So far, the scenario plays out pretty much the same either way.

But wait . . . what's that sound? *The telephones!*

While the liberal columnist is enjoying his cigar, the liberal talk show host has to defend his position to a steady stream of callers. The columnist can chose to merely bask in brilliance of his own reflection in the mirror behind his desk, while the talk show host has to spend the next few hours defending his position against arguments based on fact, reason, and logic.

The columnist's isolation allows him to protect his image as a learned man possessed of brilliant ideas. He faces a challenge only if he chooses to do so. The talk show host crumbles under the onslaught of contrarian arguments, and limps to the end of the show humiliated and bowed under the weight of fact and logic.

It would all be so much easier for the liberal talk show hosts if they just didn't have to take phone calls. Then again, after they wrapped up their "America is bad, the United Nations is good; individualism is bad, collectivism is good; capitalism is bad, a government-controlled economy is good; private medical care is bad, socialized medicine is good; Fox News is bad, CBS and CNN are infallible; minorities are bad, and the jury is out on most white people" routine, they might find it hard to fill the remaining two hours and forty-five minutes of their show.

SO . . . WHAT'S A GOOD LIBERAL TO DO?

About what? About talk radio? About the fact that pretty much the only way you can get a liberal talk show lineup on the radio is to buy the time?

Oh . . . you didn't know about that?

Well, you've no doubt heard of Air America, the great experiment in liberal talk radio network. Al Franken and Gang? Yup! That's the one. The Great Experiment in Broadcast Bankruptcy. Well, a quick look at the history of Air America illustrates why lefty-talk on the radio is pretty much a nonstarter.

First, let's lay out one fundamental difference between the Air America crew and syndicated conservative hosts such as Rush Limbaugh, Sean Hannity, Mike Gallagher, and the rest, including myself. Air America pays (or had to pay) many of its radio stations to carry their programming. I am not aware of one major daily syndicated conservative or libertarian talk show that has to pay to have its shows aired. The radio stations pay *them*.[2] A combination of very poor ratings and this pay-as-you-go business model—sometimes adding up to hundreds of thousands of dollars a year—is bound to lead to problems. Problems like, oh, *insolvency*.

There's another way you can make a success out of a liberal radio talk show: Find a liberal who's actually entertaining! Sure, there are some, though your chances of finding Faith Hill folding towels in an East Los Angeles Laundromat are much better.

For liberals with entertainment value, Ed Schultz comes to mind. Ed is entertaining and pleasant, and his show works. But Ed's handlers have to keep him sequestered somewhere in the frozen wasteland of North Dakota to make sure he doesn't get too much exposure to the real America. I suspect that if Ed ever moved to some American population center where he actually has to step over urban campers

---

[2] Simply put, their syndicators receive and sell a certain number of commercial minutes for every hour the show is aired, plus, in some cases, a cash payment.

(and their waste matter) to get home at night, and where doors have locks, he might start sounding a bit different on the radio. Plus, last time I checked, North Dakota wasn't exactly at the top of Osama's to-do list.

So talk radio doesn't work all that well for liberals, but it's terrific for conservatives and libertarians, who dominate the airwaves.

So it is, so it always will be. Right?

Not so fast. The future of talk radio depends on just who has a grip on the machinery of the federal government, and right now that grip is in the hands of a Democrat Congress and a White House that's eager to placate them. Considering the positioning of the chess pieces, let's just say that the future of talk radio isn't all that bright.

On November 8, 2006, the day after the great Republican melt-down in Congress, I started opening my show with the phrase "Counting down the last two and-one-half years of talk radio . . ." The 2008 elections may tilt the scales once and for all, but at this point I'm firmly convinced that Democrats will try to destroy talk radio.

Think about it. Why shouldn't they?

Of course, there's that little thing we call freedom of expression— but remember, we're talking Democrats here. These are people who are far more concerned with their idea of the "common good" than they are with individualism. Democrats might tell you that the effect of what is said in the public arena carries far greater consequences than any individual's right to self-expression on the so-called "public airwaves."

Hold on a minute. Before we get into the methods the Democrats will likely use to get rid of their talk radio nemeses, I need to make a point about this "public airwaves" nonsense.

As even the bush-league despots of the world have long known, if you want to control a population, you need to control that popula-tion's access to information. Perhaps you've noticed, but every time some tyrant wannabe launches an attempt to take over a government, he sends rebels or troops to the television and radio stations and to the newspapers. Step 1: Control the media. (All right, that's probably Step 2. Step 1 is usually putting the current leader out of commission.)

Well, our American political class has noticed the same thing.

When the first ten amendments to our Constitution were added, the people drafting them still had a greater appreciation for the power of the people than the power of government. By the time Marconi started tickling crystals with cat hairs, things had changed.

Our founding fathers protected our access to information unfiltered through the political process with their First Amendment guarantees of freedom of speech and freedom of the press. Back then there were only two ways that information could be passed from one individual to another. You either spoke it or you wrote it. Hence, both methods have absolute Constitutional protection.

Now, of course, you can broadcast that information; a concept unimagined by the powdered-wig crowd.

Politicians greeted the arrival of radio with more worry than wonderment. Here was a means of spreading information not only to vast numbers of people, but to vast numbers of people who can't even read! Stories of political misdeeds in Washington could spread throughout the country in a matter of hours instead of days or weeks. Political errors and misjudgments would be more difficult to contain once every American with a pulse and access to a newfangled radio heard about them.

By the time broadcasting arrived on our doorstep, the love of freedom and the preservation of the liberties of the people weren't what you would call foremost on the minds of politicians. Then as now, the acquisition and maintenance of political power came first. Whatever came second was far, far behind.

It was clear: this radio thing had to be brought under control, sooner rather than later.

On what pretext, though, could the Imperial Federal Government of the United States seize control over broadcasting? Well, let's see. The signals somehow fly through the air, and everybody has a right to their share of the air, don't they? After all, if you're denied air, you die! That must mean that *everyone* owns the air, and if that's true, then it's reasonable for them to expect their wonderful elected officials to control what flies through that air—including Fibber McGee and Molly, not to mention any future Rush Limbaughs.

Brilliant! If the people own the airwaves, the people get to say what can and cannot be broadcast there! And, of course, they'll do that through their elected officials!

And presto, the power of broadcasting was now officially controlled by the government.

The airwaves are public only because our founding fathers didn't know they existed, just as they couldn't have envisioned personal computers or Xerox machines back when they were knocking out copies of the Constitution and its amendments in pen and ink. In 1776 air was for breathing, not much else. If Thomas Jefferson and his buddies had foreseen the era of broadcasting, there's no doubt that First Amendment protections would have been guaranteed for radio and television.

Today, politicians have invented plenty of further excuses for the fact that First Amendment guarantees aren't extended to broadcasting. One favorite excuse is to say that this government control is necessitated by the fact that broadcasting frequencies are limited, and that to control their allocation and use is, somehow, to protect the people.

That's utter nonsense. Atlanta, Georgia, has one daily newspaper and forty-plus radio stations, plus about six television stations. The one daily newspaper operates free of government control and censorship. The nearly fifty broadcast outlets do not.

Consider this: Every day in America more people get their evening news from *Entertainment Tonight,* an insipid syndicated television show covering celebrity news, than from CBS, NBC and ABC combined. On the day I wrote this, one of the lead stories on ET's website was the newsbreak that a pair of sunglasses once belonging to Steve McQueen brought $70,000 at an auction.

We are, in many ways, at a point our founding fathers could never have envisioned. Today, in America, most people get their daily news from agencies that are licensed to operate and to one extent or another controlled by the federal government—thanks to the absurd concept of "public ownership of the airwaves," a fiction created to allow the government to control an emerging means of spreading information to large numbers of people in very little time.

So how will the Democrats use their power over broadcasting to destroy talk radio?

It's called the "Fairness Doctrine," and it presents so great a threat to the free expression of ideas in this country that it deserves its own chapter.

That would be the next one.

DESTROYING TALK RADIO

Detailing the Left's Plan
for the End of Conservative Talk Radio

No mistake about it: The left hates talk radio. With a blinding passion.

Liberals have finally realized that they can't enjoy widespread success in the talk radio format. They've spent millions trying, and they've failed. A number of the left's most visible icons have given it a shot, people like former New York governor Mario Cuomo. They've failed miserably. Leftist entertainers who know their way around a microphone, Hollywood stars like Alec Baldwin, have tried it. Not good. Not just not good . . . but hideous and laughable.

Liberals know—because they have consultants, who are usually smarter than they are—that talk radio is going to belong to libertarians and conservatives as long as the format is allowed to exist.

Talk radio, especially Rush Limbaugh, enabled the 1994 voter revolution. Sure, the Republicans had their Contract with America, but that contract was worthless if the people didn't know about it.

The Contract with America was taken to the people by talk radio. Intrigued by the idea of a hundred-day voting agenda, the conservative jocks yakked it up. Not that these hosts necessarily agreed with every point in the Contract. They just felt that it was a unique approach; it captured their imaginations. As a result, the American people got an in-depth education in the principles behind the Contract and the probable effect of its passage:

Bye-bye Democrats.[1]

Democrats are dedicated to making sure that such a disaster never befalls them again. They're back in power now, and in power is where they intend to stay. They will do everything in their power to make sure a ragtag and unelected band of radio talk show hosts don't wee-wee in their Cheerios again.

The only way, then, for liberals to deal with this threat to their continuing power is to get rid of it. Murder is the preferable option. And the most likely murder weapon will be something called the "Fairness Doctrine."

(Amusing, isn't it, how leftists love anything with the word "fair" in it? Liberals know that the simple-minded drones who blindly vote for them will react positively to almost any atrocity if it's sold to them as "fair." The word "fair" is almost as important to the liberal lexicon as the word "security.")

When the left first set forth to control content in broadcasting, they knew they might have a bit of a problem selling the concept that the government should control how talk from a certain perspective can be aired about a given political issue on the radio. That just smelled too much like blatant censorship, and back then people actually had a working familiarity with the concept of a free press, and were more likely than they are today to defend it.[2]

So if you can't control what is said, what's the alternative? Just make it logistically and economically uncomfortable to say it in the

---

[1] It is worth noting that if the Republicans had maintained the fervor for reform and for reducing the size and power of the Imperial Federal Government of the United States they had in 1994, they would still be controlling things in Washington.

[2] Sadly, recent studies have shown that a sizeable percentage of Americans would support government controls on what not only radio and TV stations can broadcast, but also on what newspapers can and can not print, even on opinion pages.

first place! In other words, put a price on freedom of expression—a price talk radio might very well not be willing to pay.

The Fairness Doctrine does, in fact, sound fair . . . at least on the surface. First implemented by the Federal Communications Commission in 1949, it was devised to ensure that all issues of public importance be presented on broadcast stations in a fair and balanced manner. Nobody seemed aware enough back then to ask why the government was so ready to assume the role of arbiter of fairness in broadcasting when it had never played that role in the printed media. Perhaps that's because the American people didn't see the Fairness Doctrine as a threat to the free flow of information. After all, in 1949 most Americans still got most of their news from newspapers absent any semblance of government control.

Through the years, both Democrats and Republicans have used the doctrine to harass political opponents. A Kennedy Administration official named Bill Rudner once admitted that he and his colleagues "had a massive strategy to use the Fairness Doctrine to challenge and harass the right-wing broadcasters, and hope the challenge would be so costly to them that they would be inhibited and decide it was too expensive to continue."[3]

Then again, Republicans aren't exactly squeaky-clean on this issue. As Thomas Hazlett tells us, when Richard Nixon was president, "License harassment of stations considered unfriendly to the Administration became a regular item on the agenda at White House policy meetings."[4]

This is a different era, though, and you can rest assured that when the Democrats try to breathe new life into the Fairness Doctrine,

---

[3] "Return of the Fairness Doctrine" Tony Show, *The Washington Times*, Sept. 5, 1993.

[4] "The Fairness Doctrine and The First Amendment" Thomas Hazlett, *The Public Interest*, Summer 1989. *Note:* Both the Rudner and Hazlett quotes are to be found in Heritage Foundation Executive Memorandum No. 368, "Why the Fairness Doctrine is Anything But Fair" by Adam Thierer, October 29, 1993.

their true goal will be actual fairness, not some partisan attempt to silence a radio genre they never have and never will master.

Yeah . . . and pigs fly and don't love slop.

The Fairness Doctrine survived until 1987, when it suffered a well-deserved death. The FCC, controlled at that time by Republicans, concluded that the doctrine did more to inhibit than to encourage the free flow of ideas in the broadcasting marketplace.[5] Democrats were not amused. It was as if they had some anxious premonition of what awaited them once their precious federal controls were lifted.

Sure enough, after the Doctrine was overturned, talk radio began to flourish. Across the nation, AM radio stations started switching to the talk format, and newly emerging talk show hosts started fine-tuning their acts.

The Democrats made two attempts to kill the growing threat of talk radio.

In 1987, immediately after the FCC dropped the doctrine, the Democrat Congress tried to reinstate it through legislation. No go: Reagan veto. When the Clintonistas assumed power in 1993, they made another attempt to revive the Doctrine, this time calling it the "Fairness in Broadcasting Act of 1993" (there's that "fair" word again). It never saw the light of day, dying along with many other Democrat big government dreams in the voter revolution of 1994.

Democrats foresaw their ruin in talk radio, and vowed to strike back when they had the power to do so. Now that time has come. And here's how they plan to bring about the destruction of talk radio.

Let's take a hypothetical talk show host, Vince Verbose by name. Vince is a conservative, syndicated on five hundred radio stations in all fifty states; he has about 17 million loyal listeners.

One day, Vince spends thirty minutes railing against a Democrat

---

[5] The Republicans of the twenty-first century obviously aren't cut from the same mold, having created the anti-free speech monstrosity known as the McCain-Feingold Campaign Finance Reform Act.

plan for tax increases on the rich. The word goes out via the Internet: *Vince Verbose is campaigning against a tax increase for the rich. Vince is greedy. Vince hates the poor. Vince needs to be silenced. Contact your local radio stations and demand time to present a "fair and balanced" rebuttal.*

Within twenty-four hours, the better part of five hundred radio stations get demands from local Democrat "activists" demanding time to refute the hateful things Verbose has said about the Democrats and their plans to make the rich pay their fair share.

The program directors swing into action. The day's slate of programming is pulled apart so that the person who complained can come in and present his opposing viewpoint. The pace of the programming is lost, and the advertisers aren't amused. But at least you've avoided problems with your license by responding to the equal time request.

Two days later another one of your syndicated hosts, Bob Blather, dares to say that Islam isn't the peaceful religion we're told it is.

Within minutes the Council on Islamic-American Relations is contacting imams from mosques in every one of Blather's markets. They want equal time on each and every radio station that carries Blather to deliver their "Islam is a religion of peace" lecture.

Once again the station has to clear the time, irritating listeners and angering advertisers by putting on yet another "equal time" spokesman to enjoy his fifteen minutes of fame.

Know what? It wouldn't take a week of this nonsense before the program director throws up his hands and decides to change formats. Instead of putting up with these talk radio shenanigans, they change to Hispanic programming, jock news, or garden shows.

And this is no paranoid doomsday scenario. It's starting already. At a recent meeting of the Democrat Party of Oregon, a resolution was adopted to use the power of government and the Fairness Doctrine to rein in those horrible right-wing talk show hosts.

One more thing: Sectors of the national media that are traditionally liberal, such as newspapers, magazines, and the nightly network newscasts on CNN, ABC, CBS, and NBC, would not be subject to the Fairness Doctrine. The courts have decided that the First Amendment protections relating to freedom of the press apply pretty much across the board to the printed media, and almost as broadly to broadcast programs classified as news.

This leaves one sector of the national media that would be affected by the Fairness Doctrine: talk radio (along with some TV talk shows). As luck would have it, talk radio is the only sector dominated by the right.

Funny how things work out, isn't it?

MCCAIN-FEINGOLD

There is another possible way that the left will move to silence talk radio, and that is through the use of the hideously ugly Bipartisan Campaign Finance Reform Act of 2002,[6] otherwise known as "McCain-Feingold."

McCain-Feingold puts a ban on certain ads funded by soft money for sixty days prior to a general election. This would include ads funded by corporate money that cover certain campaign issues and make references to specific political candidates, even though those ads call for neither the election nor defeat of those candidates.

So how could McCain-Feingold be used to silence a talk show host? All you'd have to do is allege in court that the host's radio program is effectively a paid advertisement for a wide range of political positions, one that mentions the names of various candidates for office repeatedly. These three-hour political ads, you'd argue, are funded by corporations and businesses who want the messages in these ads to be disseminated to the voters; the advertising they buy on these shows would amount to soft money contributions.

You don't think the Democrats could find a federal judge who would go along with that nonsense? Please. We have federal judges

---

[6] What can you say about a president who will publicly state his opinion that a bill is unconstitutional, and then sign it?

who assist developers in stealing private property for commercial development. We have federal judges who have passed on asset forfeiture laws. We have a Supreme Court that declared McCain-Feingold constitutional. And you think they wouldn't do what they could to keep us from discussing the issues behind the next election during that sixty-day time period?

What did you put in your Wheaties this morning?

If not one way, then the other. If not the Fairness Doctrine, then McCain-Feingold. Somehow, the Democrats are determined to find a way to silence talk radio.

It's a simple issue of survival.

PRESIDENT BUSH, THE DEMOCRATS, THE MEDIA, AND THE WAR ON ISLAMIC FASCISM

As you know by now, when it comes to my show, I like to mix things up. One day we're throwing cats out of airplanes. The next day we're detailing the dangers of our continued participation in the United Nations. A few days later I'll have crazed listeners waving dildos at the poor sap in our mailroom.

I don't believe there's anyone who wants to listen to serious discussions of politics day after day after day. As Brother Dave once said, man cannot live on bread alone. He must have peanut butter.

Still, this is a book, not a show. You can put it down anytime you want, and pick it up again a few days later (assuming you've bought it, that is). So before I turn you loose, I need to get a few things off my chest about President Bush and the war in Iraq.

Let's begin with terminology. The war in Iraq and Afghanistan is commonly, and erroneously, referred to as the "war on terror." The enemy here is not terror. Terror is a tactic. The enemy is radical Islam—or, if you prefer, Islamic fascism.

The Islamic fascists are dedicated to the destruction of the West.

They are zealots who truly believe that it's their destiny to bring the world under Islamic law.

There are many books out there written by people far more knowledgeable than I on this subject. Among the most prolific is Robert Spenser, whose books include:

- *Islam Unveiled: Disturbing Questions About the World's Fastest Growing Faith*

- *Onward Muslim Solders: How Jihad Still Threatens America and the West*

- *The Truth About Muhammad: Founder of the World's Most Intolerant Religion*

- *The Politically Incorrect Guide© to Islam*

- *The Myth of Islamic Intolerance: How Islamic Law Treats Non-Muslims*

And there are many others—among them Mark Steyn's amazing book *America Alone: The End of the World as We Know It,* in which he details the all-but-inevitable Muslim conquest of Europe (the future Eurabia). These excellent books and many others have established beyond a doubt that the threat of Islamic fascism is real, it's imminent, and it is largely unrecognized by the American people.

The Islamic terrorist[1] attacks of 9/11 completely changed the nature of the Bush presidency. I also believe it changed the nature of George W. Bush himself.

On September 15, 2006, I was privileged to spend nearly two hours in the Oval Office with President Bush and four other radio

---

[1] Note, please, that I do not use the word "terrorist" without the word "Islamic." "Terrorist" is only half a word.

talk show hosts.[2] The ground rules were simple. We could discuss anything we wanted with the president, but we could not take notes, nor could we quote the president directly.[3]

I left that office with two distinct impressions of George W. Bush. First, that those people (usually on the left) who judge George Bush to be ignorant are hugely mistaken. Second, that George Bush is absolutely dedicated to the cause of defending this country against any further attacks by Islamic fascists, and to destroying those who perpetrated the horrors of 9/11.

I found areas of disagreement with the president during that meeting. He believes that Islam itself is truly a peaceful religion. I do not. But he clearly believes that the course of action he has pursued in Afghanistan and Iraq was correct, despite errors made along the way.

I'm no military strategist, any more than the many in the media who have been so critical of Bush over the past four years. I do recognize, however, that mistakes were made.

Perhaps we should have kept the Iraqi army intact. Maybe we should have kept some of Saddam's lower-level officers in charge of their commands. We surely could have done more to create an atmosphere of law and order in the days after Saddam's downfall, when rampant looting turned Baghdad into an Arabian version of New Orleans after Katrina. More troops? Maybe so.

One thing I'm sure of, though, is that the Democrat Party and its fellow travelers in the mainstream media were dedicated to the cause of making sure that Bush's plans for Iraq did not come to fruition.

Democratic hatred of all things Republican began with the ill-fated Republican revolution of 1994. The Democrats simply could not believe that the voters had turned their backs on them after so

---

[2] Sean Hannity, Mike Gallagher, Michael Medved, and Laura Ingraham.

[3] The hate mail I received after I told my listeners of this session in the Oval Office was insane. The mere fact that I attended this meeting was proof positive that I was nothing but Bush's lapdog, ready to roll over and play dead at his command.

many decades of dedicated service in the cause of replacing freedom with security.

Then and there, Democrats made a vow to one day return to power in Washington, and then to make sure that they would never lose again.

In 2000, the Democrats thought they had it made. Al Gore had been bred from the cradle forward to be nothing less than president of the United States. It was his very reason for existing, his destiny.

When Gore lost Florida by so thin a margin—and when all the legal maneuvering of the Democrats failed to overturn those results— the sense of outrage and dismay in Democrat ranks only increased. Never mind that their hero, Al Gore, had failed to carry his home state. Bush had won by the closest of margins, and for that he must be destroyed. His presidency must fail.

The attacks of 9/11 did bring about a temporary reprieve in the effort to destroy the Bush presidency. For a brief period, Americans were united in their determination to avenge those attacks and to bring those responsible to justice, if not to the gallows.

The passage of time has now served to soothe the angers and fears of the American people. This, in turn, has given the Democrats free rein to continue their campaign to destroy Bush's presidency.

Most people don't know that the decision to remove Saddam Hussein from power in Iraq was made during the Clinton presidency, not the Bush administration. Saddam's removal from power became the official policy of the United States government long before 9/11 and long before George Bush took the oath of office.

All of that was forgotten, though, when President Bush sent the troops in.

The goals that President Bush set were laudable: Remove a dangerous and murderous dictator from power, and establish a beachhead for freedom in the Middle East.

Soon after the invasion of Iraq, one pundit—I can't recall which one; they seemed to breed like flies around then—said that if our efforts in Iraq were successful, history would see it as one of the most noble accomplishments in world history.

Democrats, however, were determined that no such history would ever be written.

That's right. I believe that the Democrat Party resolved early to defeat Bush's efforts to bring peace, economic liberty, and a freely elected representative government to the people of Iraq. They could pick up the pieces later, when they came to power. But success must not be achieved on Bush's watch.

Think back to some of the reactions of Middle East leaders to Bush's removal of Saddam from power.

Libyan dictator Muammar al-Qaddafi suddenly became a pussy-cat, announcing an end to his nuclear programs and playing nice with the West. The House of Saud announced broader voting privileges in the Kingdom of Saudi Arabia. Throughout the Middle East, strong-men and leaders watched events in Iraq with a wary eye. Would George Bush move beyond Iraq if he felt that any other country posed a threat? Would they be attacked if they were discovered hiding any of Saddam's weapons? Just how dedicated was the American President to creating a free nation where Saddam Hussein once ruled?

Well, it didn't take long for the Arab world to recognize that things weren't going all that well for George W. Bush. America was not unified; indeed, there were deep divisions about his policies. Democrats were calling for an exit strategy before the smoke cleared from the first attacks. American pundits were decrying the loss of civilian life. Reports of American troop successes were hard to find.

Within months, the Arab world knew that the American people weren't likely to stick this one out. Day after day they saw attacks on Bush, his secretary of defense, and virtually all aspects of the war.

The Islamic fascists, like many Americans, recognized that the American media was working from a clearly defined template. Stories that reflected American successes in Iraq, that would make the president look good, must be downplayed. Stories that would embarrass the president or demoralize our troops would be played up.

Abu Ghraib, anyone?

Day after day the stories on the network newscasts detailed bombings and death, even as day after day American troops were lauded by the Iraqi people for building schools and hospitals.

The Islamic fascists watched, and learned.

They knew that if they could just maintain a steady stream of suicide bombings resulting in the deaths of American soldiers, the American people would grow quickly tired and throw in the towel. They knew that their suicide bombings would lead the nightly newscasts, so they stepped up their campaign.

It became standard operating practice after Abu Ghraib for any Islamic terrorist being held by coalition forces to scream torture. They knew that the media would pick up the story and run with it, even without any corroborating evidence.

Here's the point: if the Democrat Party hadn't been so hell bent on destroying the Bush presidency—if the Democrats had shown a unified front with their commander in chief and our troops—who's to say that complete victory in Iraq would not have been ours by now?

Just as Islamists despise weakness, they fear a determined enemy. They stopped viewing America and George Bush as a determined enemy when the Democrats, with the eager help of the leftist media, started their attacks.

It looks now as though the Democrats are going to get what they wanted. George Bush has been discredited, and the American people have turned against the war on Islamic fascism.

In two years, while the American people are, in all probability, electing a Democrat president, the Islamic fascists will be planning their next terrorist attack on our soil. The final show of weakness by the American people—the election of a Democrat president—will vastly encourage the Islamists.

As of today, the Islamic fascists are winning. Slowly but surely, they're seeing their dream of conquering the West come true. It took a few simple bombs on trains to overthrow a government in Spain. Other European countries are scrambling to find ways to appease their growing Muslim populations.

Sooner or later, the American people will wake up to the threat posed by these murderous radicals. Will we fight? Of course we will.

By then, however, the price we'll have to pay will be so much greater than the price we would have paid for complete victory in Iraq . . . a victory that was denied by the weakness and desire for revenge among Democrats and their media friends.

Remember one thing about these Islamic fascists.

They shoot schoolchildren in the back.

NO WAY IN HELL

This is the most useless chapter in this book. Useless because its topic is something that just ain't gonna happen.

If there's any testament to the widespread dementia that courses through some of my listeners, it's the all-too-frequent e-mails suggesting that I run for president. These people need professional help.

(Then again, when you think of Barack Obamamania . . .)

First, a reality check, on slim chance that any of you are actually serious:

There is no way in hell I could ever get elected. None. I was a horrible student all the way through my undergraduate years in school. I had a lower-than-C average in high school. I flunked out of college after the first semester of my sophomore year. Did I do anything exciting with my time waiting to get another chance at college? Oh, yeah: I pumped gas and delivered newspapers. I've been a department store assistant buyer in the fine jewelry and carpet departments, loaded trucks, sold insurance and chemicals, worked in an employment agency, and worked for the U.S. Postal Service. Add to that the fact that I've done things that would be considered crimes in thirteen states and the District of Columbia[1], and that's one helluva presidential resume, isn't it?

Let's face it. I'd be better off if I'd worked at a fancy law firm, drafting papers for an illegal tax avoidance scheme that cost the tax-

---

[1] The statute has run on all of them. Trust me on this one.

payers millions of dollars; or if I'd gone to Vietnam, applied a few Band-Aids to some scratches, scammed some Purple Hearts, and then come home to accuse our troops of atrocities.

There's also the problem of compensation. I make more than the president. And I'd like to keep it that way.

So I'm going to put this Boortz for President stuff to rest. Well . . . at least the serious part.

On the other hand, I've often thought it might be fun to take a stab at the Libertarian Party nomination. At least that way I know I wouldn't win. (Then again, the Libertarians aren't very fond of me now —a little something about my stance on the war in Iraq—so I'll have to kiss that little daydream goodbye.)

Still . . .

If lightning *did* strike, what would I try to accomplish? Just for the fun of it, I decided to pull together a platform, full of my pet ideas. (Yes, what follows is a blatant exercise in runaway egotism. My guess, though, is that you're going to see one or more of these platform items show up on someone else's campaign brochure before it's all over.)

REPEAL THE SIXTEENTH AMENDMENT AND ENACT THE FAIRTAX

There's a reason Marx and Engels included a progressive income tax in their Communist Manifesto "to do" list. Our current tax scheme is a convoluted and impossible-to-understand system of income confiscation and redistribution, created by politicians to facilitate vote-buying and to enable the constant expansion of the size of government.

As your president, I would dedicate my term to the passage of the FairTax Act and to the repeal of the Sixteenth Amendment, which enabled our income tax system.

Obviously we don't have the space here to go through a full description and discussion of the FairTax. Bottom line: The FairTax eliminates all corporate and personal income and payroll taxes, estate taxes, and capital gains taxes, and replaces them with one inclusive national retail sales tax. You can get all the information you need at Fairtax.org or by reading *The FairTax Book,* written by Congressman John Linder and yours truly. The book debuted at number one on the *New York Times* bestseller list, so don't worry—nobody's going to think you're a crank for being interested.

REPEAL THE SEVENTEENTH AMENDMENT

Very few Americans realize this (quiz your children!), but we didn't always vote for our U.S. senators.

Under our Constitution as originally ratified, senators were appointed by the state legislatures. The idea was that the members of the House of Representatives would represent the people of the United States, and the senators would represent the interests of the state governments.

In 1913,[2] the Seventeenth Amendment changed all that. From that point on, senators were elected by the people.

Things have been pretty much going downhill ever since.

The principal problem with the Seventeenth Amendment is that it leaves the fifty states with no official representation in Washington. If the nation of Angola has some sort of a beef with our national government, it has an official representative—the ambassador from Angola—to meet with our State Department officials and smooth things over. If the state of Arkansas has a problem with Washington— a huge unfunded mandate, for instance—there's no "Ambassador from Arkansas" to make the point. The Arkansas senators are elected by the people, as are the members of the House; the state government has no specific representative to take up its case.

Our founding fathers clearly felt that most governance should be

---

[2] The State of Alabama didn't ratify the Seventeenth Amendment until 2002. That would be about ninety years late. Things are really up to speed in Alabama.

at the local level. Today, we've failed at that goal. With no official representation inside the Beltway, the state governments have no real ability to help restrain the flow of government power from the local to the national level.

The repeal of the Seventeenth Amendment would help correct this imbalance, vastly strengthening the state governments' hand in Washington. In that sense power would begin to shift from the federal level to the state level, bringing us closer to the system of semi-sovereign states that was envisioned by our founders.

Before he left public office, Senator Zell Miller of Georgia actually introduced a resolution calling for a Constitutional amendment repealing the Seventeenth. Smart man.

APPOINT A FEDERAL TENTH AMENDMENT COMMISSION

"The powers not delegated to the United States by the Constitution, nor prohibited by it to the States, are reserved for the States respectively, or to the people."

Here again, the theme is limiting the power of the federal government and keeping as much government as possible at the local level.

Citizens feel more connected to those who wield power at the local level than they do to their U.S. senators and congressmen. They see their local politicians at church, in the grocery stores, on the streets, and at sporting events. Local politicians have a smaller support and voter base, and clearly understand that they're far more accountable to the voters than their counterparts insulated behind the marble entrances of the House and Senate office buildings in Washington.

This is precisely why our founders wanted most governance to be local, rather than national. Hence the Tenth Amendment.

Today, most government comes from Washington. Our local politicians may be free to locate schools and set speed limits, but when the serious lawmaking starts, all eyes are on the U.S. Capitol.

Though the Constitution grants a defined list of specific powers to the federal government, it is routinely ignored. When the Feds want to assume a new power or responsibility, they simply do it. And it's time to stop the bleeding. When was the last time you heard of anyone on the House or Senate floor citing the Tenth Amendment to complain about some overreaching new federal law?

Never? Yeah, me too.

My proposal, then, would be to establish a Tenth Amendment Commission, made up of an equal number of representatives of state governments and the federal government. After meeting for one year, the committee would present a report detailing a list of regulatory and legislative powers assumed over the years by the federal government that should be returned to the local level.

The result would be to bring governance back where it belongs— to the local level, and closer to the people.

ELIMINATE THE DEPARTMENT OF EDUCATION

This was one of the promises the Republicans made during the 1993 political campaign. It's a shame they didn't follow through.

Since the creation of the U.S. Department of Education, we've seen two trends at work. First, more and more of the power over our educational processes has flowed to the bureaucrats and politicians in Washington. Second, the amount of actual learning in our government schools has been on a steady decline.

I'm a little tired of hearing that the solution to our education problems is simply more parental involvement. The fact is, the more our educational system is controlled by the federal government, the more estranged they're going to feel, and the less likely they will be to become engaged.

For the best interest of our children, we need to get rid of the Department of Education—and return the control of our local schools to the communities.

(While we're talking education, by the way, I'll repeat the importance of encouraging school choice programs at the local level. As I've said, competition improves the quality of virtually any product or service—including education. The federal government should remove all regulatory barriers to fostering school competition through voucher programs. And yes, this does include religious schools.)

EXTEND FIRST AMENDMENT RIGHTS TO THE BROADCAST MEDIA

This one is so simple, even a government school social studies teacher could grasp it.

Most Americans get their daily dose of news from the broadcast media. This means that most Americans are getting their news from organizations licensed by the federal government.

This is not good.

I would call for a Constitutional amendment granting full First Amendment rights to the broadcast media in the United States, and to the Internet.

This would surely bring cries of outrage from "activists" who are concerned about such issues as political correctness, whether or not some speech may be "offensive," and whether a given speaker or writer is showing the requisite amount of "sensitivity."

I would tell these people to go away.

REFORM HEALTH CARE

Do you remember the last time you had to go stand in line to renew your driver's license or to buy tags? How about the last time you had to pay a visit to the local Social Security office?

Great . . . now drag up all the emotions that go along with that memory. That is the future of health care in this country.

I'm absolutely convinced that socialized medicine in the United

States is inevitable. The American people have fully embraced the idea that the responsibility for their health care should belong to someone else—either their employer or the government.

As president (you know, I'm starting to get into this!) I would immediately take steps to introduce as much competition into the healthcare market place as possible. Here are just a few suggestions:

1. Transfer all employer-held health insurance plans to employee ownership and control. This will force individuals to comparison shop for health insurance, thus introducing an element of competition into the health insurance marketplace.

2. Enable private collectives to purchase group health insurance plans.

3. Encourage states to end costly health insurance mandates. There is no reason that a sixty-year-old couple should be forced to buy a health insurance policy with maternity benefits. A company that pays only the unexpected expenses connected with a pregnancy and childbirth should be able to market its insurance policy for a lot less. Likewise, there is no reason for a non-drinker who doesn't use illegal drugs to have to pay for a policy that covers treatment for alcohol and drug abuse. The latest suggestion for a mandate is coverage for obesity treatment. Imagine the cost.

4. Allow hospital emergency rooms to turn away freeloaders with non–life threatening injuries. The law that requires an emergency room to treat everyone who comes through the door, regardless of their ability to pay, is a disaster. Too many people are using the hideously expensive emergency facilities at hospitals for the sniffles or the abrasion they suffered scratching off their lottery tickets.

5. Deny federal medical funds to any state whose laws limit competition in the medical field. There is no reason in the

world that an optometrist shouldn't be able to use simple drops for some procedure that simply doesn't require the services of a more highly trained, and thus more expensive, ophthalmologist.

6. Grant more health-care privileges to nurse assistants and other medical personnel. They can diagnose a simple sore throat or the flu as well as anyone with seven years of medical training.

7. Instruct the FDA to prioritize making more drugs available over the counter.

8. Make tax-free medical savings plans available to every citizen.

9. Grant full tax deductibility for all medical expenses, including preventative care.

10. Encourage a "loser pays" system for all medical malpractice lawsuits. (More on that below.)

11. End the state licensing of doctors. (This one is controversial, so we'll devote the next section to it.)

And that's just the beginning; once those reforms are in place, we'll assess the results and take it from there.

ENCOURAGE STATES TO END PROFESSIONAL LICENSING REQUIREMENTS

In the government pages of your local phone book, you'll find a list of phone numbers for professional licensing boards, usually under the heading "Secretary of State."

There is no reason for the state to be in the business of licensing all of these professions. This is something that should clearly be handled by the private marketplace.

Outrages abound in the operation of these licensing boards. In Texas and many other states, it would be illegal for an unlicensed individual to charge you for advice on whether or not a certain pillow would look good on your couch. In Louisiana, you can't even arrange flowers without a license. What's more, the people who decide whether or not you get that license are people who arrange flowers for a living. So you're asking them for license to go into competition with them! Yeah . . . that makes sense. Let me know how that works out for you.

As president, I would push for a system where licensing of professionals is handled through private licensing boards.

My general policy in all matters governmental would be to default to freedom. When the question is whether to encourage freedom and individual liberty, or to increase the regulatory power of government, I will always favor freedom. I'm generally unmoved by arguments that some people may abuse that freedom and suffer as a consequence. Freedom means you're free to make decisions that will hurt you. The government isn't your nanny. We all need to grow up and take responsibility for our actions.

Let's take a look at the two biggies: law and medicine.

My position is that people should be able to decide to receive medical services from whomever they choose, regardless of their background. If an individual wants to choose a medical practitioner responsibly, he should look for a doctor with appropriate private accreditation. Let the American Medical Association set up an accreditation process for doctors in all specialties. That way, when a consumer sees "AMA" after a doctor's name, he'll know he's dealing with a competent professional. The state shouldn't stand in the way of a person's choice of medical practitioners—not when a private accreditation system would work just as well.

You might be interested in knowing that for the first 150 years in this nation's history, we did not license doctors—or lawyers, for that matter. Somehow we survived.

As for lawyers, same thing. Let the American Bar Association put that "ABA" behind those they deem to be qualified, and then let the consumer make his free choice.

Know this: Most of the government's professional licensing requirements are designed to limit competition, not to protect the consumer.

Competition lowers prices while improving services. Consumers should accept responsibility for their choices.

START A LOSER-PAYS SYSTEM FOR FEDERAL LAWSUITS

Our system of tort law has become a crapshoot. Treasure hunters have no trouble finding seamy lawyers who are eager to file lawsuits over any perceived grievance. Plaintiff's lawyers and defendants know that if they manage to get a case to trial there's an excellent chance that they'll end up with an idiot jury that will award some damages "just because the plaintiff got hurt."

It doesn't matter whether or not the plaintiff caused his own injuries. The fact that he got hurt, regardless of causation, is often enough. All too frequently you'll hear some juror say, "Well, after all, they're insured. Isn't that what insurance is for?"

Defense attorneys recognize the potential for a bad verdict from a rogue jury, so often they recommend that their clients settle just to avoid the costs of going to trial. Plaintiff's lawyers know this, so they often file suit even when they know the defendant didn't really do anything wrong.

This is a fundamentally unjust situation. To address the problem, I would push for a "loser-pays" system at the federal level. Under such a system, those who file a lawsuit in the federal courts—and lose—are required to pay the defendant's legal expenses.

You win, they lose. They win, you lose.

I once had a character come into my law office with a can of soda. The top of the can carried a different brand name than the label on the side of the can.

He wanted to sue.

"What are your damages?"

"Well, I dunno. But the label is wrong."

"How were you hurt by this?"

"Well, I wasn't exactly hurt, but if we sue them, can't we get something?"

"Get the hell out of my office."

END THE WAR ON DRUGS

You know how I feel on this, so I'll make it simple:

Put me in office, and the very first thing I'll do is order a survey of all non-violent drug offenders currently serving time in prison. Those with no other criminal record would be pardoned.

The second thing I would do is instruct my drug "czar" to convert all federal drug programs from the law enforcement approach to a treatment-based approach. Much of the money saved would be returned to the taxpayers.

EXPEDITE EXECUTIONS

As president, I would make sure our country does not eliminate the death penalty, but continues to embrace it. Some people just don't deserve to draw another breath.

What I would do is establish a special federal capital court with exclusive jurisdiction over death penalty appeals. A judge from this court would be assigned to sit with the presiding judge for the sole purpose of monitoring the trial and any death penalty issues involved.

After conviction, the defense lawyer would be required to file any appeal with this judge within two weeks of sentencing. This judge would then present the appeal to a three-judge panel of which he is a member. The panel would vote within one week, and if the sentence is upheld, the criminal would take the eternal celestial dirt nap one week after that.

From sentence to execution in one month: Just watch those crime rates drop.

Finally, I would find an equitable way to punish any holier-than-thou nations who choose to extradite criminals back to this country because of our death penalty.

A CRASH PROGRAM FOR ENERGY INDEPENDENCE

The best way to emasculate the Islamic terrorists is to deprive them of the funding they need to carry forth their goals.

As president, I would initiate a Manhattan Project–type effort to bring energy independence to the United States. If we made it a priority, we could have Arab sheikhs begging for oil buyers in a very short period of time.

I would immediately, by Executive Order if possible, bring about oil drilling in the section of the Alaskan National Wildlife Refuge (ANWR) that was specifically set aside for that purpose.[3] I would also lift restrictions on drilling for gas and oil off the Florida Gulf Coast. It's time for Florida to become part of the solution, not part of the problem.

Subject to appropriate environmental protections, we would also immediately enable the private exploitation of the shale oil reserves in Utah and other Western States, and encourage private efforts at coal gasification in the East.

We would also have safe, modern nuclear power plants sprouting across the countryside like Starbucks coffee shops.

IMPLEMENT TERM LIMITS

Our professional politicians haven't impressed me much lately, so it would be time to implement term limits. After two terms, senators would have to step down and allow state legislatures to come up with

---

[3] The eco-radicals don't want you to know this, but the section of ANWR set aside for oil exploration would be comparable to a quarter sitting in the corner of a 9 x 12-foot rug.

new blood. Ditto for members of Congress: Give them three terms—six years—in office, then send them back home to earn an honest living.

REPLACE OUR ELECTORAL SYSTEM WITH A PARLIAMENTARY MODEL

The United States is not well-served by this absurd presidential beauty contest we carry out every four years. Let's face it. The voters of this country just aren't prepared to make an informed choice about which candidate is best qualified to run the show for the next four years. Just because you have a nice head of hair and don't sweat all that much on camera doesn't mean you're the best choice for commander in chief.

To understand the vapidity of the average voter, look at the Barack Obamamania that emerged in the fall of 2006. Here was a man who has accomplished little, if anything, in his limited years in elected office, yet suddenly he was being hailed as the great hope of the Democrat Party. Sure, he has a pretty face. Sure, he has a nice story about being a first-generation American. That's not enough to be an effective president.

I would propose a Constitutional amendment calling for the members of the House of Representatives to nominate one person to serve as president for the following six years. That nomination would be subject to confirmation by the Senate.

Under this system, the representatives elected by the people would make the nomination; the senators appointed by the state legislatures would ratify that choice. Both the people and the state governments would have a say in who serves the single six-year term.

This plan has the added advantage of focusing the voters on the one body in Washington were the power truly lies: the House of Representatives.

What most voters don't realize is that they can change the complexion of our government completely, every two years, simply by changing the makeup of the House. Why? Because the House has the sole power to originate all spending bills, as well as all tax bills. Our country is ill-served when the voters concentrate their attention and energies on the presidential beauty contest, while ignoring the races where real differences can be made.

PLACE NEW RESTRICTIONS ON VOTING

Given that the Constitution grants no actual right to vote in federal elections, I would move immediately to set qualifications for those who *do* want to head to the polls on Election Day. Bear in mind, under my new plan the highest federal office the people could vote for would be congressman. Those who wanted to make their voices known on who should represent them in the U.S. Senate would have to deal with their legislative candidates at home.

MAKE THE TAXPAYER'S ADDENDUM
A REQUIRED ADDITION TO EVERY LAW

I actually managed to have a bill establishing the Taxpayer's Addendum introduced in Georgia's General Assembly years ago.

It went nowhere.

But such details are unlikely to stop a guy like me. So I'll take the improbable event of my election to bring this concept to the federal government.

It's a simple provision: Every time a congressman or senator co-sponsors a spending bill, he would be obliged to affix his signature to an addendum reading:

> I, _____, in sponsoring/co-sponsoring this bill, do hereby affirm that I believe it is more important that the United States federal government seize the money appropriated herein from the taxpayers to fund this bill, than to allow the taxpayers who actually earned this money to retain it for their own needs.

After all, every time a member of Congress votes to spend one dollar of federal funds, that member effectively states that the federal government has a greater need for that money than did the person who earned it.

When Congress approved that half-million dollars for the restoration of Lawrence Welk's birthplace, for instance, the members who supported the appropriation were telling taxpayers that this restoration was more important than anything they could have spent that money on—including paying their bills, saving for the down payment on a house, putting their children in private school, booking a family vacation, or anything else.

If a member of Congress cannot sign this simple statement, he should simply refuse to sponsor the bill, or vote against it.

ENACT SEVERE RESTRICTIONS ON THE USE OF EMINENT DOMAIN

No society based on freedom and economic liberty has ever survived once that society began to ignore the property rights of individuals.

But apparently that little history lesson has escaped our friends in the judicial branch of government. In the 2005 case of *Kelo v. City of New London,* the Supreme Court of the United States decided that property rights in America should take a back seat to the needs of politicians and developers.

As things stand now, a developer can approach a local politician and suggest that more tax revenues could be generated from a particular piece of privately held property if the politician would seize that property through eminent domain and turn it over to the developer. The opportunity for increased tax revenues, according to the Supreme Court, amounts to a "public use."

The people of this country have made it abundantly clear that they're not at all happy with this ruling—or with eminent domain abuse in general. The politicians, on the other hand, love it.

I would move immediately to remove any federal funding from any state or local government that willingly participates in eminent domain abuse of this kind.

END ASSET FORFEITURES WITHOUT DUE PROCESS

Property rights are human rights. Property has no rights. Humans have a right to property. Property should not be taken away from citizens without due process of law.

Several years ago there was a gentleman in Memphis, Tennessee, who made a few extra bucks every year selling plants at a local gas station. Every spring the routine was the same. The man would take several thousand dollars in cash and head for the Memphis airport. There he would buy a one-way ticket to Mobile, Alabama. When he arrived in Mobile he would rent a truck and use the cash to fill that truck up with all sorts of nice green plants. He would then drive overnight back to Memphis to set up shop at the gas station. Every year he made several thousand dollars doing this.

One year, the agent who sold him his ticket at the Memphis airport became suspicious. Here was a man buying a one-way ticket to the Gulf Coast with cash. Hmmmmmm. The police were notified, the man questioned. He consented to a search. They found his money and confiscated it.

He was not charged with a crime. He was not arrested. They just took his money, on the assumption that it was going to be used to buy drugs.

This kind of highway robbery has also been approved by the Supreme Court. By now, I assume you aren't all that shocked.

When questioned about such behavior, police and their defenders will offer the ridiculous explanation that they're engaging in no due process rights. Why? Because they aren't taking action against the individual, but against the cash. If the man wants his cash back, they say, let him sue the government and prove he wasn't going to do anything illegal with it.

If this doesn't amount to being found guilty without due process, I don't know what does.

Put me in office, and I'll bring such federal asset forfeiture actions to an end.

GET THE UNITED STATES OUT OF THE UNITED NATIONS

You know where I stand: Since its formation, the United Nations has been an essentially anti-American institution. It's a club that petty, tinhorn dictators from around the world use to slam the greatest country this world has ever had the privilege to host. We pay most of the bills and take most of the heat.

This has to end.

I would propose that the United States give the UN an eviction notice. They should be given five years to vacate their East River digs and move elsewhere.

Beyond that, a suggestion: Perhaps the world community would like to seize Haiti and give it to the United Nations? If the UN would like to prove its value as a peacekeeping body, perhaps it would like to begin by moving into that international basket case of a nation and giving it the old college try.

FORM A NEW LEAGUE OF FREEDOM

I do recognize that the world needs some kind of international forum for the resolution of disputes and for addressing problems facing the international community.

I would propose, therefore, an agency to replace the United Nations. As soon as the UN moves out of its headquarters, the new International League of Freedom should move in. This new international organization would be modeled loosely after the UN, but with one key difference: Its membership would be restricted to nations whose governments are elected by the people in free and open elections, and where a certain set of rights, modeled after our Constitution's Bill of Rights, are protected.

PRIVATIZE SOCIAL SECURITY

Anyone who doubts that contemporary Americans actually fear freedom need look no further than the debate over Social Security privatization.

Social Security is not a retirement plan. It is an income redistribution plan designed to buy votes. If any private entrepreneur in any state in the nation were to devise a savings, disability, and investment program modeled after Social Security, he would be arrested and prosecuted for felony fraud.

The federal government should not promote a scam that would constitute a crime if promoted by a private company.

Instead, I would propose that Social Security be converted to a system of privately held accounts. The people who earned this money should not be forced to donate it to a sham retirement program that does more to rob them and their heirs of their hard-earned money then it does to pave the way to a comfortable retirement. I would also propose that during the transition period all current Social Security benefits to retirees and to those soon-to-retire be guaranteed by law.

STRENGTHEN OUR BORDER PROTECTIONS

I would expand the mission of the Coast Guard to protect all borders, on land and on sea. Further, I would fund the expanded mission of the Coast Guard with money saved from the end of the war on drugs.

The invasion of illegal immigrants into our workforce must be stopped—now.

I would also propose a system that would give American employers unable to find enough legal residents to staff their workplaces the opportunity to import guest workers from other countries. These workers would be required to have guest worker permits that can only be issued in their home countries. When brought to America for their temporary work assignments, they would be paid by closely regulated employment agencies hired by the employers. No direct payments of any kind could be made by the employer to the employees. All pay would go through the agency. The employer and/or the agency would be responsible for assisting the guest worker in finding temporary housing.

Once a guest worker's employment period ended, he would be provided transportation back to his country.

Sanctions against employers who employed, housed and paid guest workers or illegal aliens outside of the agency system would be punitive.

START A NETWORK OF ECONOMIC REFUGEE CAMPS

All federal subsidies for welfare housing would cease, as would various other social service and welfare programs for the so-called "poor."

In the place of these programs, we would establish a chain of economic refugee zones on abandoned military bases. There would be no gates to keep people in, or to keep them out.

Any person in this country who finds himself unable to cope, to feed or clothe himself, or to deal with his drug or alcohol addiction could report to or ask to be transported to one of these "Opportunity Zones." There they would be provided with a place to live, food to eat, health care, and the basic necessities of life. They would also receive job training, drug or alcohol rehabilitation, and other forms of counseling. There would also be a wide range of job placement services available.

Once the individual felt prepared to work and to provide for himself, he would receive a small sum of cash and be transported to the city of his choice.

RIDES ON AIR FORCE ONE

Every time I flew somewhere for a speech or official visit, we would give an ordinary taxpaying American citizen the opportunity to grab a friend and ride along on Air Force One. We could choose them by location and lottery. It's the greatest private jet out there—and the taxpayers paid for it. They ought to get a chance to use it!

(Notice I said *citizen*.)

OKAY, I'M EXHAUSTED

If you want any more out of me you're going to have to give me a second term.

As self-aggrandizing as this chapter may have sounded, there was a method to my madness. I wanted to set forth an election agenda that would excite the passions of our more thoughtful, open-minded voters, and do the country some genuine good—regardless of which poor sap tried to use it as a genuine springboard to office.

Because any candidate who tried would never be elected. Not in this country, anyway.

Oh, well. We can dream, can't we?

THE DOLLAR BILL
SAVINGS PROGRAM

I don't want you to finish this book and send it to join that great stack of finished reading material under your bed without giving you something that can truly change your life. I'm serious. I've ranted and raved for umpteen pages about things that please me, things that irritate me, things that amuse me, and things that outrage me. Hopefully you've been amused, pleased, outraged, and irritated by what I've written. Let's add insulted and offended. It would be truly sad if I went through all of this effort and didn't manage to put one sentence somewhere in this book that didn't either insult you or offend you. These days, Americans spend so much time looking for an excuse to claim victim status at some perceived insult or offense that I feel duty-bound to provide every one of you the prize you've sought so ardently.

Now it's time to do something nice.

If you'll finish this chapter before putting the book away, and if you'll consider giving serious consideration to what I am going to suggest, I guarantee that you'll be pleasantly surprised at the very least, and greatly rewarded at best.

In the early 1980s, I signed on to a three-day skiing trip from Atlanta to Vail, Colorado. Not having large amounts of cash to throw around, I opted to save a few bucks by agreeing to a roommate on the trip.

My dreams of some paperwork snafu[1] that would billet me with some long-and-blond flat-belly were dashed when Bill came in and started unpacking. A construction worker from Atlanta,[2] Bill was a great guy, and he was very excited about his first ski trip to Colorado.

When you live in Atlanta, a ski trip to Colorado is your dream; a ski trip to some quarter-mile slope covered with brown slush in North Carolina is your reality. Most Atlanta skiers learn fast how to survive the impact of some out-of-control good old boy zipping down the slope in what we call the "Birmingham stance," then crashing full speed into a lift line. In those days my favorite ski jacket bore a legend I'll never forget: "I hear banjo music, ski faster."

Bill felt compelled to explain to me just how he'd managed to save enough money to come to Colorado. It was simple: He never spent a dollar bill.

Bill explained his savings scheme to me, and on my return to Atlanta I put it into practice. It worked. I had tried every imaginable way to save money. Budgets, piggy banks[3]—you name it, I tried it and I failed. I'd actually come to the conclusion that it was impossible for me to save any money, because I barely had enough to pay my bills in the first place. The truth is that the ski trip was a freebie because I had promoted it on the radio. Maybe if I'd promoted it a bit harder I would have had my own room . . . but I'm glad it didn't work out that way.

Well, I tried Bill's plan, and it worked—better than I ever thought possible. I've mentioned it on the air many times since I met Bill, and every time I do I end up with letters from people who tried it and

---

[1] It's an acronym, and if you don't know what it stands for you will be rewarded if you try to find out.

[2] Remember, this was around 1983 or so. Today the construction worker from Atlanta would be named Guillermo and would not likely be found on the ski slopes of Vail.

[3] Do Muslim children have piggy banks? Look . . . someone has to ask the question.

wanted to thank me. So, in a parting act of supreme goodwill, I'm going to share it with you.

The plan is simple: You never spend a dollar bill. Okay . . . almost never. If you need to leave a one- or two-dollar tip for an obliging waitress or valet parking attendant, that's fine. Tolls are allowed, too. Other than that, don't spend your dollars. Period.

Every morning when you leave your home for work or school, check your stash to make sure that there are no dollar bills anywhere. You can carry all the fives, tens, twenties, fifties, and hundreds you want. But *no dollar bills.*

If you want to stop at the local convenience store to pick up a cup of coffee on the way to work, fine. That coffee's going to cost more than a buck, so the smallest denomination you can use to pay for it would be a five. Let's say you get $3.50 in change. The fifty cents goes in your pocket; you can spend it later. The three dollar bills get put away. You are not to touch them until you get home that evening. For all practical purposes, they cease to exist.

Later, it's time for your coffee break. You head to that coffee shop on the first floor—the one with that cashier with the dark brown makeup under her eyes—for another cup of coffee and a bagel. The tab is $3.25. You pull out another five, put the seventy-five cents in change in your pocket, and put the dollar bill away.

Neal, I can't put that dollar away. I won't have enough for lunch!

Fine! Then don't get that coffee and bagel. Save the five for lunch. You won't die. Besides, there's probably free coffee in your company coffee cave anyway.

Get it? Every time you spend money, you have to make a decision. You know you'll have to burn a few dollar bills. So, instead, put them in your back pocket, or in that zippered compartment in your purse. Wherever you put it, that dollar bill ceases to exist.

The payoff comes when you get home at night. You take the dollar bills out of their designated hiding place and stuff them into a box or can. There they stay. For the first month, don't count them. You add your day's collection of dollar bills to the stash, and you just let them sit there.

I've coerced people into trying this savings plan who swore on their mother's urn that there was no way in the world they could possibly save any money. They just didn't make enough. The bills wouldn't get paid. Saving any money was just impossible. From time to time, I've even offered to match the first month's savings, just to get a close friend or colleague to give the plan a try. (*Close friend,* I said. Not you, pal.)

The big payoff for me comes when a friend comes to me after the first month to tell me he's counted up the dollar bills. There's a look of amazement and excitement in his eye every time. He can't believe what he's done.

"How much did you have?"

"Neal, you won't believe it. I had a hundred and forty dollars in that can!"

For someone like that, who thought he'd never make enough to save any money, that $140 seems to come out of nowhere. Add it up and you have about $1,680 for the year. There's your Christmas shopping or a good hunk of your property taxes for the next year. Or there's a mighty nice trip to Vail to bust your buns on the slopes.

My daughter, Laura, thought it was great sport to make fun of me for stuffing those dollar bills into coffee tins during her high school years. When she opened her high school graduation present—a virtual brick of tightly bound dollar bills, thousands in all—she stopped laughing.

It works. It works every single time. I have never had one person give this savings plan an honest try who didn't report amazing and unexpected success.

There's a bigger lesson to be learned here, too. Perhaps you've already figured it out.

The average head of household in this country has nearly $10,000 in credit card debt. You know how it feels to receive your credit card bill at the end of the month and be stunned by the total: *How did it ever get that high?* There's that huge balance, all that accruing interest, and you can't do much beyond paying the minimum! *By the time I get this balance paid off,* you think, *I'm going to be shopping for a nursing home somewhere.* Yet month after month it continues: The balance grows, you keep paying the minimum . . . and somewhere a bankruptcy lawyer awaits your call.

How does that balance grow so steadily? Exactly the same way your shoebox stash of dollar bills gets so big: one dollar at a time. A buck here, two bucks there, and suddenly at the end of the month you can't believe how much you've spent—or saved.

Earlier, I ventured that the most destructive influence at work in this country today is the institution of government schools. Well, credit cards are sneaking right up behind them. Millions of Americans have been robbed of their economic independence by those little pieces of plastic.

If that's true of you, it's time for you to reclaim your economic liberty. I've talked on the air about how many of us need to develop an escape plan—a plan we can follow to help us flee the growing oppressiveness of taxes and government regulation. You'll never be free to enjoy your years of peak earning capacity (not to mention your retirement years) if you're up to your ears in unmanageable credit card debt.

The dollar bill savings plan demonstrates one of my fundamental beliefs about this country. Our problems have a way of creeping up on us, little by little, dollar by dollar, over time. But the solutions can be accomplished the very same way—painlessly—if we just take the time, and discipline, to make them right.

Well, somebody had to say it. I'm thankful you gave me the opportunity.

ACKNOWLEDGMENTS

It's dangerous to put an acknowledgments section in a book: You just know you're going to leave some people out, causing them never to forgive you.

There are some people I want to thank, though, so I'll have to take the risk.

Topping the list are Belinda Skelton, Royal Marshall, Ken Rogers, Bryan Gainey, and Laura Nunemaker for doing the hard behind-the-scenes work while I run my mouth. Special thanks to Pete "The Pig Farmer" Spriggs for his deft handling of the nation's number one radio station, Atlanta's Newstalk 750, WSB. Thanks also to Pete's predecessor, Greg "Bugsy" Moceri, who went on to become the best talk radio consultant in the business. Special thanks to Cox Radio's executive vice president and COO, Marc Morgan, who aided and abetted me as I ran from the law.

My gratitude to Ramona Rideout and Paul Douglas for their hard work schlepping my syndication.

Special thanks to CB Hackworth, who deftly worked the magic of Lexis-Nexis every time I needed to nail down a date, quotation, or statistic, and to Cal Morgan at HarperCollins, who edited my long-winded rantings to a manageable manuscript.

I also want to thank some of my colleagues in talk radio who have remained friends even as we sometimes battle one another for ratings and stations. Sean Hannity tops this list. When Sean and I competed against each other in Atlanta before the days of syndication, we used to pick up the phone and talk to each other during newsbreaks. There but for hair go I. When he becomes president, he tells me, I can still call him Sean.

And a special note to Jack Swanson: If I'm such a damned good talk show host, why aren't I on any of your San Francisco radio stations? No book signing for you!